D1112885

MALT WHISKY

The revised edition of Malt Whisky is dedicated to Dr Nicholas Morgan, to mark his 20 years in the whisky industry, and in gratitude for 20 years of help and friendship.

CHARLES MacLEAN

MALT WHISKY

PHOTOGRAPHS BY JASON LOWE

MITCHELL BEAZLEY

Malt Whisky by Charles MacLean

First published in Great Britain in 1997 by Mitchell Beazley,
an imprint of Octopus Publishing Group, Endeavour House,
189 Shaftesbury Avenue, London, WC2H 8JY.

Copyright © Octopus Publishing Group Limited 1997, 1998, 2002, 2006, 2010
Text copyright © Charles MacLean 1997, 1998, 2002, 2006, 2010

Reprinted 1997, 1998
Revised 2002, 2006, 2010

First published in paperback in 2006
All rights reserved.
No part of this publication may be reproduced or used in any form or by any means,
electronic or mechanical, including photocopying, recording or by any information
storage and retrieval system, without the prior written permission of the publisher.

Charles MacLean has asserted his moral rights as author of this work.

A CIP catalogue record of this book is available from the British Library.

ISBN-13: 978 1 84533 570 0

All photography by Jason Lowe, with the exception of the following:
Alamy/Jim Henderson 120; /World History Archive 42. Corbis/Bettmann 45. George
Bernard 25, 27, 29, 32 left, 32 centre left, 32 centre right, 32 right, 34, 47. George
Bernard/Bernard Photo Productions 24. Getty Images/Matthew Peyton 105; /The
Conservative Party Archive 39. Octopus Publishing Group/Miller's at millersonline.com/
Lyon & Turnbull 40. ScotlandsImages.com/Crown Copyright 2007, The National Archives
of Scotland 20. TopFoto/Sarah Fabian-Baddiel/HIP 15. Whyte and Mackay Ltd. 49.

The publishers would also like to thank everyone who supplied whisky labels.

For the 2010 edition:
Commissioning Editor: Hilary Lumsden
Executive Art Editor: Juliette Norsworthy
Managing Editor: Georgina Atsiaris
Design: Two Associates, London
Typeset in ITC Garamond and Gill Sans
Printed and bound in China

CONTENTS

FOREWORD

No one knows who first conceived the simple but ever wondrous idea of converting the humble barley grain into spirit but all agree it has been a collective gift from our Celtic forefathers. Perhaps they knew only too well that after a cheerful summer would surely come the dank drip or icy cold and snow of winter. Their foremost guard to ensure survival was the water of life – uisge beatha – itself.

That distillation in earliest times was an art, cultivated as much in remote Highland glens as in devout Lowland abbeys, cannot be denied. Nor can the claim be resisted that, on August 24, 1494, Friar John Cor of Lindores Abbey in Fife converted eight bolls of barley malt into aqua vitae for his sovereign, King James IV; the first record of distilled spirit in Scotland.

Now, more than 500 years on, Scotch whisky has established itself as a gift to discerning drinkers throughout the world; with care it improves from birth; it traces its original line through fire and water, themselves the chief elements of creation. It can be enjoyed as a single malt and yet will blend easily with brotherly spirits from across Scotland. It will never fail to offer a challenge to those most wise parts of the human body – the senses of taste and satisfaction.

That is why I commend this remarkable book. You may well be encouraged to try out the marvellous range of flavours and styles, then perhaps be inspired to come and visit the source. You will then realise how profound, through the medium of malt whisky, is Scotland's contribution to humanity.

THE EARL OF ELGIN AND KINCARDINE KT

INTRODUCTION

The genesis of this book was a talk I gave in Brussels in September 1995 to mark the launch of the Scotch Single Malt Whisky Society of Belgium. In it I attempted to answer the question: "Why are all malt whiskies different?" Borrowing Winston Churchill's description of the Soviet Union, I said that malt whisky was "a riddle, wrapped in a mystery, cloaked in an enigma". The riddle is the product itself, its taste and smell; the mystery is how it comes to be like this, made as it is from the simplest ingredients – malted barley and water; and the enigma is why so simple a product cannot be made elsewhere in the world.

Happily the conundrum cannot be solved, but in this book I have set about unwrapping the mystery and exploring the enigma from a variety of different angles, but always with the original question in mind. Thus, my rapid canter through the history of Scotch whisky pauses only to look at how flavour might have been affected by, for example, innovations in still design or taxation. My consideration of ingredients and the production process continually asks: "What contribution to flavour does each stage make, relative to the others?" My exploration of the differences between malts from one region of Scotland or another looks at flavour through the glass of geography.

Scotland is at the heart of the matter, for malt whisky is the quintessence of Scotland. It recollects the land of its birth with every sip – peat hags and bog myrtle, the sun on the loch, the rain on the mountain, white beaches and salt spray: the fugitive aromas of the land itself. It also speaks of the people of Scotland, the tough farmers who developed the art of distillation, the intrepid "smugglers" who kept the still-fires burning in the face of the law, the remarkable entrepreneurs who built a world market for Scotch in the later decades of the nineteenth century.

And in its effects, malt whisky epitomises the inherent dichotomy of the Scottish psyche – at once passionate and rational, romantic and ironic, mystical and sceptical, heroic and craven, full of laughter and despair.

As JP McCondach wrote in The Channering Worm: "Much abused, by its addicts and traducers alike, it is a complicated simple, the whisky, pure in essence, but diverse in effects; and against it none can prevail".

ACKNOWLEDGMENTS

BIBLIOGRAPHICAL

This book owes a debt to many other books published on its subject. An extended list appears in the bibliography – alas, there is not room to list the general historical, scientific and topographical texts consulted – but I should like to single out a handful of sources that I have referred to in the text.

First, six relatively recent books which have made major contributions to the history of Scotch: Michael S Moss and John R Hume's The Making of Scotch Whisky [1981] is the leading account of the subject, Charles Craig's Scotch Whisky Industry Review [1994], an infallible archive of dates and details, the late Dr RB Weir's The History of the Distillers Company 1877 to 1939 [1995], Gavin D Smith's engaging A-Z of Whisky [1997], Misako Udo's exhaustive The Scotch Whisky Distilleries [2006] and C Anne Wilson's intriguing Water of Life [2006].

It would be immodest of me to add my own *Scotch Whisky: A Liquid History* [2003] and *Whiskypedia* [2009] to this list, but I have used both in revising and updating this edition of *Malt Whisky*. I have also used the invaluable *Malt Whisky Yearbook* [2010 edition], edited by Ingvar Ronde, an up-to date mine of information about the subject. The "classical" authorities begin with Alfred Barnard's *The Whisky Distilleries of the United Kingdom* [1887], an engaging account of his tour to every distillery in the kingdom, and *The Manufacture of Spirit as Conducted at the Various Distilleries of the United Kingdom* by JA Nettleton [1898], the "bible" for production practice. My "desert island" book is *Whisky* by Aeneas Macdonald [1930, re-issued, with a revealing introduction by Ian Buxton in 2006]; other favourites are Sir Robert Bruce-Lockhart's *Scotch* [1951], Professor RJS McDowall's *The Whiskies of Scotland* [1967] and Professor David Daiches's *Scotch Whisky, Its Past and Present* [1969]. All have been reprinted.

PERSONAL

In earlier editions of this book I listed 39 people who had been especially generous with help for *Malt Whisky*. All but seven of those named have now retired from the whisky industry – a telling indication of how time passes. I take the opportunity now to thank those who have supported me (materially and intellectually; with laughter and learning) over the years since the first edition:

Rob Allanson (*Whisky Magazine*), Jon Allen (writer), Michael Alexander (Diageo), Raymond Armstrong (Bladnoch distillery), Helen Arthur (writer), Iain Baxter (Inver House Distillers), Michael Beamish (Tullibardine distillery), Giuseppe Begnoni (Whisky Paradise), Jim Beveridge (Diageo), Dave Broom (writer), Alex Bruce (Adelphi distillery), Rob Bruce (Whyte & Mackay), Ulf Buxrud (Malt Maniacs), Ian Buxton (writer), Ian Chapman (Gordon & Macphail), Geraldine Coates (writer), Trevor Cowan (SMWS), David Cox (Edrington), Ronnie Cox (Berry Bros & Rudd), Jason Craig (Edrington), Katharine Crisp (Burn Stewart Distillers), Douglas Cruikshank (Chivas Bros), Bob Dalgarno (The Macallan distillery), Raymond Davidson (Glencairn Crystal), Gordon Doctor (Ian Macleod Distillers), Rob Draper (SingleMalt TV), Jonathan Driver (consultant), Campbell Evans (Scotch Whisky Association), John Finnie (Balgonie House), Andrew Ford (Diageo), Ken Grier (Edrington), David Grant (Wm Grant & Sons), John and George Grant (Glenfarclas distillery), Kenny Grant (Glen Garioch distillery), Alan Gray (analyst), Micky Heads (Ardbeg distillery), Johannes van den Heuvel (Malt Maniacs), Justin Hicklin (Hicklin Slade), Robbie Hughes (Glengoyne distillery), Olivier Humbrecht (Malt Maniacs), David Hume (Wm Grant & Sons), Kai Ivalo (SMWS), Christine Jones (archivist), Richard Joynson (Loch Fyne Whiskies), Mike Keillor (Morrison Bowmore), Davin de

Kergommeaux (Malt Maniacs), Fred and Stewart Laing (Douglas Laing & Co), Mari Laidlaw (Morrison Bowmore), Keith Law (Diageo), Paul Lockyer (Diageo), Ian Logan (Chivas Bros), Graham Logie (Lagavulin distillery), Dr Bill Lumsden (Glenmorangie), David Mair (Wm Grant & Sons), Neil Mackinlay (Inver House Distillers), Stephen Marshall (John Dewar & Sons), Alexander McCall Smith (writer), Frank McHardy (Springbank distillery), Rowan McKenzie (Inver House Distillers), Alastair McIntosh (Scotch Whisky Experience), John McLellan (Kilchoman distillery), Marcin Miller (Quercus Communications), Glen Moore (Morrison Bowmore), Douglas Murray (Diageo), Martine Nouet (writer), Hans Offringer (writer), Silvio Preno (The Vintners Rooms), Lucy Pritchard (Diageo), John Ramsay (Edrington), Andrew Rankin (Morrison Bowmore), Donald Renwick (Royal Lochnagar Distillery), Mark Reynier (Bruichladdich distillery), Captain Stewart Robertson (S.Y. Grampus), Stuart Robertson (Huntly distillery), Maureen Robinson (Diageo), Ingvar Ronde (publisher), Colin Ross (Ben Nevis distillery), Ian Russell, (archivist), Peter and Leonard Russell (Ian Maclead Distillers), Professor Alan Rutherford (Heriot Watt University), Graham Scott (NEVIS Design), Jacqui Seargeant (archivist), Euan Shand (Duncan Taylor), Sukhinder Singh (The Whisky Exchange), Charlie Smith (Talisker distillery), Gavin Smith (writer), David Stewart (Wm Grant & Sons), Kier Sword (Royal Mile Whiskies), Douglas and Willie Taylor (Speyside Cooperage), Hamish Torrie (Glenmorangie), Gerry Tosh (Edrington), David and Michael Urquhart (Gordon & Macphail), Serge Valentin (Malt Maniacs), Billy Walker (BenRiach distillery), Mark Watt (Duncan Taylor), Ian Williams (Cardhu distillery), David Williamson (Scotch Whisky Association), Anthony and Cathy Wills (Kilchoman distillery), Allan Winchester (Chivas Bros) and Vanessa Wright (Chivas Bros).

CHARLES MACLEAN, EDINBURGH, 2011

HISTORY

Some historians believe that the Latin *aqua vitae*, meaning "the water of life" was translated by the Romans during their occupation of Britain from *uisge beatha* which is the Gaelic for whisky. The same evocative expression is applied in other languages, for instance *eau de vie* in French and *akvavit* in Danish. All these terms describe alcohol that has been concentrated by distillation.

In the 1930s, the popular Scottish novelist Neil Gunn imagined the discovery of distilling whisky to have been made accidentally. He described the picture of an ancient Celt observing the steam from his vat of fermented gruel condensing into an ardent spirit.

"It is purer than any water from any well. When cold it is colder to the fingers than ice. A marvellous transformation... But in the mouth, what is this? The gums tingle, the throat burns, down into the belly fire passes, and thence outward to the finger-tips, to the feet, and finally to the head... Clearly it was not water he had drunk: it was life."

In this opening chapter we will follow the often dramatic and undeniably romantic history of the evolution of the whisky industry, from its simple origins as a mainstay in the crofter's year, to the massive, international industry it is today.

ABOVE This was the first label that used Arthur Bell & Sons as the brand name.

LEFT The production water for Glengoyne distillery runs off the Campsie Fells through a picturesque sandstone gorge.

From our perspective – that of the modern consumer – the history of Scotch whisky has two important threads.

First, flavour. Early stills were crude, and the spirit they produced can scarcely be dignified by the description "potable". The "marvellous transformation" imagined by Neil Gunn (*see* previous page) in his description of the discovery of whisky by an ancient Celt, would have been more like a sharp blow to the head. Indeed, the Scots word "skelp", which means just this, derives from the Gaelic *sgailc*, that is "a bumper of spirits taken before breakfast" – a morning dram.

Second, price. Whisky is made from the cheapest, most elemental of ingredients – water and barley – and is produced by a simple process. Puritan instincts dictate that those things that give us pleasure should be paid for and this was first put into practice by the imposition of tax by a Puritan parliament in 1644.

Subsequent governments have not looked back, and developments in the history of Scotch whisky have often been brought about by excise duty, or its avoidance, by a search for quality and flavour at an acceptable price and by vigorous, pioneering marketing all over the world. The Scotch malt whisky made today is of higher quality than ever before.

HUMID VAPOURS

One peers in vain into the gloom of the Celtic twilight for the smoke of the earliest distillers' fires. One tradition holds that the mysteries of distilling were borne across the Irish Sea by the Gaelic-speaking Celts who founded the Kingdom of Dalriada on Scotland's western seaboard in the early sixth century, known to history as the Scots. The Scots Gaelic for *aqua vitae* is *uisge beatha*, (pronounced "ooshkie bayahah") which was abbreviated to *uiskie* in the seventeenth century, and to *whiskie* by 1715. The modern spelling – whisky – first appears as late as 1736. The Ancient Irish, it is maintained, were taught how to distil by St Patrick, two centuries before they arrived in Scotland, and he had learned the secrets during his years at Auxerre in central France, before his mission to Ireland, which commenced in 432. When English armies invaded Ireland in 1170, they found monastic distilleries in several parts of the country.

Some authorities hold that the secrets of distilling were brought to Europe from the Middle East in about 1150 by the Moors. Certainly, the Middle East was the cradle of medical and chemical knowledge. Kemi was an early name for Egypt, and it is claimed that potable spirits were created here before 3,000 BC, probably

"The admirable essence... an emanation of the divinity, an element newly revealed to man but hid from antiquity, because the human race was then too young to need this beverage destined to revive the energies of modern decrepitude."

Raymond Lully
1236-1315

ABOVE Stones weighted to the roof prevent the thatch being blown away on a traditional croft in Skye.

made from grapes or flowers, rather than grain. Further east, the Chinese, Tibetans, Indians and Sinhalese distilled from rice, millet, fermented mare's milk, coconuts and palm sap.

The Old Testament mentions *maaim haaim*, which "made human hearts joyful", and has been translated as *aqua vitae*. Proverbs xx.1 states: "Wine is a mocker, strong drink is raging". I have even heard it argued that the "Holy Spirit" should be understood literally, that Jesus Christ learned the secrets of distilling from his earthly father, St Joseph the Carpenter (or cooper?) and that the turning of water into wine at the marriage in Cana was in fact the turning of wine into brandy!

The Alexandrian Greeks distilled turpentine from pine resin; in the fourth century BC Aristotle described how "sea water may be made potable by distillation: wine and other liquids can be submitted to the same process. After they have been converted into humid vapours they return again to liquids". He also entertained the notion that those made drunk with "strong drink" fell on the back of their heads, while those intoxicated by wine fell on their faces! The equipment used was primitive – for example, sweet water was collected from boiling sea water by hanging sponges in the steam; in the first century AD Pliny the

Elder mentions hanging fleeces over boiling resin to catch the vapours and make turpentine. However, nowhere in classical literature is reference made to the convivial drinking of spirits – and the Romans were no strangers to revelry. The truth is that most distillates were used as medicines or perfumes.

THE ADMIRABLE ESSENCE

It seems that the secrets of distilling were lost to mainland Europe during the Dark Ages, even supposing they had been known here in the first place. They were rediscovered or revived by Arnold de Villa Nova, a thirteenth century Moorish scholar, born in Spain and educated in Sicily, who taught alchemy, medicine and astronomy at Avignon and Montpellier. Arnold has been described as the "Father of Distilling", for as well as studying the "distillation" of nitric, hydrochloric and sulphuric acids, he distilled wine and named the result *eau de vie* and *aqua vitae* – "the water of life".

His contemporary and pupil, Raymond Lully, is credited with attributing the name "alcohol" to distilled spirits – the word comes from the Arabic *al kohl*, which means both "a mind-altering drug" and a "genie or spirit".

BELOW Highland Park distillery, Orkney.

Theophrastus Bombast von Hohenheim (aka "Paracelsus" 1490–1541), the most celebrated of all medieval alchemist/physicians, often refers to alcohol.

Although there were a few aristocratic dabblers in science, the earliest European distillers were generally monks and their interest in distilling was primarily medicinal. They applied the process first to wine and infusions of herbs, and later, in the colder climates of northern and western Europe, where grapes did not flourish, to fermented mashes of cereals. Famous contemporary liqueurs like Benedictine, (invented at the Abbey of Fécamp, Normandy in 1510) and Chartreuse (made by Carthusian monks at Voiron, near Grenoble, from a recipe given to them in 1605), continue this tradition.

The distillation of cereal mashes was not unknown to the Ancients. Edward Gibbon, in his historical masterpiece, *The Decline and Fall of the Roman Empire*, recounts how one Maximin headed an embassy to Attila the Hun from Constantinople in 448 AD, during which they encountered "a certain liquor named *camus*, which according to the report of Priscus, was distilled from barley".

RIGHT An excerpt from the Exchequer Roll, 1494, the first written reference to distilled spirits in Scotland.

AQUA VITAE

The first record of distilled spirit in Scotland is found in an Exchequer Roll of 1494, where it is written "To Friar John Cor, by order of the King, to make aquavitae, VIII bolls of malt". The king was James IV (1488–1513), the best loved of all the ill-fated House of Stuart. It has been suggested that he got a taste for *aqua vitae* – or *uisge beatha* as it was known in the Gaelic tongue – in Islay where he had been campaigning the year before. Be that as it may, Friar Cor was of the Benedictine Order at Lindores Abbey in Fife; eight bolls amounts to 1,900 lbs or 870 kg, and this quantity of malt would make around 1,250 bottles of today's whisky. A further Exchequer Roll entry, on 22nd December 1497 while the King was lodging in Dundee, records the payment of nine shillings to a barber (ie. surgeon), for *aqua vitae*.

In 1505, the Guild of Surgeon-Barbers of Edinburgh was created, the ancestor of the modern Royal College of Surgeons of Edinburgh. Among the privileges granted to them by Seal

---

■ **1494** First recorded mention of *aqua vitae* in Scotland   ■ **1505** Guild of Surgeon-Barbers of Edinburgh is granted a monopoly for making *aqua vitae*

of Cause of the Town Council was the exclusive right to "mak and sell *aqua vitae* within the burgh" – further evidence of its connection with medical uses. Some say that the surgeons used *aqua vitae* for preserving parts of the body prior to dissection.

The invention of effective ways of condensing the spirit that came off when a mildly alcoholic wash was boiled, and the discovery of the advantages of concentrating this spirit by further distillation, was crucial to producing a potable liquid, rather than medicine or embalming fluid. Early alembics were small and relied upon the surrounding air to cool and condense the vapours. During the fifteenth century the benefit of cooling the condenser in a tub of water was recognised, but it was only in the middle years of the sixteenth century that this tube was coiled into a "worm" within the cooling tub. At about the same time the still head was elongated into a pear shape, which increased the reflux of condensate back into the body of the still, permitting better separation of spirit from water and reducing the carry-over of noxious impurities. These were major breakthroughs in the production of better quality spirit.

In 1560 the monasteries were dissolved in Scotland, although not as ruthlessly as in England, and there was a move away from the cloister into the community by numerous monks whose knowledge of distilling was eagerly embraced by the laity. From this time, wherever suitable cereals were grown, domestic distilling became part of the farming year, as brewing had long been. Indeed, so widespread had the practice become by 1579 that, in anticipation of a poor harvest and food shortages, an Act of Parliament restricted the manufacture of *aqua vitae* throughout the land, limiting it to "Earls, Lords, Barons and Gentlemen for their own use".

Fynes Moryson, a late-Elizabethan travel writer, records that three kinds of spirit were distilled in the Western Isles, graded for strength and quality by the number of times they were distilled. They were *usquebaugh* (distilled twice), *trestarig* (distilled three times) and *usquebaugh-baul*, (distilled four times); also termed

Some say that the surgeons used aqua vitae for preserving parts of the body prior to dissection.

■ **1527** *The Vetuose Boke of Distyllacyon* by Heironymous Braunschweig is published in English, the first book on the subject   ■ **1579** Act of the Scottish Parliament restricts the making of *aqua vitae*, on account of poor harvests

RIGHT Early stills were charged by removing the head. This one dates from the late seventeenth century.

simplex, composita and *perfectissima*. Raphael Holinshed in his *Chronicles* of 1577 – famous as one of Shakespeare's sources – distinguishes the same three grades, and stresses the medicinal value of the spirit:

> "*Being moderately taken it cutteth fleume, it lighteneth the mynd, it quickeneth the spirits, it cureth the hydropsie, it pounceth the stone, it repelleth the gravel, it puffeth away ventositie, it kepyth and preserveth the eyes from dazelying, the tongue from lispying, the teeth from chatterying, the throte from rattlying, the weasan from stieflying, the stomach from womblying, the harte from swellying, the belie from wirtching, the guts from rumblying, the hands from shivering, the sinews from shrinkying, the veynes from crumplying, the bones from akying, the marrow from soakying, and truly it is a sovereign liquor, if it be orderlie taken.*"

■ **1590** Fynes Moryson records the exporting of *aqua vitae* to Ireland   ■ **1609** The statutes of Iona "legalise" the distilling of whisky in the Highlands and Islands   ■ **1618** Earliest reference to *uisge* being drunk, at the funeral of a Highland chief

These early forms of whisky were made from a mixture of whatever cereals came to hand most readily – oats and wheat as well as more than one kind of barley. Furthermore, it is certain that much of the spirit was "compounded" (ie. mixed with herbs, sugar and spices) and even "rectified" (re-distilled with botanical additions, in the same way that gin is made). Some authorities, including the great lexicographer Dr Johnson in his *Dictionary* (1755), go so far as to define usquebaugh as "a compounded distilled spirit, being drawn on aromaticks". By the late sixteenth century production was such that Scotch *aqua vitae* or *uisge beatha* was being exported to Ireland and to France.

UISGE BEATHA

Loosely defined though it might have been, employing varying ingredients with varying flavours from district to district, the Water of Life was an established part of the social life and economy of Scotland by the early seventeenth century. It was made on farms and in castles up and down the land, especially in the Highlands, during the autumn and winter months when the grain had been harvested. This pattern persisted until modern times. The high protein barley husks and spent grains were also an important form of animal feed during the sparse winter months. The spirit was made on small stills of between 20 and 50 gallons (90 and 220 litres) capacity with cylindrical bodies, charged by removing their heads, which were either domed or conical. This was a part-time cottage industry with only a handful of dedicated "distilleries".

The quantity of whisky made by each household or community depended upon the surplus grain available, but there was usually enough to supply local needs, with some left over to contribute to rents and even to export to the Lowlands, England and France. Contemporary references to Scotch spirits are few – a Highland funeral here, a wedding there, rewards for recruits to the army – yet production was sufficient to persuade the Scottish Parliament to impose the first excise tax on spirits in 1644, at the rate of 2/8d (Scots) per Scots pint (in English measures, about 7d per gallon), in order to raise money for the army of the Covenant ranged

■ **1655** Robert Haig rebuked by the Kirk for distilling on the Sabbath   ■ **1644** An Act of the Scottish Parliament is passed, imposing duty on spirits to raise money for the army of the Covenant against Charles I. This tax was retained after the Restoration of the monarchy and has been with us ever since, despite being universally resented.

The first distillery mentioned in an official document was that at Ferintosh, on the Black Isle, established by Duncan Forbes of Culloden in about 1670. Forbes was a prominent Whig and a supporter of William of Orange and as a result his distillery was sacked by supporters of James II in 1689. Once the rising had been quelled, he claimed compensation and was granted the privilege of distilling whisky duty free "from grain grown on his own estate... upon payment of an annual sum of 400 merks" (about £22). The dispensation remained in force for 95 years, and made the Forbes family a fortune. They bought neighbouring lands, built three more distilleries on the estate and began to produce whisky in large quantities, and to sell it all over Scotland.

So successful were they that the very word "Ferintosh" became synonymous with quality. By the late 1760s Ferintosh distillery was producing almost two-thirds of the legally distilled whisky in Scotland – some 90,000 gallons (409,000 litres) annually. The Forbes family was reputed to be making an annual profit of £18,000 – equivalent to about £2 million per annum in today's money. In 1784 the Government terminated the privilege with a lump sum payment of £21,000, an event lamented by Robert Burns:

> "Thee Ferintosh! O sadly lost!
> Scotland lament frae coast to coast!
> Now colic grip, an' barkin' hoast
> May kill us a';
> For loyal Forbes' charter'd boast
> Is ta'en awa."

PEAT-REEK AND FIREWATER

Following the union of the parliaments of England and Scotland in 1707, duty on excisable liquors was levied at the same rate as in England and a Scottish Excise Board, manned by English

■ **1655** Excise duty is reduced to 2d per gallon ■ **1661** Act imposed stating that two ounces of bullion be paid to the Mint for each ten gallon barrel of *aqua vitae* exported ■ **1688** The first attempt is made to charge duty according to the strength of the spirit ■ **1713** The English malt tax is extended to Scotland

DOCTOR PROSODY

LEFT A satirical scene depicting Johnson and Boswell in a smuggler's lair at the time of their Hebridean tour.

officials, was established in Edinburgh. Six years later the English malt tax was extended to Scotland (although at half the English rate) in the face of vehement opposition from Scottish MPs, who claimed this was in breach of the Act of Union.

This and other vindictive measures fuelled support for the First Jacobite Rising of 1715, which petered out later the same year after the Battle of Sheriffmuir. When the Malt Tax was increased in 1725 there were serious riots in Glasgow, but the ultimate effect of this was to reduce the quantity of ale, which was the staple drink of the populace, and increase the consumption of whisky. Legal output doubled, then tripled in the mid-1720s to nearly 155,000 gallons (700,000 litres). Following the Gin Act of 1736, which did not apply to Scotland, production again increased.

This growth was made possible by the use of mixed cereals; unmalted barley and wheat as well as malted barley. There was a dramatic increase in small and medium-sized distilleries all over the country and, towards the end of the century, a rise in the number of Lowland manufactories, mainly owned by the Haig and Stein families. Domestic stills were exempt from duty, so long as they used home-grown grains and produced for domestic

■ 1725 Walpole introduces a measure to tax malt in Scotland at the English rate, 6d per bushel, resulting in the Shawfield Riots in Glasgow ■ 1736 The year of the Porteous Riot in Edinburgh, when Captain Porteous was lynched after he ordered the City Guard to fire into the crowd

consumption only. It was illegal to sell the whisky, although it was itself a currency in the Highlands, often being used for part-payment of rents.

Crop failure in 1757 led to a ban on distilling throughout Britain which continued until 1760, and forced most of the registered distilleries out of business. Home stills were unaffected by the ban and began to meet the demand for whisky. These were the beginnings of the "smuggling" era.

To counter the rise in the illicit trade, and the competition from the duty-free output of the Ferintosh distilleries which, as we have seen, were producing two thirds of the legal whisky in Scotland by 1770, many legal distilleries had to resort to fraud in their excise declarations. The government passed a series of increasingly draconian measures in the attempt to prevent this, forbidding distilling in wash stills of less than 400 gallons (1,818 litres) capacity and ordering that the heads of stills should be padlocked and sealed, to prevent the stills being used without the authorities' knowledge. This simply encouraged smuggling and discouraged producers from taking out licences. Hugo Arnot estimated in his *History of Edinburgh*, that there were 400 illicit stills in the city in 1777 and only eight licensed. Led by the Haig and Stein families, by now the major producers of legal whisky, the registered distillers formed a monopoly to flood the Lowland market with raw and fiery, but cheap, grain spirit. The unpleasant flavour of most of the whisky produced at this time was made palatable, certainly amongst the gentry and in many public houses, by mixing it with other ingredients such as lemon and spices, or with warm water and sugar, and serving it as "punch" or "toddy".

In 1777 the Steins experimented with exporting 2,000 gallons (9,100 litres) of their rough spirit to London for rectification and compounding into gin. This was hugely successful; within five years the export had grown to nearly 184,000 gallons (835,360 litres). The 1783 harvest was disastrous, however, and the Highlands were gripped by famine. Distilling was banned in many places and duty was again raised. Rioters sacked the Haig distillery

---

■ **1751** Gilcomston distillery, Aberdeen is founded   ■ **1757** Distilling is banned (until 1760) on account of bad harvests   ■ **1774** All wash stills less than 400 gallons (1,818 litres) and spirit stills less than 100 gallons (455 litres) are prohibited   ■ **1779** All duties are increased by five per cent; malt duty by 15 per cent; private distilling permitted in two gallon (nine litre) stills

at Canonmills in Edinburgh, suspecting that it was using grain and vegetables which might otherwise have fed the poor.

William Pitt's Wash Act of 1784 cut duty, and allied it to still capacity and to the amount of wash that could be distilled off each day. It also introduced the Highland Line, making different provisions for distilleries located above and below the line. Highland distillers were favoured with lower tax and were allowed to use smaller stills (minimum 20 gallons or 91 litres capacity), which they charged with weak washes and worked off slowly, producing flavoursome whisky. However, the Act insisted that they use only locally grown grain and forbade them to export their product outwith the region. The Lowland distillers responded to

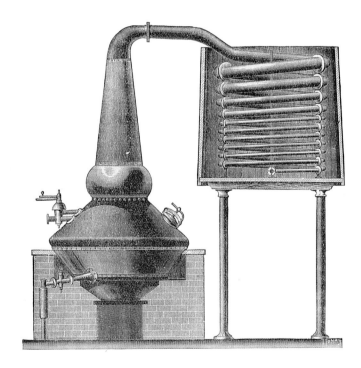

LEFT Engraving of a pot still with worm tub attached, circa 1870s..

■ **1781** Private distilling is made illegal for the first time. Until now, distilling for domestic consumption, free of duty, had been permitted ■ **1784** The Wash Act defines the Highland Line, lowers duty and pegs it to still capacity; riots occur at Haig's Canonmills distillery, Edinburgh

the Act by using stronger, thicker washes and developing a new kind of still – shallow and wide-bodied, with a large base and tall head – which could be worked off in a matter of minutes. Since there is less fractionation in rapid distilling, the quality of Lowland whisky was further impaired. Highland whisky was infinitely preferable but it was not available legally in the Lowlands.

THE SMUGGLING ERA

The benefits that maturation brought to wine were generally recognised by about 1740, and it is safe to suppose that Highland connoisseurs will have experimented successfully with laying down casks of whisky, at least by the late eighteenth century. The majority of spirit however was sold "straight from the still mouth" and in 1814 public houses in Glasgow proudly advertised that they were selling whisky distilled from that summer's barley, less than six weeks after the Highland harvest had been taken in. Such whisky was reckoned to be "wholesome, palatable and medicinal in moderation", while Lowland whisky was judged "obnoxiously the reverse"! A contemporary observer remarked: "Whisky in those days being chiefly drawn from the flat-bottomed stills of Kilbagie, Kennerpans and Lochryan was only fitted for the most vulgar and fire-loving palates; but when a little of the real mountain dew from Glenlivet or Arran could be obtained, which was a matter of difficulty and danger, it was sure to be presented to guests with as sparing a hand as the finest Maraschino is now offered by some laced lacquey... at the close of a first class repast."

Lowland distillers survived by making gut-rot, and Highland distillers were not legally permitted to sell their better product below the Highland Line.

By the 1790s the situation was impossible. Lowland distillers survived by making rot-gut, and Highland distillers were not legally permitted to sell their better product below the Highland Line. The powerful English distillers dropped their prices to quell the flow of whisky flooding south and put pressure on the government to drive out the Scots. They succeeded in this in 1788. The Government imposed excise duties on everything they could think of, including bricks, candles, calico, paper, salt, soap, hides and leather, in order to prosecute the war against France, and when they could no longer be increased in number, they were

■ **1788** Lowland Licence Act requires Lowland distillers to give 12 months notice of supplying the English market. This effectively prevents them from making whisky for at least a year. Many go bankrupt as a result

LEFT A report on
smuggling whisky
from The Scotsman
newspaper, March 1823.

The United Associate Congregation in St Andrew's, gave a unanimous call on Wednesday last to Mr Ebenezer Halley, preacher of the gospel, to be their minister. The reverend Mr Thom of Anstruther preached, and the reverend Mr Taylor of Ceres presided.

ILLICIT DISTILLATION.—On the evening of the 4th inst. Mr Samuel Milligan, Supervisor of Excise, Paisley, received information that an illicit distillery was at work in a cottage adjoining the Mansion House of Carrdonald. Mr Milligan immediately proceeded to the spot, accompanied by Messrs A. Clerk, E. Cameron, P. M'Lellan, H. Cogan, A. Lang, W. Shorman, and W. Foreman, officers of excise, when they detected a private distillery, carried on with systematic regularity, consisting of one still, contents 60 gallons, one still head, one worm, one worm tub, one mash tun, two wash tuns and 100 gallons of worts, &c. all of which were effectually destroyed. Two of the smugglers were taken before one of his Majesty's Justices of the Peace, for the county of Renfrew, and they having failed to pay the penalty of L30, each were committed to the jail of Paisley. Mr Milligan's exertions in banishing the baneful traffic from our doors, have been indefatigable, for which he deserves the praise of every good member of society.

FIFE CAUSE.—Appeals have been presented to the House of Lords against the decision of the Judges of the Court of Session in Scotland, which lately (confirming the judgment of the Jury Court upon the " issue" directed by the House of Lords to be tried, which was to establish, whether the deeds executed by the late Earl of Fife were his deeds or not) found that these were not his lordship's deeds, and gave the cause

■ **1793** War breaks out with France; tax on whisky trebles in the Lowlands to £9 per annum per gallon of still capacity

raised in rate. Meanwhile the smugglers became bolder, often condoned by the landowners, from whose ranks Justices of the Peace were appointed, and who themselves benefited from the illicit trade by being able to increase rents with some hope of obtaining payment.

An official report of 1790 describes smugglers as "travelling in bands of 50, 80, or 100 or 150 horses remarkably stout and fleet and having the audacity to go in this formidable manner in the open day upon the public high roads and through the streets of such towns and villages as they have occasion to pass."

The Government was bereft of ideas about how to cope with the situation. Duty was tripled in 1793 to £9 per gallon of still capacity, doubled again in 1795 and again in 1800. Further increases took place in 1804, 1811 and 1814. The Small Stills Act of 1816 abolished the Highland Line and permitted the use throughout Scotland of stills of not less than 40 gallons (180 litres) capacity. It also allowed weaker washes and reduced duty by about a third. As a result, the number of legal distilleries increased from 12 to 57 in the Highlands by 1819, and from 24 to 68 in the Lowlands.

There was growing concern among landowners in the Highlands about the growth of violent crime, mostly associated with food shortages, evictions and land clearances for sheep parks, but much of it blamed on the lawless smugglers. Also, improved communications with the Lowlands encouraged a number of lairds to establish their own legal distilleries which, of course, competed with the smugglers. The Fourth Duke of Gordon, one of the most powerful landowners in the northeast, addressed the House of Lords on the subject in 1820, urging a further reduction of duty and a more moderate attitude towards legal distillers, in return for which he pledged that the landowners would cooperate with the excise officers in putting down smuggling.

A Commission of Inquiry into the Revenue was set up, under the chairmanship of Lord Wallace, and based on its findings the Excise Act of 1823 more than halved duty on spirits to 2/5d per gallon and set the licence fee at £10 per annum. The Act

---

■ **1795** Tax on whisky doubles to £18; in 1797 tax trebles again to £54 per annum ■ **1800** Tax doubles again to £108; by 1803 it was £162 per annum per gallon of still capacity ■ **1811** Duty on spirits exported to England increases by 2/- per gallon ■ **1814** Excise Act prohibits stills under 500 gallons capacity in the Highlands, amounting to an interdict on distilling there; Matthew Gloag establishes his grocer's business in Perth

sanctioned thin washes, introduced duty-free warehousing for
export spirits, and opened the export trade to all. These changes
laid the foundations of the modern whisky industry.

No longer was it necessary to design and operate stills
primarily to avoid paying tax; no longer need there be a
difference in quality between legally produced whisky and illicit
whisky and no longer was it so desirable to work outside the
law. Distillers could now choose their own method of working;
what strength of wash to use and what size and design of still
would produce the best whisky.

BLENDED WHISKY

Between 1823 and 1825 the number of licensed distilleries in
Scotland rose from 125 to 329; 100 of these would not last beyond
ten years. Many of the newly entered distillers were former
smugglers, although this was not without its dangers from jealous
neighbours. Among the first to take out a licence was George
Smith of Glenlivet, a remote district of Speyside, where there
were as many as 200 illicit stills operating in the early 1820s. His
neighbours warned him that they would burn the new distillery to
the ground – a fate that befell several others – and he was obliged
to carry a pair of hair-trigger pistols in his belt for some years.

New distilleries were often built on sites which had formerly
been used by smugglers, not only on account of the water supply,
but also because of established connections with local farms for
the supply of grain, and the disposal of draff. Similarly, distilleries
were often built near drovers' inns, which had long been a source
of custom before the days of licensed distilling.

Some landowners in the Highlands also set up distilleries on
their estates, notably Lord Lovat at Beauly, the Duke of Argyll at
Campbeltown, (where 27 distilleries were established between
1823 and 1837), Mackenzie of Seaforth in Lewis and Campbell
of Shawfield in Islay. All hoped that these ventures would be
profitable since smuggling had been suppressed – convictions in
magistrates' courts fell from 14,000 in 1823 to 85 in 1832. However,
the sharp increase in production from almost three million gallons

*Distilleries were
often built near
drovers' inns,
which had long
been a source
of custom
before the days
of licensed
distilling.*

■ **1816** Sykes hydrometer is adopted for measuring alcoholic strength; Small Stills Act is introduced
■ **1822** Illicit Distillation (Scotland) Act abolishes the Highland/Lowland distinction and dramatically increases
penalties for illicit distilling   ■ **1823** The Excise Act reduces duty to 2/- per gallon, imposed in an annual
licence fee of £10. This massively stimulates legal distilling   ■ **1826** Robert Stein takes out a patent for a
continuous still

ABOVE FROM LEFT
Andrew Usher II (1826-98); William Teacher (1810/11-1876); Arthur Bell (1825-1900); John Dewar (1806-80).

(13.5 million litres) in 1823 to ten million gallons (45.5 million litres) in 1828 was nowhere near matched by demand. Most of this was grain whisky, made in the Lowlands by the large distillers and exported to England for rectification. Ninety per cent of malt whisky was consumed in Scotland.

A general trade depression in 1829 combined with pressure from the English brewers and distillers to persuade the Duke of Wellington's government to increase duty on spirits and to remove duty on beer in the 1830 Budget. The Lowland grain distillers were undaunted by this. Several of them had been experimenting successfully with continuous distillation. This process used stills which were radically different and had been patented firstly by Robert Stein of Kilbagie in 1827 and perfected by Aeneas Coffey, former Inspector General of Excise in Dublin, in 1830. Although expensive to install, such stills were cheap and simple to control. They produced strong (94 to 96% ABV), pure and bland spirit at a furious rate, since they did not have to be cleaned and re-charged after each batch. In the Highlands, meanwhile, there was widespread distress owing to bad harvests from the late 1830s to about 1850, compounded by the potato blight in the mid-1840s. Between 1835 and 1844, the number of licensed distilleries fell from 230 to 169 and many firms were forced into liquidation.

Distillers large and small sold their products in bulk, by the cask. Patent-still grain whisky had a market among poorer people in the Central Lowlands, but the majority of it went south of the

■ **1827** George Ballantine founds his business as a grocer and spirit dealer in Edinburgh ■ **1830** William Teacher opens a licensed grocer's in Glasgow ■ **1830** Aeneas Coffey patents his continuous still for grain whisky ■ **1836** The Parnell Commission of Enquiry into the Liquor Trade is held; the first Coffey still in Scotland is installed at Grange distillery, Alloa ■ **1839** James Chivas founds his firm of grocers and wine merchants in Aberdeen ■ **1846** John Dewar establishes his own business as a wine and spirits merchant in Perth

border to England for rectification into gin. Some malt distillers appointed agents; most sold direct to wine and spirits merchants, who sold the whisky to their customers in stoneware jars holding eight and ten gallons (45.5 litres) or, increasingly after 1845, in glass bottles. Prior to this glass was prohibitively expensive but in that year the duty on it was abolished.

Many spirits merchants were also grocers, selling tea and coffee and general provisions as well as alcohol, and generally known as "Italian Warehousemen". Almost all of the great names in the whisky industry began as such. Matthew Gloag, whose grandson created The Famous Grouse blend, had his own shop by about 1814. Charles Mackinlay was an apprentice with the tea, wine and spirit merchant Walker, Johnston & Co in 1824. Johnnie Walker opened his grocer's shop in Kilmarnock in 1820, George Ballantine in Edinburgh in 1827. In 1828, John Dewar walked to Perth to work in a relative's wine and spirit shop. Arthur Bell was first employed as a travelling salesman by Thomas Sandeman, wine merchant in Perth in the 1830s. James Chivas and his brother arrived in Aberdeen in 1836; James went to work in a wine and spirits shop, which he took over in 1841.

The random mixing of whiskies from various different distilleries had long been practised – even the mixing of whisky with other spirits or herbs – but this was invariably in the interest of producing a cheaper drink, of debatable quality. Nevertheless it is safe to suppose that some spirits merchants did experiment with mixing whiskies for the more discriminating end of the market. In 1853 the mixing together of whiskies of different ages from the same distillery, called vatting, was permitted before duty had to be paid.

The same year Andrew Usher and Company, the Edinburgh-based agent for Smith's Glenlivet, put the first true brand of Scotch whisky on the market. It was called Usher's Old Vatted Glenlivet and became one of the most popular whiskies of its day.

The blending of several different malts with cheaper, blander grain whisky was the next logical step, and was pioneered by Andrew Usher II, Charles Mackinlay and WP Lowrie. Gladstone's

■ **1847** Charles Mackinlay & Co is established   ■ **1851** Arthur Bell becomes a partner in the firm he had joined in the mid-1830s and was later to own   ■ **1853** Andrew Usher creates the first true blended whisky; tax increases to 4/3d per proof gallon   ■ **1856** The First Trade Agreement between grain distillers is reached   ■ **1860** Gladstone's Spirits Act raises duty to 10/- per gallon, but allows blending in bond, which leads to a dramatic increase in blending

RIGHT Usher's warehouse, in Edinburgh for "Old Vatted Glenlivet", circa 1890..

Spirits Act of 1860 allowed blending under bond, which made it possible to produce blended whisky in substantial volumes for the first time. Blended whisky had three great virtues: it had broader appeal than the strongly flavoured, smoky malts or fiery grain whiskies of the day; it could be made up to a formula so that its flavour remained consistent; and it was cheap to produce.

The coming of the railway both facilitated the spirits dealers' access to supplies of whisky for "fillings", and allowed them to send their products to a wider market. The Edinburgh to Glasgow railway opened in 1842 and by 1846 the capital was linked to Newcastle. In 1850, the line between Perth and Aberdeen was laid, and in 1854 a branch line to Huntly and later to Keith, in the heart of the whisky country, was added.

The repeal of the Navigation Acts in 1845 also opened up the export market to the colonies and dominions, and within ten years grain whisky was being exported to Canada, India, New Zealand and South Africa in relatively large quantities, mainly for consumption by expatriate Scots. Blended whisky would soon follow and from then onwards the fortunes of distillers – of both malt and grain whisky – were tied to the blenders.

By the end of the century and right through to the late 1970s, around 99 per cent of the malt whisky made went for blending. Blended whisky put Scotch onto the world stage.

Sir Robert Usher, Andrew Usher II's son, wrote in 1908: "Before 1860 very little Scotch whisky was sent for sale in England [ie.

■ **1863** John Dewar begins to use paper labels   ■ **1867** Alexander Walker trademarks his slanting label (still in use)   ■ **1869** Cragganmore distillery built   ■ **1875** Glenglassaugh distillery built   ■ **1876** Glenlossie distillery built

as such and not for rectification into gin], but after that the trade increased in leaps and bounds." Sir Winston Churchill, a keen whisky drinker, supported this view in 1945: "My father would never have drunk whisky except when shooting on a moor or in some very dull, chilly place. He lived in the age of brandy and soda."

With the advent of blending, it became possible to create a consistent product economically in large quantities with broad appeal in terms of flavour. Because blended whisky brings together the varied and variable products of several distilleries, it is possible to achieve consistency of flavour. And since customers could now rely on their favourite blend tasting the same, time and again, the door was opened to branding and large scale marketing. What is more, the extensive development of railway networks in Europe and the USA, and the fast, reliable steamship services to connect with these networks, made a world market possible. Scotch whisky was poised to conquer the world.

And since customers could now rely on their favourite blend tasting the same, the door was opened to branding and large scale marketing.

THE WHISKY BOOM

The 1870s and 1880s was an era of great confidence in Scotland. Glasgow was "the second city of the Empire"; following the example of the Queen-Empress, all things Scottish became fashionable; hundreds of well-to-do and influential Englishmen travelled north each autumn to fish and shoot.

The era produced a large number of remarkably able Scots: Lord Lister, the "Father of Antiseptics"; Lord Kelvin, "the architect of nineteenth-century physics"; Alexander Graham Bell; Sir William Arroll (builder of "the eighth wonder of the world", the Forth Railway Bridge); David Livingstone; Sir Thomas Lipton (inventor of multiple retailing) and Sir William Burrell the shipping magnate, to name but a few.

Their like was matched by their contemporaries in the whisky trade, many of whose brands are still household names today; men like John and Thomas Dewar (Dewar's White Label), James Buchanan (The Buchanan Blend), Alexander Walker (Johnnie Walker), Peter Mackie (White Horse) and Thomas Sandeman

■ **1877** The Distillers Company Limited is founded ■ **1879** "Black Bottle" is registered by Gordon Graham & Co, Aberdeen ■ **1880** Johnnie Walker's London office opens; a court rules that the name "The Glenlivet" may only be used by George and JG Smith

(VAT 69). Their ability and vigour was phenomenal, and their efforts were greatly assisted by nature in the form of a tiny louse, *Phylloxera vastatrix*. From the mid-1860s the vineyards of France were devastated by this pest, and during the 1880s those in Grande Champagne, the vineyards supplying the great Cognac houses, were ruined, thus ceasing production of Cognac and denying the English middle classes their favourite tipple – brandy and soda. Blended whisky, also drunk with soda, was there to replace it.

Not all buyers of bulk whisky were as scrupulous as the blending companies. As whisky became more popular, pubs and spirits shops catering for the poorer classes in the major cities bought the cheapest spirit they could lay their hands on and added substances to it to make it palatable. There was no legislation to control this and no minimum age limit at which the spirit must be sold. Prune wine and sherry essence were added to counteract fusel-oil; glycerine, burnt sugar and green tea to give body and colour; tartaric and acetic acid, sugar, pineapple and other fruit essences to add sweetness and flavour. More ominous additions were acetic ether, turpentine, varnish, naphtha (the source of methyl alcohol) and even sulphuric acid to help with beading and alcoholic affect.

This was all perfectly legal, although by the 1870s it was giving grave cause for concern. Charles Cameron, editor of *The North British Daily Mail*, and himself a doctor, undertook it upon himself to investigate and expose the worst excesses of adulteration in Glasgow. He recruited the help of Dr James Gray, an analytical chemist, and together they collected samples of whisky from numerous establishments in the city, publishing their results in the *Mail* between April and October 1872. There were howls of protest from the licensed trade and others and the affair quickly petered out. Further samples were analysed by the industrial chemist RR Tatlock for the Inland Revenue but showed nothing untoward, so it may be assumed that the practice ceased.

One effect it did have, though, was in the area of branding and marketing. Over the next two decades there was a greatly

---

■ **1882** James Whyte and Charles Mackay establish themselves as whisky merchants and register their own brand, "Whyte & Mackay Special Reserve"; William Sanderson creates "Vat 69"; James Buchanan creates "The Buchanan Blend", aka "Black & White"

LEFT The distinctive pagoda roofs of Strathisla distillery.

increased use of bottles, with driven corks sealed with metal capsules. The words "pure", "wholesome", "fine old", and so on, were often used on whisky labels. Distillers, blenders and merchants' names became more conspicuous and testimonials from public analysts were common.

During the 1860s many malt whisky distilleries were rebuilt and modernised, and production doubled during the decade. The first new distillery to take advantage of the Strathspey railway was built at Cragganmore on Speyside. A new peak was reached in 1877, and this led to a further spate of building and reconstruction, on a scale not seen for half a century. Eleven distilleries were opened

■ **1883** James Logan Mackie creates "White Horse'" ■ **1885** Arthur Bell's sons take control of the business

"The notion that we can possibly develop a palate for whisky is guaranteed to produce a smile of derision in any company except that of a few Scottish lairds, farmers, gamekeepers and baillies, relics of a vanished age of gold when the vintages of the north had their students and lovers."

Aeneas
MacDonald
Whisky
1930

during the 1870s and 1880s, mostly by blending companies, to secure supplies of fillings. However, the high productivity of the continuous still brought problems of over-capacity and thus market instability.

In 1877 the principal grain whisky producers – Port Dundas, Carsebridge, Cameron Bridge, Glenochil, Cambus and Kirkliston Distilleries – amalgamated to form the Distillers Company Limited (DCL), in order to achieve self-regulation and prevent trade wars. The DCL would later play a crucial role in the history of the Scotch whisky industry.

Between 1884 and 1888 a brief but general depression led to several amalgamations and take-overs which strengthened the ties between blenders and distillers. In 1885 spirits generated just under £14 million for the Exchequer – nearly one sixth of the entire national revenue, and more than enough to pay for the Royal Navy at the height of the Empire!

Such was the demand for blended whisky in the 1890s, and so safe was the industry regarded by investors, that distillery construction amounted to a mania. Speyside was the preferred location; the delicate, sweet, complex style of "Glenlivet" whiskies, as Speysides were generically referred to at the time, suited the needs of blenders better that the more robust west coast malts or the blander Lowlanders.

One of the achievements of the pioneers was to tailor blends to appeal to southern or overseas palates. Smoothness was read as a sign of quality in a blend, and the malts of Speyside bestowed such mellowness. Increasing emphasis was placed on the benefit of maturation in ex-sherry casks, to achieve the same goal. Two decades before, the demand was for powerful, peaty, spicy Island and Campbeltown malts, which could "cover" a high proportion of grain whisky, which in some cases made up to 95 per cent of a blend. Only a handful of malts were promoted as "singles", such as Smith's Glenlivet, Glen Grant, Highland Park and Bowmore.

The demand for lightly peated malts led to the development of the high, pagoda-roofed kilns that allow more ventilation and

---

■ **1887** Highland Distilleries is founded   ■ **1893** "Dimple"/"Pinch" is first registered as a brand by Haig & Haig

LEFT A poster for the Conservative Party from the 1909 General Election, objecting to Lloyd George's budget 1909.

which have since become the architectural motif of malt whisky distilleries. The whisky commentator Alfred Barnard observed during his tour of distilleries in the late 1880s, "It is considered [that the height of the roofs is] of great advantage where peats are used solely, as it gives the malt a delicate aroma without having to use coke to prevent the flavour being too pronounced." Even at that date peat was the universal fuel for drying the malt. Barnard

■ **1894** "The Grouse Brand" is introduced by Matthew Gloag II. By 1900 it had been re-named "The Famous Grouse" ■ **1899** Pattison, Elder & Company of Leith collapses

ABOVE The
characteristic Haig's
"Pinch" or "Dimple"
bottle; the first bottle
shape to be patented in
the USA.

found only two distilleries in the Highlands which dried their malt over a mixture of coke and peat, and two more where coke was the principal fuel used.

We cannot know for certain but this does suggest that the Highland malt whisky drunk by our forebears must have been more phenolic than anything we know today, although I have tasted a Macallan distilled as long ago as 1874 which had little or no discernible smoky character.

In the late 1880s pot still malt whisky accounted for 37 per cent of the spirits made in Scotland; the remainder was patent still grain spirit. The domination of the market by the grain whisky producers and the blenders, and the practice of using very little malt in some blends, made the independent malt distillers nervous. In 1890 they sought to limit the definition of Scotch whisky to the product of the pot still. A Select Committee was set up under the chairmanship of Sir Lionel Playfair which found against them and allowed blended whisky to be described as Scotch. All looked rosy for the blenders. But the bubble was bound to burst; stocks were built up to absurd levels and output jumped from 19 million gallons (85 million litres) in 1889 to almost twice that in ten years.

And burst it did, dramatically, with the collapse of the most flamboyant of the blending companies: Pattison, Elder & Company of Leith. Even in an age of extrovert entrepreneurs, the controlling directors, Walter and Robert Pattison, were reckoned to take conspicuous consumption too far. In 1898 they were said to have spent £60,000 on advertising. One of the company's stunts was to train 500 grey parrots to recite "Pattisons' is best". Robert Pattison spent a fortune on his mansion near Peebles, some 35 kilometres (19 miles) from Edinburgh, and if he missed the last train home, it was said that he simply hired another!

To finance their operations the brothers sold stock and bought it back at inflated prices by obtaining Bills of Exchange which were later discounted. They also over-valued property and paid dividends from capital. By the time liquidation proceedings began in December 1898, there was a shortfall of £500,000; their assets were worth less than half this amount.

■ **1900** Duty per proof gallon is raised to 11/-   ■ **1904** Arthur Bell & Sons introduces "Bell's Special Reserve"   ■ **1905** Islington Borough Council instigates the "What is Whisky?" case   ■ **1906** Dewar's introduces "White Label"

MALT WHISKY

It is likely that the whisky boom of the 1890s would have expended itself without the collapse of Pattisons of Leith. Stocks and production levels were completely out of balance with sales, and besides this there was a dramatic downturn in the British economy after 1900. The number of operating distilleries dropped from 161 in 1899 to 132 in 1908, and during these years it became increasingly difficult to sell at a profit the large stocks of mature malt whisky accumulated during the 1890s. The malt distillers were nervous about their complete reliance upon the blenders being able to win new customers, and looked back wistfully to the days when they controlled the industry.

In an effort to regain some of that control they stepped up their demand that the term whisky was limited to malt whisky only, and during 1903 orchestrated a campaign in the press promoting their case. Not surprisingly, the blenders supported the grain whisky producers. The debate smouldered on through 1904 and 1905; then, in October that year, the London Borough of Islington raised a prosecution under the Food & Drugs Act 1875 against two wine and spirit merchants for retailing whisky "not of the nature, substance and quality demanded". Their blends contained only ten per cent malt to 90 per cent grain, although this proportion was not uncommon for cheaper blends, even those made by reputable companies. In spite of the DCL paying for the defence, the case was lost and in February 1908, on the petition of all parties (malt distillers, grain distillers and blenders), a Royal Commission was set up to investigate Whisky and Other Potable Spirits. It reported in July 1909 that the term "Scotch whisky" embraced malt, grain and blended whisky, no matter how little malt was in the blend.

By the time the "What is Whisky?" question had been answered, the industry had a far graver problem to face. In April 1909, Lloyd George, Liberal Chancellor of the Exchequer and himself a teetotaller from a strict Temperance family, presented his "People's Budget". Among other major reforms, this introduced old-age pensions, unemployment benefit and national insurance, and – partly to pay for these measures – increased duty on spirits by

■ **1908** The Royal Commission on Whisky decides that grain and malt (and thus blended) can be described as "Whisky" ■ **1909** Johnnie Walker introduces "Red Label" and "Black Label"; the People's Budget raises tax to 14/9d

RIGHT
Advertisement
for Pattison's
Scotch Whisky,
from *The Graphic*,
London 1898.

■ **1913** William Manera Bergius of Teacher's invents the replaceable stopper cork   ■ **1915** The Central Control Board (Liquor Traffic) is set up; Buchanan's and Dewar's merge

a third. Peter Mackie of White Horse commented, "The whole framing of the Budget is that of a faddist and a crank and not a statesman. But what can one expect of a Welsh country solicitor, without any commercial training, as Chancellor of the Exchequer in a large country like this?" The Budget was thrown out by the House of Lords, but the Prime Minister, Herbert Asquith, went to the country looking for a mandate to limit the power of the Upper House in relation to finance. He won the election with a majority of two, and the Budget was passed. One contemporary observer later noted: "From that date the home trade began to sicken, and there has been a continual if irregular decline ever since."

Matters were to get worse. In August 1914, the First World War broke out, and when victory was not secured by Christmas, as expected, the British Expeditionary Force became bogged down in Flanders and so short of shells that it amounted to a national scandal. The Government sought a scapegoat, and came up with the notion that munitions workers – prosperous in comparison with their pre-war condition – were producing insufficient arms because they were drinking too much strong liquor, which was leading to inefficiency and absenteeism. This ridiculous argument was supported by the fact that the consumption of whisky had increased with the rise in wages.

"Drink is doing more damage in the war than all the German submarines put together," said Lloyd George, and proposed that duty be doubled. When faced with a rebellion in the House, he established the Central Control Board (Liquor Traffic) which more or less took over management of the whisky trade. In 1916 it cut pot still production by 30 per cent, and the following year banned it altogether. It also ruled that the strength at which spirits were sold should be 40% ABV, and 26% ABV in "munitions areas", which embraced all the large centres of population.

In 1918 exports were forbidden, duty was doubled (to £1.10/- per proof gallon) and prices were fixed, so that the producers could not pass the tax on to the consumer. Whisky consumption in the home market dropped to ten million gallons (45 million

In 1918 exports were forbidden, duty was doubled and prices were fixed, so that producers could not pass the tax on to the consumer.

■ **1917** The Whisky Association is formed

43

litres) and although the ban on distilling was lifted in 1919, overall production fell to 13 million gallons (59 million litres).

PROHIBITION

In the autumn of 1920, the world economy slipped into a recession which would last for the rest of the decade. The same year the US government moved to prohibit the import of alcoholic beverages, except under special licence for medicinal purposes, and banned distilling in the USA. The ban was not lifted until 1933.

Paradoxically, Prohibition laid the foundations for the phenomenal success of Scotch whisky in the USA since it stimulated demand for quality liquor. Whisky companies appointed agents in the Caribbean, who imported Scotch legally and then ran it into the USA, illegally, in small, fast boats. Whisky imports to the Bahamas, for instance, soared from 119,000 gallons (540,000 litres) in 1918 to more than 386,000 gallons (1.75 million litres) in 1922. The tiny French colonies of St Pierre and Miquelon imported 119,000 gallons (53,900 litres) of Scotch in 1922 – described as "quite a respectable quantity for a population of 6,000 people"!

Such "moonshine" whiskey as was made in the USA was of poor quality, so demand for good Scotch was enormous. A well-known bootlegger was Captain Bill McCoy, employed by Berry Bros & Rudd as an agent for Cutty Sark; his name became synonymous with good whisky – "The Real McCoy".

Most of the Scotch that found its way into the illegal bars and speakeasies in the eastern States was heavily diluted by the owners of such establishments. For this reason, the bootleggers preferred dark-coloured, strongly flavoured whiskies, which could be diluted without too much loss of flavour. The heavy malts of Campbeltown were especially favoured, and the distillers of what had once been able to describe itself as the "Whisky Capital", readily shipped their product direct to the Caribbean. Unfortunately, the demand severely stretched their resources and they began, disastrously, to sacrifice quality for quantity. Some 16 Campbeltown distilleries disappeared in the 1920s.

■ **1918** Duty doubles to 30/- following the Bonar Law   ■ **1919** Duty is increased to 50/- by Austen Chamberlain

LEFT An illegal speakeasy in New York during Prohibition.

THE TURBULENT YEARS

At this time very little whisky was bottled and sold as single malt: almost the entire production went into blends. Such quantities as were made available were most commonly bottled by spirits merchants and independent bottlers, notably Gordon & Macphail of Elgin and William Cadenhead of Aberdeen, and had only a local market. There were some exceptions to this general rule – Cardhu (formerly Cardow), Craigellachie, Glenfarclas, The Glenlivet, Glenmorangie, Glen Grant, Highland Park, Lagavulin,

■ **1920** Chamberlain increases duty to 72/6d per gallon; Prohibition in the USA   ■ **1923** "Cutty Sark" introduced by Berry Bros & Rudd

Laphroaig, Macallan and Talisker for example, were all bottled by their proprietors in limited quantities but they were hard to come by. Many private customers continued to buy in bulk, by the stoneware jar or by the cask as their fathers and grandfathers had done, most commonly in "quarters" holding ten gallons, or "octaves" of five gallons. In his classic *Notes on a Cellar Book* (1921) Professor George Saintsbury recollects that, during his days in Edinburgh before the First World War, "I used to endeavour to supply my cask with, and to keep independent jars of, the following: Clyne Lish, Smith's Glenlivet, Glen Grant, Talisker and one of the Islay brands – Lagavulin, Ardbeg, Caol Ila, etc... Ben Nevis is less definite in flavour than any of these, but blends very well. Glendronach, an Aberdeenshire whisky, of which I did not think much forty years ago, improved greatly later; and I used to try both of these in my cask."

Until 1913 all bottles were sealed with driven corks, like wine bottles. That year William Manera Bergius, who became managing director of William Teacher and Sons in 1923, invented the replaceable "stopper cork" and for decades Teacher's Highland Cream was sold with the slogan "Bury the Corkscrew". In 1926 White Horse Distillers introduced the screw cap (originally made from Bakelite, an innovation which doubled the sales of the brand in six months. Production of malt whisky also advanced at this time from 5.6 million gallons (25.5 million litres) in 1927 to 8.7 million gallons (39.5 million litres) in 1930, but this was at the expense of considerable price cutting. The Depression badly affected sales; in 1930 DCL reduced production by 25 per cent. By 1932 output had dwindled to under ten million litres, less than half of the previous year's total. That year all malt distilleries closed except Glenlivet and Glen Grant.

In the early 1930s Sir Alexander Walker, Chairman of Johnnie Walker, commented: "A complete stoppage of production would, I think, let the Government and the Chancellor know the effect of their indifferent policy, and stimulate farmers and others interested in the industry to take a stronger action than they have hitherto done." In fact, nothing was done.

Prohibition was lifted by President Roosevelt in 1933, (though Congress imposed a high import duty until 1935) and there was a slow recovery in the UK economy after 1934. Total whisky production was up to 25 million gallons (114 million litres) by 1935, and 30 million gallons (136 million litres) by 1938. The outbreak of war in 1939 brought another increase in duty (10/- per proof gallon), and the lack of foreign grain supplies, owing to the cordon imposed by German U-boats, forced the closure of all the grain distilleries in 1941. Some 72 malt distilleries remained in operation in 1941; 44 in 1942 and none in 1943/44. By 1943, the pre-war price of a bottle of whisky had been doubled by duty from 13/6 to 27/-.

Even before the end of hostilities, the War Cabinet was aware of whisky's importance as a dollar earner, reducing the nation's debt to the USA. In a famous memo of 1945, Winston Churchill wrote: "On no account reduce the barley for whisky. This takes years to mature and is an invaluable export and dollar producer." But the Labour Government which was elected the following year was committed to intervention in the economy and, although it released more barley, it raised duty yet again by 31 per cent by 1948. By 1950 there were adequate stocks of barley to resume production at pre-war levels, but mature stock was now low. Long-closed distilleries began to be re-commissioned (such as Tamdhu, Blair Athol, Pulteney and Bladnoch); in 1949 the first new distillery was built since 1900 at Tullibardine. DCL increased the number of stills in its malt whisky distilleries by more than half.

BELOW Buchanan's "Black & White" advertisement for Christmas 1948.

To friends everywhere we send Greetings and all Best Wishes for

A MERRY CHRISTMAS AND A GOOD NEW YEAR

"BLACK & WHITE"
SCOTCH WHISKY

JAMES BUCHANAN & CO. LTD., SCOTCH WHISKY DISTILLERS, GLASGOW & LONDON

■ **1936** Hiram Walker acquires George Ballantine & Co   ■ **1939** Duty increases by 10/- to 82/6d per proof gallon and to 97/6d in 1940   ■ **1941** *SS Politician*, carrying a cargo of Scotch, founders off the island of Eriskay. The event was immortalised by Sir Compton Mackenzie in *Whisky Galore*   ■ **1945** Scotch production is limited to half of what it had been in 1939; distilling is permitted on Sundays for the first time since 1823   ■ **1953** Formal controls on barley allocations cease, but rationing of whisky in the market remains until 1959; "Chivas Regal" is launched

Expansion, refurbishment and new building continued during the 1960s and Glenturret, Benriach, Jura, and Caperdonich were all reopened. Tomintoul, Tamnavulin, Loch Lomond, Deanston, Glen Flagler, Ben Wyvis and Ladyburn were built. Glenfarclas doubled in size, as did Bunnahabhain, Dalmore, Fettercairn, Knockdhu, Glen Spey and Tomatin. It was an era without parallel since Victorian times and expansion continued until 1976, with four newly built distilleries: Braes of Glenlivet (now called "Braeval"), Allt-a-Bhainne, Pittyvaich and Auchroisk.

In 1975/76 there was a sharp slump in the fortunes of the whisky industry, brought about by the oil crisis and the end of the Vietnam War, which had boosted the US economy. Recovery picked up in 1977, but by 1979 the world economy was moving into a deep recession. Demand for Scotch dipped in promising new markets such as Europe and Japan while in the USA sales fell by over four million gallons (18.2 million litres) between 1978 and 1980. The situation was exacerbated at home by an increase of VAT from eight to 15 per cent, which combined with higher duty to add £1.20 to the price of a bottle by 1982.

In 1983 and 1985 DCL closed 21 of its 45 distilleries. Fourteen of these never went back into production. Other owners followed suit: a further eight distilleries were closed between 1981 and 1986, most mothballed rather than dismantled.

THE FUTURE FOR BOLD JOHN BARLEYCORN

Until the 1980s single malt whiskies remained scarce outside Scotland, and many were only available in the district of their manufacture. The impetus towards promoting single malts – long recognised as the finest expression of Scotch whisky – came from the independent whisky companies, which felt threatened by the shrinking number of independent blenders. The larger corporations were historically opposed to promoting malt whiskies as so much of their success had been built on blends.

In 1963 the directors of William Grant & Sons, owner of Glenfiddich distillery, had resolved to set aside stock with a view to promoting its whisky as a single malt. Other independents

■ **1957** The price of a standard bottle of Scotch in the home market rises to £1.87   ■ **1960** The Scotch Whisky Association is formed to provide legal status in foreign courts   ■ **1962** International Distillers and Vintners formed by a merger of W&A Gilbey, Justerini & Brooks and United Vintners   ■ **1970** Glenlivet & Glen Grant Distillers merge with Hill Thomson and Longmorn-Glenlivet to become (in 1972) The Glenlivet Distillers Ltd   ■ **1975** Whitbread buys Long John International from Shenley Industries

followed suit, notably Macallan and Glenmorangie in the late 1970s – and by the early 1980s DCL had quietly launched its "Malt Whisky Cellar"; single malts from Lagavulin, Linkwood, Rosebank, Royal Lochnagar and Talisker distilleries. In 1980 a symposium of whisky companies estimated that exports of single malts should rise by eight to ten per cent over the next five years. In fact the growth was almost twice that, and the increase has been steady ever since at about half that rate. During the same period, blended whisky sales have declined in the traditional markets.

Perhaps the greatest impetus to the sector was given by United Distillers in 1988 when the company launched its "Classic Malts" range aided by a substantial promotional budget. This comprised six whiskies of differing styles, displaying regional diversity: Cragganmore, Dalwhinnie, Glenkinchie, Lagavulin, Oban and Talisker. Similarly Allied Distillers repackaged Laphroaig, Miltonduff and Glendronach whilst the Chivas & Glenlivet Group followed suit in 1994 with Longmorn, Glen Keith, Strathisla and BenRiach, naming it the "Heritage Selection". Leading malt whiskies, such as Glenfiddich, Glenmorangie, The Glenlivet and The Macallan are now promoted with massive annual advertising budgets.

Never before have so many malt whiskies been so widely available. Never has so much malt whisky been enjoyed by so many people.

LEFT The first bottle of whisky in the world to break the six figure price barrier was revealed on October 14th 2010 by The Dalmore distillery which has sold two bottles for £100,000 each.

■ **1979** VAT is increased to 15 per cent, between 1980 and 1985; Hiram Walker attempts to take over Highland Distilleries ■ **1987** DCL becomes United Distillers; Allied Distillers is founded to head Allied Brewers' spirits operations; United Malt and Grain Distillers is formed to take over Scottish Malt Distillers and Scottish Grain Distillers ■ **1988** The "Keepers of the Quaich" is founded to promote Scotch; United Distillers launches "Classic Malts" range ■ **1994** 500th anniversary of the first recorded mention of whisky

HOW WHISKY IS MADE

Every malt whisky tastes different from the next. Indeed, every cask of malt whisky from the same distillery tastes slightly different from its neighbour, even if it came from the same still run. This wonderful diversity of flavours comes from three sources: the raw materials (water, malted barley and yeast), the production process (mashing, fermenting and distilling) and maturation.

So complex are the inter-relationships between these elements that they still defy scientists. Men who have worked all their lives at the craft of distilling still disagree about the contribution made by each stage or ingredient, relative to the rest.

Maurice Walsh, novelist, wrote in his introduction to Marshall Robb's book, *Scotch Whisky* (1950): "I knew one small town with seven distilleries and I knew an expert who could distinguish the seven by bouquet alone. The seven distilleries were on one mile of a highland river; they used the same water, peat and malt, and the methods of brewing and distillation were identical, yet each spirit had its own individual bouquet. One, the best, mellowed perfectly in seven years; another, the least good, not 100 yards away, was still liquid fire at the end of ten years." Here we will explore the alchemy that makes each malt whisky so different.

ABOVE The manhole in the side of the still is used for cleaning the interior.

LEFT Onion-shaped stills at Highland Park distillery.

WATER

Folklore and tradition hold that it is the water with which an individual malt whisky is made that distinguishes it from other malts. Even today, many distillery workers view their water with superstitious awe, while management goes to great lengths to protect and preserve the source and its purity, buying up the catchment area and controlling land use.

HARD AND SOFT WATER

It is frequently stated that the best malt whisky is made from soft water (ie. water with a low pH value). "Soft water which rises through peat and runs over granite" is a time-worn marketing claim. In truth, the usefulness of granite is that, being so hard, it imparts no minerals whatsoever to any water percolating through or running over it, and many well-known distilleries pipe their water from wells and springs before it has a chance to make contact with peat. What is more, some of the most famous names employ hard water – Glenmorangie, Glenkinchie and Highland Park, for example – and plausibly claim that the additional minerals in hard water impart spiciness to the finished product. Certain minerals, such as calcium, magnesium and zinc, are deemed to be essential for good fermentations, although adequate amounts of them are usually obtained from the malt itself.

Water makes its impact during fermentation; its main influence may be on spirit yield, rather than flavour. But, the two are linked. I have been told by many distillers that high yields mitigate against flavoursome whiskies. It may be that micro-organisms in the water work upon the barley and yeast to reduce the yield and enhance the flavour. Certainly, high bacterial and mineral levels can affect the process of fermentation, as with brewing beer.

A water with a low pH value will not necessarily make better whisky, although the distinguished whisky expert Professor McDowall argues that, since soft water is a far better solvent than hard water, it is capable of extracting much more from the malt during mashing. "Tea made with the hard water of London is much better than the same tea made with soft water which is known to extract the bitter oxalic acid from it. This may produce irritation of the urinary tract in some persons, especially if they are not accustomed to it... At one time the town council of Kirkaldy concluded that tea was indeed more harmful than whisky!" One might add, since water's capacity to dissolve

LEFT Taking samples of water from the spring that supplies Strathisla distillery.

solubles is enhanced if it contains carbon dioxide and by the presence of acid-producing bacteria, that come from peat, soft peaty water is best.

PEATY WATER

Many experts still maintain that the use of peaty water, especially in Islay, contributes character to the product. According to the authority on distilling, JA Nettleton, the use of "moss-water" by Highland and Western distilleries makes it possible to continue to save spirit at considerably lower strengths: 48% to 51% ABV, rather than 74% to 75% ABV (*see* page 78). "The evidence [of experienced distillery operatives] tends to support the view that – where presumably identical mashing materials are used, and where the fermenting and distilling routine is the same, and nothing differs except the quality of the water – this great difference of 50 or 60 degrees is compulsory... Mysterious influences are ascribed to the use of moss-water. It is certain that spirits are collected at extremely low strengths, and that they are full-bodied and feinty... the flavour and other characteristics are approved of by connoisseurs." So it seems that collecting at low strengths may have more to do with the style of whisky desired than the use of moss-water.

PURITY

Distillers agree that the most important factor as regards water is its purity; it is essential that water be as free from organic and mineral impurity – from micro-organisms, organic matter, minerals dissolved or in suspension – as possible. Some distilleries put their production water through a UV unit to kill any *E. coli* that might be present, but no distilleries use distilled water, although this is one of the potential sacrifices the Scotch whisky industry may be forced to make to the European Community in its ever-increasing march towards uniformity in industry.

Many distillers maintain that the influence of water is neutral, that the best distilling water will contribute very little flavour to the whisky it makes. Soft water (more or less rain-water) is almost as pure as distilled water, so long as it does not pass through air-borne pollution. In fact most of Scotland's water is famously soft, especially in the Highlands. The absence of any near neighbour from whom air-borne pollution might travel, combines with the prevailing westerly and southwesterly winds to ensure total purity.

VOLUME AND TEMPERATURE

The two other water-related factors that influence the choice of a distillery site are the amount of water available and its temperature. Whisky distilleries require a great deal of water, for cooling the condensers and cleaning the plant, as well as for producing and reducing the spirit. A copious supply is essential; if the water source dries up, even temporarily, the distillery shuts down. This has led to the demise of many established distilleries.

The temperature of the water in the condenser affects the amount of contact the spirit vapour has with the copper from which the condenser is made. Copper is a purifier: if the cooling water in the condenser is warm, the vapour takes longer to liquefy so has more contact with copper and emerges purer and lighter. On the other hand, if the distiller wants a heavier, more "traditional" spirit he must make sure the cooling water is truly cold. In the days when they received a dram of spirit before going on shift, distillery workers used to prefer the whisky made during the dead of winter, when the cooling water was very cold, to that made in the summer: it had more "character".

Distilling was traditionally a winter activity, on account of this and the fact that, before the recent climate changes, water levels were generally lower during July and August. Still today, most distilleries will time their "silent season" (when the site closes for maintenance and holidays) during the summer months.

BARLEY

Malted barley is the principal raw material in the production of malt whisky and therefore its quality and consistency is of considerable importance to distillers. Barley is graded on a scale of one to nine, and only the top three grades are suitable for malting (ie. the top 20 per cent), since only this portion has the capacity to germinate and grow.

Quality in barley is defined by maltsters as:

High starch content. It is the starch that turns into sugar, and thence into alcohol: high starch yields more alcohol.

Low protein content (less than 1.5 per cent). The higher the protein the lower the starch.

Low nitrogen content (less than 1.7 per cent). High nitrogen indicates high protein. Nitrogen is also the active ingredient in fertilisers, which creates something of a problem for farmers. To obtain a high yield, they must fertilize, if they fertilize too much their barley will be unsuitable for malting.

High likelihood of germination. As we will see, germination is a pre-requisite for malting, so the capability of the grain to germinate is essential.

LEFT "Bold John Barleycorn". Research into the best varieties is extensive and continuous.

ABOVE Sunlight shines over carefully spread out, moistened barley as it awaits germination.

Well-ripened, plump and dry. Maltsters tell farmers to leave the crop until it is absolutely ripe and can wait no longer and then to leave it for another three days. Barley with more than about 16 per cent moisture content is likely to go mouldy in storage. This is not the decisive factor it once was, since most barley is artificially dried now.

Considering these quality constraints, one has sympathy for the farmer, especially in the Highlands, where poor soil gives low yields, and where late summer gales can ruin a crop. But this is just the climate and husbandry that produce the best barley for malting.

Maltsters maintain vehemently that it makes no difference where the barley comes from, so long as it meets the specification outlined above. Yet there is a general feeling among distillers that Scottish barley is best. Tradition, romanticism and marketing hyperbole all play their part in this. In the "What is Whisky?" case of 1909, malt distillers attempted to have the definition of Scotch limited to being a product made from Scottish barley. At that time many malt distilleries bought their supplies locally, from individual farms, and sometimes only from specified fields on certain farms. At the same time the grain distillers were importing barley from California, Denmark and even Australia. Today some barley still comes from England and abroad, although Scotland grows more than enough to meet the whisky industry's needs. The problem with buying from abroad is that the quality can be variable, and it is difficult to send back if unsuitable.

The distillers' feeling that Scottish barley is best has some support in reason. Cold northern winters kill bugs in the ground, thus avoiding the need for harmful pesticides, and long northern hours of daylight help to concentrate flavour. Think of the difference between the flavoursome raspberries grown in Scotland and the flabby, tasteless apologies-for-raspberries grown in warmer climes. However, late harvests mean that the crop is sometimes cut wet, and since the technology to dry it without killing the embryo was not readily available to farmers in the past, it quickly went mouldy and was useless.

Maltsters and distillers buy either straight from the farm, which guarantees tonnage but not quality; on the "spot market", which gives access to the pick of the crop but can be volatile, or by specifying to a grain merchant exactly what is required. The last is the most common way of buying, although some maltsters resent having to pay a middle man.

Distilleries will buy malt from all over Scotland, to spread the risk of local bad harvests, and specify their requirements as to quality, quantity and degree of peating for the whole year. The grain merchant dries and stores the barley and sells it in lots from 500 to 2,000 tonnes.

There is a general feeling among distillers that Scottish barley is best. Tradition, romanticism and marketing hyperbole all play a part in this.

BARLEY VARIETIES

Before the Second World War barley was purchased as Scotch or English, with small quantities originally coming from Denmark, California, Australia and elsewhere. Today the UK is divided into five barley regions; Northwest (including Northern Ireland and North Wales), Northeast, Central, Southwest and Southeast. Until the 1950s two barley varieties dominated the market: Spatt Archer and Plumage Archer. Then a number of different hybrid varieties began to appear, including Proctor, Pioneer, Maris Otter (a hybrid of the first two and the most important malting barley of the

1970s), and finally, Golden Promise. This latter variety, introduced in 1966, was especially popular in some quarters. It thrived on upland farms, gave higher yields (385 to 395 litres/85 to 87 gallons of alcohol per tonne) and germinated quickly and evenly.

But Golden Promise was superseded by further new varieties that yielded increased alcohol levels, and that were not so vulnerable to mildew and disease. The 1980s saw Halcyon, Pipkin and Puffin come and go, and these were in turn replaced in the 1990s by Optic, Chariot and Derkardo. Currently, the most popular varieties are Optic and Oxbridge (producing up to 420 litres/92 gallons of alcohol per tonne). The Macallan and Glengoyne distilleries, which long remained loyal to Golden Promise, now have difficulty obtaining supplies.

Does it make any difference which variety the distiller uses? There are hundreds to choose from, and more hybrids appear every year, rigorously tested over a dozen years or more before being recommended by the Institute of Brewing, which publishes an annual list of approved and provisionally approved varieties, deemed to be commercially viable for malting, brewing and distilling. These varieties are vigorously promoted by maltsters if they meet the strict requirements necessary for their production techniques.

The given wisdom – supported by many chemists – is that the barley variety makes no difference to flavour. They argue that the distilling process is so fierce, and the level of alcohol so high, that any flavour an individual variety of barley might impart is blown away. Some varieties yield more esters than others; winter barley is less estery than that grown in summer, and some Highland distilleries will not use it. Also many distillers today are concerned that the new varieties sacrifice flavour to alcohol yield and resistance to disease, and that they change too quickly as more hybrids are developed.

In 1967 Professor McDowall, the industry commentator, remarked that the modern practice of using fat barley for the maximum yield might reduce the flavour of modern whisky. Recently a distillery manager told me of a variety for which he had to run the foreshots for an hour and a half before spirit could start to be saved, where he would normally expect to run foreshots for only half of that time.

From this it appears that the barley used by the maltster does make a difference to production. And although it is difficult to quantify, it is likely that the variety makes a contribution to overall flavour of the spirit, albeit small and subtle.

LEFT Yeast is pitched into the washback to start the fermentation process.

YEAST

The only other ingredient in malt whisky is yeast, a subject that is passed over silently by whisky writers and marketing people alike. Yeasts are micro-organisms related to fungi. The cells are invisible to the naked eye; one gramme of yeast contains in the region of 10,000 million cells! There are countless strains of yeasts blowing around in the air and multiplying all around us, wherever conditions are right. About 1,000 of these are in regular commercial use, but only a few strains are appropriate for making whisky. Some make bread; the French and Spanish words for yeast are *levure* and *levadura*, both derived from the Latin, "to lift" (ie. cause dough to rise). Others make beer – our word "yeast" comes from the Dutch "*gist*" (foam), and it must be said that the Germans and the Dutch pioneered the scientific study of this mysterious substance in the nineteenth century, when the best

59

brains in Europe, including Louis Pasteur, debated whether the stuff was animal, vegetable or mineral. Interestingly, the yeasts sought by beer brewers impart a bitter flavour to bread and not enough alcohol to whisky.

Like mushroom spores, yeast cells can exist for years in a somnolent state, only arousing themselves when the right food (broadly, sugars) and conditions (warm and wet) present themselves. Then they run riot, gobbling up the sugars like piranha fish, recreating themselves, doubling their number in two hours – called "budding". At the same time they generate carbon dioxide and, most importantly from the brewers' or distillers' point of view, produce alcohol at a prodigious rate.

The speed and violence of the fermentation (*see* page 72) is remarkable. Yeast is "pitched" at 2.2 per cent of the weight of the malt mashed, so a typical mash of eight tonnes will take about 175 kilogrammes of yeast. The reaction starts, visibly, within a couple of hours and can be over in 50 hours as the saccharine malty solution, called "wash", seethes and foams. In days gone by, when yeasts were more unpredictable, the whole fermenting vessel (called a "washback") could rock like a ship in a stormy sea. Small boys were employed to fight back the foam with heather "flails" or brooms. In modern distilleries washbacks are fitted with mechanical switchers.

Scotch whisky distillers today use a cultured yeast, grown from a single cell, which produces a reliable and consistent fermentation. In the past brewers' yeast was also used, but this has become less reliable, and has been abandoned. The yeast is either liquid, dried or (mostly) solid, like cheese.

YEAST'S CONTRIBUTION TO FLAVOUR

What contribution does yeast make to the flavour of the finished product? As well as alcohol (ethanol), yeast produces small quantities of other compounds, known as congeners, including a wide range of esters, aldehydes, acids and higher alcohols, which contribute to flavour.

It used to be claimed that distillers' yeast (cultured) maximised yield of alcohol, while brewers' yeast developed flavour. Some, notably Macallan distillery, maintained that a "cocktail" of several yeasts, both distillers' and brewers' developed complexity. Scottish distillers are silent about this now they have abandoned brewers' yeast!

MALTING

ABOVE Drum maltings at Port Ellen, Islay. Such automatic systems have largely replaced traditional floor maltings.

The malting process makes a vital contribution to the flavour of Scotch whisky. Like most seeds, barley has two parts; the embryo, which is the living structure that will grow into a new plant, and the endosperm, a store of starch which will feed the young plant until it can fend for itself.

During germination the barley seed produces enzymes. The main ones are cytase, which breaks down the cell walls and makes the starch accessible for growth, and amylase (also called diastase), which converts the starch into its soluble form, dextrin. During the mashing process, the amylase converts the dextrin into maltose, a soluble sugar.

Malting is, effectively, controlled germination. The craft of the maltster is to allow the germination to progress to a point where the cell walls have been broken down, but before the starch begins to be used by the growing plant. He stops the growth by drying the "green malt" (ie. after it has germinated) in a kiln.

STEEPING

Dry barley has less than 12 per cent moisture. This must be raised to 46 per cent for the enzymes to be activated, so after it has been carefully cleaned, the barley is immersed in water three times, with air rests in between, over two to three days.

The actual length of time depends upon the temperature of the water, the size of the grains and their capacity for absorption. While the grains are submerged they are constantly aerated to ensure equal uptake of water and avoid "clumping". If the maltster understeeps he can spray the grain, but this leads to an uneven water uptake. If he oversteeps, the grain can be dried out by a tumble-drying process.

BELOW Floor maltings where the germinating barley is turned over by hand.

GERMINATING

In traditional floor maltings, the damp grain is then spread out on a concrete floor to a depth of about 30 centimetres and soon each grain sprouts a tiny rootlet. This generates heat, particularly close to the floor, so the barley has to be regularly turned with wooden shovels and rakes to keep the temperature even and prevent the little roots becoming entangled. The task is called "turning the piece", and goes on for about a week, or less in hot weather. The grains lose moisture at the rate of 0.5 per cent each day, and are spread out more thinly until the rootlets begin to wither and the grain – now referred to as "green malt" – becomes mealy. Maltsters call this "modification", and can gauge the progress made by biting the grain to taste its sweetness and rubbing it to assess its texture; if the grain is chalky and smooth it is ready, if lumps remain it is under-modified. The degree of modification may make a difference to the overall flavour of the whisky, although maltsters argue that the number of under-modified and over-modified grains balance out.

Having your own maltings allows for greater control of the flavour sought. The process is slower and more natural and does not force germination. Bowmore, Laphroaig, Springbank, Balvenie and Highland Park all swear by it. The last tried using commercial maltsters, supplying them with Orcadian peat, but this was not a success. All make around 20 per cent of their requirement, and buy in the rest.

The problems with floor malting are the limitation it necessarily imposes upon the amount of malt that can be made at a time, the labour intensive nature of the process and the variable nature of the malt thus created. For these reasons, floor maltings have been largely replaced by pneumatic malting systems. The term simply means that air is passed through the grain to control its temperature and by doing this the batch size can be greatly increased.

There are three pneumatic systems: Saladin Boxes, named after its late nineteenth century inventor, Charles Saladin, Rotary Drums and Steep, Germinate and Kilning Vessels (SGKVs). The Saladin system comprises a long concrete or metal trench fitted with revolving rakes, which pass up and down it, turning the piece, and a perforated bed, through which humidified air can be blown through the grain. Typically it can process 200 tonnes per batch. Drum maltings hold from nine to 50 tonnes of grain, which is turned by gravity, as the drum rotates (which it does nine times a day). Humidity and temperature are controlled by

Having your own maltings allows for greater control of the flavour sought. The process is slower and more natural and does not force germinaiton.

internal sprays and by blowing air through the grain. SGKVs
were developed in the late 1970s at Moray Firth maltings
in order to achieve the whole malting operation in a single
vessel. Several hybrid vessels have been created which can
perform the same process.

KILNING

In the kiln the green malt is spread out evenly on a perforated
metal floor with a furnace below. There are two kinds of modern
kilns; direct fired, where the gases of combustion pass through the
malt bed, and indirect fired, where the air is heated by oil-fired
burners or steam-heated radiators, before it passes through the
malt. The kilns have tapering roofs to draw out the heat from the
furnace and since the nineteenth century they have been capped
with the pagoda-style roofs which have become the architectural
trade-mark of malt whisky distilleries.

The first stage of the kilning process is the free drying phase,
which evaporates moisture on the surface of the green malt. Hot
air at 60°C to 65°C (140°F to 149°F) is driven through the layer of
malt (the volume of air is more important than the temperature).
When peat is used, it is thrown into the furnace at this stage.
The temperature must be kept below 60°C (140°F) or the
phenols in the peat that lend the whisky its smoky characteristics
are destroyed. The lower the temperature is, the higher the
level of peatiness communicated to the malt. Next there is the
forced drying phase, during which the temperature is increased
to 70°C to 75°C (158°F to 167°F) and the air flow reduced. By
now the moisture content of the malt will have reduced to
about five per cent.

Finally there may be a cooling phase, where the temperature
is lowered to about 30°C (86°F) to prevent further curing of
the malt. The whole exercise takes between 20 and 48 hours,
depending on what type of kilning process is being used, the
size of the kiln and the amount of malt.

The fuel used during the kilning process makes a significant
contribution to the flavour of the whisky. When peat was the
only fuel available to Highland distillers their malts tended to
have a dominant smokiness. The advent of the railways brought
steady supplies of coke and coal allowing maltsters alternatives
to peat. This gave them far greater control over the final flavour
of their whisky and by the 1870s the distilleries on Speyside were
producing more lightly peated malts than previously, in the style
known as "Glenlivet".

PEAT

Peat is acidic, decayed vegetation made from bog plants such as sphagnum moss, heather, sedges and grasses – the composition varies according to the peat bog's location. For peat to develop, there must be high rainfall, a cold atmosphere and poor soil drainage or aeration. The waterlogged ground cannot break down the vegetation, so a thickening layer of peat develops. Some ancient peat bogs are up to 10,000 years old and the peat layer can run to a depth of nine metres (29.5 feet).

Traditionally peat was the abundant, free fuel of the Highlands. Hard work to "win", or cut – although a good cutter can win about 1,000 peats a day – and not terribly efficient in terms of the heat it produces, peat was an economic necessity for Highland malt distilleries, which usually had their own peat bogs.

LEFT Peat banks can be found all over the West Highlands and islands of Scotland. Some bogs are up to 10,000 years old.

65

In May or June the distillery workforce would cut the year's
requirement; no mean task, considering that a single crofting
family could use 15,000 peats a year for domestic purposes. Once
cut the peats were laid out on the heather around the peat bank
for a fortnight or so, and then stacked in small pyramids called
cas bhic, Gaelic for "little feet", to dry thoroughly for a year.

By the 1930s distilleries were casting farther afield to win
their peats. Glenmorangie workers, for example, went north
to Forsinard in Sutherland and lodged with local crofters and
shepherds; the work was hard, but the parties were legendary!
Many Speyside distilleries bought in peat from Pitsligo in
Aberdeenshire, which was hard and coal-like and gave off
a penetrating aroma.

The nature of peat varies from place to place, according to its
paleobotany – the successive layers and types of plants present.
Lowland peats, for example, contain more vegetable matter, have
a looser, softer texture, burn more rapidly and give off more dust.
Peat bogs close to the sea become saturated with salt spray, and
in some cases contain strands of seaweed, from winter storms. In
Orkney, peat is graded into "fog", the rooty top layer, "yarphie",
the small roots and "moss", the deepest, darkest layer. Highland
Park distillery prefers its peat to have heather roots in it.

It is now possible to control the degree of peating during
the kilning of the malt much more accurately than it was in the
past. The amount is measured by the concentration of phenolic
compounds in the smoke. Intensity of peating falls into three
broad categories: lightly peated (one to five parts per million
[ppm] total phenols); medium peated (ten to 20ppm) and heavily
peated (30 to 50ppm). Different companies use slightly different
measures. Some distilleries, Glengoyne for example, specify no
peating at all while an average Highland malt will be peated
to about two ppm. Medium peating is favoured by some:
Highland Park and Talisker peat to around 15ppm and Ardmore
to around 20ppm. Others, notably the smokier Islays, prefer
between 35 and 50ppm (the heaviest peated of all is Octomore
from Bruichladdich at over 100ppm). All distilleries blend non-
peated with peated malt to achieve the required phenolic level.
An exception to this was Malt Mill distillery within Lagavulin
(1908 to 1960), which used only peated malt in an effort to
replicate the whisky of days gone by.

Highland malts used to be more heavily peated than they
are today, but the trend since the Second World War has been
away from very smoky malts.

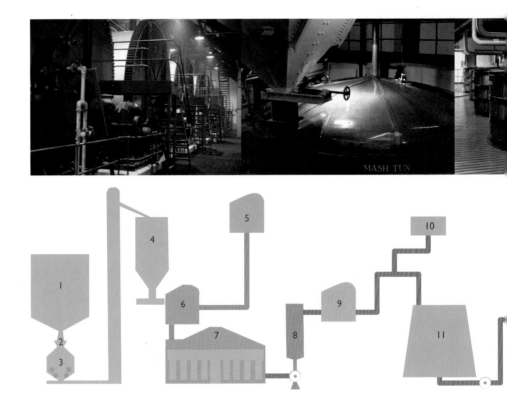

MASH TUN

After MALTING (above) and screening, new deliveries of malt are held in the MALT BIN (1) before passing to the DRESSING MACHINE (2), to remove shoots and rootlets, and into the MILL (3). Here rollers crack the husks and grind the malt.

The resulting grist then moves into the GRIST HOPPER (4) where it is stored before being "mashed". Mashing extracts soluble starch from the malt. It also activates the enzyme amylase which converts the starch to maltose. The process begins in the MASHING MACHINE (6) where the grist is mixed with hot water from the WATER TANK (5). The mixture is then run off into the MASH TUN (7), a large circular vessel usually covered to conserve heat and made from either stainless steel or cast iron. Mash tuns have perforated floors to allow the maltose-rich liquor, or "worts" to pass through into the UNDERBACK (8).

The worts are chilled through a COOLER (9) before being pumped into the fermenting vessel, called the WASHBACK (11). Here YEAST is added (10) and the frothing liquid, or "wash", is turned into alcohol and carbon dioxide over a period of two to three days.

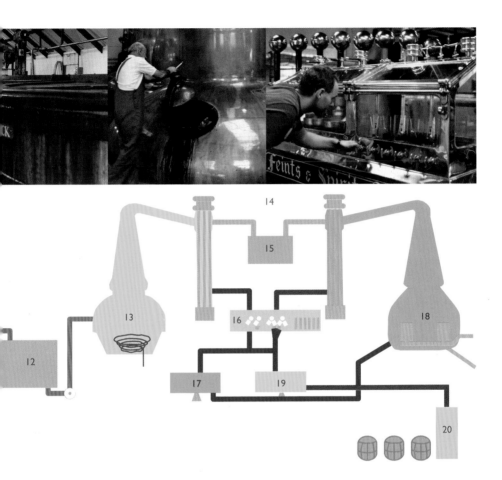

Distillation, the heart of the process, follows. This takes place in two copper stills. After fermentation, the wash passes through the WASH CHARGER (12), into the WASH STILL (13) for the first distillation. In the still, the wash is brought to the boil and the alcoholic vapours (that are boiling at a lower temperature) are driven off. The resulting vapours become liquid again as they pass through the CONDENSER (14), a bundle of copper pipes within a water jacket. Cold water from a TANK (15) flows through the pipes, surrounded by the vapours. The distillate from the wash, called low wines, then passes through the SPIRIT SAFE (16) to the LOW WINES AND FEINTS RECEIVER (17). This distillation process is repeated in the LOW WINES STILL (18), but this time the stillman monitors

its progress carefully as it runs through the spirit safe. He must judge exactly when to start and stop saving spirit: start collecting too early and pungent, impure foreshots will be included; collect too late and the oily feints will spoil the spirit. He wants only the "heart of the run", and this will only amount to about a third of the spirit distilled. This good spirit is directed to the INTERMEDIATE SPIRIT RECEIVER – ISR (19). The remaining foreshots and feints are directed to join the low wines in the low wines and feints receiver. The good spirit passes from the ISR to the SPIRIT VAT (20), where it is reduced in strength with water, before being filled into casks. Only once it has been matured for three years may it be called Scotch whisky.

MASHING

The process for making malt whisky begins with "mashing". Articulated trucks, typically bearing loads of 5,000 tonnes of malt from one of the central maltings, arrive at the distillery several times a week and deposit their cargo in the towering silos of the grain store.

At the maltsters the malt will have been "dressed", that is, passed over a reverberating wire-mesh that removes the "culm" or withered shoots and rootlets produced during malting. These, together with other waste products of the distilling process, are later recycled and used as cattle-feed; a valuable source of nutrition for livestock during the winter.

At the distillery the malt is tested for moisture (12 per cent maximum is allowed), viability for germination (it must be 99 per cent viable) and insect infestation (which can destroy a hopper-full in a matter of hours) before the load is accepted. Then the malt is screened to remove any remaining dust, stones and small grains. When it is required, the malt is loaded in hundredweight (50kg) lots into the mill hopper, which has two sets of rollers; one to crack the husks, the other to grind the malt. It must produce ten per cent flour, 20 per cent husk and 70 per cent grist and these proportions are checked carefully. If it is too fine the "mash tun" will not drain quickly enough, if too coarse, the liquor will drain too fast and maximum extraction will not occur.

THE MASH TUN

The grist is then mashed with hot water, in order to extract the maximum amount of soluble starch. Mashing also awakens the enzyme amylase once more, that had been deactivated by the maltster during kilning, and this allows it to complete the conversion of starch into maltose.

Mashing takes place in a large circular vessel, known as a mash tun. It is usually covered, often with copper, to conserve heat and is made from stainless steel or cast iron. Mash tuns have perforated floors, through which the liquor, called 'worts', can be drained off after the mashing is complete. They also contain revolving mechanical rakes that periodically stir the mash. Mash tuns hold from one tonne (Edradour) to 15 tonnes (Miltonduff), their size being related

BELOW Mash tun rakes are used to ensure that the conversion of starch into maltose is as efficient as possible.

MASH TUN

LEFT A copper-covered mash tun at Bowmore. The capacity of such vessels varies from one to 15 tonnes.

to the capacity of the fermenting vessels they will go on to fill. A tonne of malt is expected to produce 5,000 litres of worts. Many distilleries have adopted "Lauter tuns", a German invention widely used by brewers, that increase extraction. This system was first introduced at Tomatin distillery.

Three waters or "extractions" are used in the mashing process. The first, which is the third water left from the previous mashing, is heated to around 63 to 64°C (147°F), mixed with the grist in a mashing machine then filled into the mash tun. The optimum heat at which the enzymes will break down the starch is known as the "strike point". This is vital, for if the water is too hot, it will kill the enzymes, if too cool, the amount of grist will have to be reduced. After about 20 minutes the rotating rakes with which the tun is fitted begin to revolve and stir the worts, which are then drained off through the holes in the floor into the "underback".

The second extraction water is then pumped into the mash tun, this time at 70°C (158°F). It is stirred, left for 30 minutes and then emptied into the underback. The third extraction water, called "sparge", goes into the mash tun at 85°C (185°F). It takes about 15 minutes to fill and settle and then it is pumped into the hot water tank to be used as the first water of the next mashing. It contains only about one per cent sugar. The residue of husks and spent grains left in the bottom of the mash tun, called "draff", makes excellent cattle feed.

The warm worts then pass from the underback through a heat exchanger to reduce their temperature to below 20°C (68°F). This is vital. If the worts are not cooled the maltose would decompose and the yeast would then be killed off.

71

FERMENTING

ABOVE Oregon
pine washbacks at
Bowmore. While
traditionalists insist that
wooden washbacks add
a beneficial esteriness
to the spirit, stainless
steel vessels are far
easier to clean.

Fermentation takes place in a "washback" – a large vat of between 220 gallon (1,000 litre) capacity, such as at Edradour, and 15,178 gallon (69,000 litre) capacity, such as at Tamnavulin. These are made of larch or pine (Oregon pine is a favourite as it grows tall and has a tight grain with few knots) or stainless steel.

Fermentation in whisky production is similar to that for brewing beer, with one difference: the process is non-sterile. The principles of fermentation are fairly simple: yeast requires oxygen to breath, and as it is denied oxygen in the atmosphere, the yeast extracts it from the sugars, decomposing the worts into alcohol and carbon dioxide. The worts are pumped through the heat exchanger into the washback, filling it about two-thirds full. Then a carefully measured amount of yeast is pitched, usually in solution and usually added as the worts enter the back. From now on the worts become "wash". During the first phase of the fermentation process, known as the log phase and typically lasting a couple of hours, the yeast gets used to its surroundings.

In the second phase of fermentation the yeast cells multiply rapidly, consuming the sugars of the wash and turning the mixture into carbon dioxide and alcohol. It lasts about 34 hours and the reaction causes the wash to seethe and froth, often violently, and can make the washback groan and rock on its mooring-bolts. The temperature of the wash increases to about 35°C (95°F).

In the final phase, the wash calms down as the alcohol inhibits the activity of the yeast cells and there is a dramatic increase in the growth of bacteria. The latter is important, for it makes a second, bacteriological, fermentation possible. The bacteria come mainly from the malt and are basically lactic acid (*lactobacillus*); their effect is to lower the pH (ie. the degree of acidity), and allow further flavours to develop. Enough time must be allowed for the bacterial fermentation to take place. The spirit produced from wash that has been fermented for only two days has a cereal-like character, while that fermented for longer develops greater complexity. At least 60 hours is required to achieve this. By the time fermentation is complete, the wash is at between 5% to 8% ABV, acidity has increased and about 85 per cent of the solids in the wash have been converted to alcohol, carbon dioxide and new yeast cells. The last 15 per cent pass over with the wash into the wash still.

The washbacks must be well cleaned between fermentations, as excessive bacterial infestation can render the yeast useless. Sterility is one of the advantages of stainless steel washbacks; wooden ones have a limited life – albeit of about 40 years.

As with so many of the age-old debates in whisky making, traditionalists believe that wooden washbacks do have advantages. Some distillers maintain that there is a beneficial reaction between the alcohol and the bacteria that lurk in the wood – for it is impossible to sterilise wooden washbacks completely. Some experienced distillers insist that well-seasoned wooden washbacks may increase esteriness in the spirit. Others maintain that wood's principal role is to insulate the fermenting wash during the winter months. Whatever, there seems little doubt that wood does have some effect, whether for good or bad is not clear. Bowmore distillery, for one, believes in the positive properties of wood – they re-instated wooden washbacks, having replaced them many years before with stainless steel vessels.

With clean washbacks, low temperature, slow fermentation, pure water and (most important) modern barley varieties, the distillery maximises its yield of alcohol. Distillery managers are now expected to extract around 420 litres (92 gallons) of alcohol per tonne of malt, but a second fermentation, although it may increase flavour and complexity, can reduce this.

In the second phase of fermemtation the yeast cells multiply rapidly, consuming the sugars of the wash and turning the mixture into carbon dioxide and water.

ABOVE Boil-ball and lantern-shaped stills at Strathisla. "Boil-ball" refers to the spherical chambers between the body and head of the still that encourage heavier vapours to fall back as reflux for re-distillation.

DISTILLING

Distillation separates the alcohol in the wash from the water, and concentrates it. It does this by the action of heat and condensation; alcohol has a lower boiling point than water, so rises as vapour when heated. It is turned back into liquid by passing through a simple condenser.

The vessels in which this takes place are pot stills, large copper kettles, which have narrow necks (called the "lyne arm" or "lye pipe") that curve and enter the condenser, sometimes located in the open air outside the stillhouse. Traditionally the condenser was a coiled pipe of decreasing diameter immersed in a tub of cold water, known as the "worm". Only 15 distilleries still have worm tubs. Most use "shell and tube" condensers, where the shell contains the vapour and the tubes within it the cooling water.

Malt whisky making requires two stills, termed the wash or "singling" still and the "low wines" or "doubling" still. Occasionally, a third still is installed. Distilleries that had only one still performed the functions of wash and low wines stills in sequence. Wash stills are typically longer than low wines stills, as they must hold a greater quantity of liquor. The largest, such as that at Glenfarclas, hold 6,599 gallons (30,000 litres) and the smallest such as at Kilchoman just under 600 gallons (2,700 litres). They are usually filled to about two-thirds capacity.

STILL DESIGN

Stills come in three basic designs; the "plain" or "onion" (the most common), the "boil-ball" and the "lantern" shape. The way these designs are interpreted – as to capacity, height, method of heating, angle of the lyne arm etc. – differs from one distillery to another, and varies the quantity of volatiles that will end up in the spirit. Thus, very tall stills (as found at Glenmorangie), will only allow the lighter, more volatile vapours to be collected. Heavier vapours fall back as reflux and are distilled again. A similar function is performed by boil-balls, the spherical chambers between the body and the head of the still. To increase reflux some distilleries attach "purifiers" or "return pipes" to the still head; others angle the lyne arm upwards. Since 1874, Dalmore distillery's low wines stills have had water jackets around their necks to achieve the same purpose.

Another key aspect of still design is the area of copper that comes into contact with the wash and low wines. Copper dissolves easily and has an important influence on the quality of the spirit, since it removes sulphury or vegetable aromas by chemical reaction. This is especially important during the first distillation. Generally, the smaller the still, the greater the surface area of copper per unit of distilled vapour, while a narrow neck tends to increase the velocity of the ascending vapours and reduce contact with the copper.

During the 1960s and '70s, all but a handful of distilleries replaced direct firing (with naked flame) with indirect firing (via steam-heated coils or pans within the body of the still, not unlike the element in an electric kettle). This allows for easier heat control. To prevent solid particles in the wash sticking to the bottom of the still and scorching, direct-fired wash stills are fitted with 'rummagers' – revolving arms that drag heavy, copper, chain-mail around their bases. Those distillers with such stills – Macallan, Glenfarclas, Glenfiddich and Springbank distilleries – believe that the small areas of copper exposed by the rummagers contribute beneficially to flavour. Macallan went back to direct firing after experimenting with indirect heating. One industry analyst wrote, in 1903, that the former was a method preferred by many of the best whisky distillers.

BELOW Monitoring the unique "German helmet"-shaped stills at Glen Grant.

THE FIRST DISTILLATION

The first stage of the distillation process extracts the alcohol from the wash. It starts with the wash being pumped from the washback to the wash charger and thence to the wash still, which is charged to between half and two-thirds capacity, in order to allow for the expansion of the wash and the froth which builds up as it is heated. The wash will be at about 8% ABV and at 26°C to 32°C (79°F to 92°F).

When the still has been filled, the heat is turned up high and the wash is raised to

ABOVE The stillman at work. By carefully watching the distillate flow into the spirit safe he can judge when to start collecting the new-make spirit.

boiling point. After a short time it begins to froth up within the vessel, which is equipped with two "sight glasses" so that the operator can see how it is behaving. He does not want too much foaming, that might carry over the neck of the still and into the distillate. Also, the top of the lyne arm tends to wear out, depositing white flakes of sulphur in the "low wines", the term given to the first alcohol run. So the stillman turns down the heat as soon as the wash begins to froth.

Frothing was a grave problem in days gone by, especially before sight glasses had been developed. The stillman had to judge the level of the wash by swinging a suspended wooden ball against the side of the still to "sound" the charge. Until recently, soap was often added to the wash to act as a surfactant and reduce frothing. Although I have never heard the trick acknowledged, some claim that it is still being used.

The longer the wash has spent fermenting, the less frisky it will be. A wash that has been left over the weekend will settle in 15 minutes; one that has not been allowed to rest and complete its secondary fermentation may take over an hour. It is said to have "come in" when it settles and ceases to cover the lower sight glass. Once this has happened the stillman will start gradually turning up the heat again. He repeats this a couple of times – to "break the head" of froth – then steadily distils off the low wines, trying to keep the wash level between the two sight glasses. Gradual and carefully regulated heat is important; extreme action increases the deposit of oily, yeasty matter in the neck and worm, and this in turn is said to increase the presence of furfurol, a compound that has an unpleasant burnt and acrid taste. However this residue is not removed from the still during its weekly clean as a certain amount is good for flavour.

The rate at which the first alcohol run is produced depends on the size and shape of the still, the strength of the wash and the style of the condenser. A wash still of 6,599 gallons (30,000 litre) capacity, charged with 4,399 gallons (20,000 litres), will remove alcohol and water at about 220 to 330 gallons (1,000 to 1,500 litres) per hour. At the end of the run about a third of the wash will have become low wines.

The still is run until the remaining liquid is at 1% ABV, then the steam is turned off or the fire dampened down. The high-protein residue, known as "pot ale", "burnt ale" or "spent wash" and containing about four per cent solids, is drained off, evaporated into a syrup (45 to 50 per cent solids) and combined with the draff left after mashing to turn into "dark grains", for livestock fodder.

The low wines are at about 21% ABV. They pass to the "low wines and feints charger", where their strength is raised to at least 28% ABV by the "feints" and "foreshots" (*see* page 78) already in the charger. This is important, as whisky does not fractionate if the low wines are under 28% ABV. A fair amount of feints and foreshots circulate time and again and are never saved as spirit. Although this is inefficient, it is important for fractionation.

THE SECOND DISTILLATION

The second stage of distilling further purifies and concentrates the spirit. As well as pure ethyl alcohol and water, the low wines contain a large number of less pure alcohols and oils. These are mainly esters, aldehydes, furfurol and other compounds of hydrogen, oxygen and carbon. Hundreds of these organic chemicals have been identified in malt whisky, and chemists acknowledge that there are hundreds more which have yet to be isolated. They are known collectively as congeners or congenerics (USA). Although they are impurities, they give malt whisky its flavour and so must not be eliminated altogether. The skill is to include just the right amount of them in the final spirit saved.

Such impure alcohols are distilled off at the early and late stages of the second distillation. The early runnings are called "foreshots" and the later ones "feints" or "after-shots". Only the middle fraction of the distillate is saved and this is known as the "cut".

The cut must be judged precisely as too many undesirable compounds or congeners would render the spirit undrinkable. The stillman's art is to create a spirit containing sufficient quantities of these higher alcohols to ensure the whisky's distinctive taste.

Foreshots will begin to run when the temperature reaches 84°C (183°F) – if they "come over" sooner, a longer and stronger run of spirit can be expected. Foreshots are of high alcoholic strength and pungent, owing to the impurities they contain. The stillman watches them flow into the "spirit safe", a brass-bound glass-fronted box. He tests for purity by adding water. This is called the "demisting test"; if the spirit goes cloudy when water is added it is not pure. The stillman also checks the strength with a hydrometer. He lets the spirit run into the low wines and feints receiver for re-distillation until it clears, when he directs the flow to be saved by manipulating a spout within the spirit safe. Some distilleries dispense with tests in the spirit safe, preferring to run the foreshots for a specified time.

The breadth of the cut – just how much foreshots and feints are saved – has a profound effect on the flavour of the finished product.

The moment the stillman makes the cut varies and is based upon the demisting point. However in all cases the spirit will have declined in strength to 72% to 75% ABV; this usually takes 15 to 30 minutes. As we will see, the moment of the first cut is crucial to the character of the end product.

The first running of the second distillation is rich in highly desirable, aromatic esters (once, of course, any impurities are expelled). Fragrant, fruity and reminiscent of pear-drops, bananas and roses they are valuable flavour enhancers in malt whisky. There are at least 100 individual esters present – the most important from an aromatic/chemical point of view being isoamyl acetate and ethyl caprylate. About half way through the second spirit run another family of aromatics begins to emerge from the spirit. These are feints, and as the run proceeds they increase in intensity, while the esters decrease.

To start with, feints are pleasant and biscuity, then they become more porridge-like and leathery, after which they pass through a brief honey phase. Soon after this they deteriorate rapidly into unpleasant aromas reminiscent of sweat, stale fish and vomit. In the language of chemistry, the acceptable cereal feints are organo-nitrogen compounds, while the unacceptable feints are organo-sulphur compounds. The aromatic intensity of the latter can be very strong (detectable one part in a trillion!) and is often described as sulphury, rubbery or egg-like.

Because feints rise in intensity, the stillman is obliged to stop collecting spirit before they become unpleasant, even though the alcoholic strength is still high. This is the end of the cut and is crucial to the overall flavour of the spirit because some of the heavier feints will be now present. The longer the stillman leaves it before he stops saving the spirit, the more feinty and robust will be his whisky, but if he cuts too early the spirit will not have the essential character that identifies it as whisky.

Distillers are often secretive about the strength at which they stop collecting the spirit. Some, particularly on Speyside where they look for a lighter whisky character, cut as high as 69% ABV; others, looking for a heavier whisky, leave it as low as 60% ABV. Alas, the decision is sometimes left to accountants rather than seekers for excellence.

The third key aromatic group in malt whisky is the phenols. We have already investigated their origin in peat (*see* page 66). Phenolic compounds begin to become apparent in the distillate about a third of the way through the cut, but unlike the other two key aromatics, they neither rise in intensity nor decline noticeably. Some blenders measure the balance of esters, feints and phenols and then grade the whiskies accordingly.

As the run proceeds the temperature rises to 100°C (212°F), which is the boiling point of the de-alcoholised low wines. The rate at which the still is run influences the purity and flavour of the spirit. Feints can surge if the still is run too hard and blow over into the distillate, introducing coarse and rank flavours into the spirit. Indeed, a rich estery fragrance in the stillhouse is an indication that the stills are being run too fast. Some stills even have meters to control the steam automatically, and to ensure a steady flow at the rate required, which might vary between nine and 23 gallons (41 and 104 litres) per minute. It is desirable to rest the stills between changes to let the copper recover, as a well-rested still produces a lighter spirit.

The breadth of the cut – just how many foreshots and feints are saved – has a profound effect on the flavour of the finished product. The later part of the second distillation joins the early part in the low wines and feints receiver to undergo re-distillation, and the still is then run down to 1% ABV. This is called "spent lees" and goes to waste. The feints and spirits produced by the second distillation amount to between one twelfth and one thirteenth of the bulk of the original wash in the still.

FILLING

From the low wines still the spirit saved goes into the "intermediate spirit receiver". The average strength varies, but is usually around 70% ABV. There are rumours of a company, some years ago, that insisted that the average strength in the spirit receiver was 63.5% ABV. This unfortunately implies that it saved an unusually large amount of feints.

Until it has matured for at least three years the saved spirit cannot be legally called whisky. At the distillery it is known as "new-make spirit" (or "clearic" by the men who make it). This is pumped from the still house to the filling store, and from there either into a road tanker, to be transported elsewhere for maturation, or into casks on site. Prior to filling, the spirit is usually reduced in strength to 63.5% ABV, the optimum strength for maturing. Some distilleries fill at higher strength in order to reduce the number of casks required, but the price is that the spirit takes longer to mature.

The new-make spirit is filled into second-hand casks that will usually have held either bourbon or sherry, and in some cases port or other wines. The first incumbent seasons the wood and extracts more obvious flavours deriving from the wood in ways that are beneficial to whisky. The wood also absorbs wine residues, that are extracted by the maturing whisky and become part of its flavour. The cask increases complexity, enhances fragrance and delicacy, creates astringency, lends colour, develops complexity and integrates other flavours. As Dr Jim Swan, chemical analyst and the leading authority on maturation, puts it: "The transformation that takes place during maturation is as much of a metamorphosis as caterpillar to butterfly."

OPPOSITE Re-racking, ie. emptying one cask into another, at Caol Ila, Islay.

BELOW Casks wait to be filled at Bunnahabhain.

WOOD AND MATURATION

Just how crucial the contribution made by maturation is to the final product has only been fully recognised by scientists in recent years, although it was well appreciated by connoisseurs long ago. Contemporary sensory scientists estimate that maturation can account for between 60 and 80 per cent of the flavour of malt whisky. The "can" is there because of the many factors that are involved during the course of maturation: the nature and history of the cask; the style of warehouse in which it lies; its geographical location; the microclimate in which the spirit matures, and for how long. We will consider each of these factors in turn.

Whisky casks – the generic term is "cask" whatever the size or previous use – are always made of oak. They have to be, by law, and experimental maturations in other woods (chestnut for example) have not been successful.

There are about a dozen species of oak commonly used for the maturation of wines and spirits around the world. Whisky is matured almost entirely in *Quercus alba* (American white oak) with a percentage of European oak, *Quercus robur*. The latter are sessile oaks and the casks used currently are mainly Spanish. However, before the First World War many casks came from the Baltic port of Memel. Ancient oak from England was also used in the past but as it is prone to leakage and cracks, had to be split rather than sawn to create watertight stave joins.

While the European species give resinous characteristics and produce more fragrance and astringency, often to a fault, new American oak imparts sharp, turpentine-like or pine-like aromas to the whisky. All trees suitable for making casks must be at least 80 years old.

Oakwood is ideal for maturing whisky because of its intricate chemistry. It contains cellulose (which contributes little during maturation), hemicellulose (which caramelises, adding sweetness and colour), lignin (a good blending agent, pulling the flavours together, increasing complexity and producing vanilla-like notes), tannins (which produce astringency, fragrance and delicacy) and wood extractives (bourbon, sherry, etc. – *see* below). Oakwood also facilitates oxidation, which removes harshness, increases fruitiness and adds complexity, while the charring that the casks undergo removes undesirable off-notes.

BELOW Bending a cask hoop at Speyside Cooperage.

CASKS

New oak imparts a dominant woody flavour – as found in some New World Chardonnays. This is undesirable in Scotch whisky, so second-hand casks are always used. It has to be said that the tradition of filling second-hand casks originated in good Scots parsimony. A hundred years ago, casks and barrels of one kind or another were used as containers for every conceivable material – from butter and salt, to nails and fish – so were available cheap. Experimentation soon showed that ex-sherry casks gave the best flavour to the malt whisky made at that time. Two kinds of cask are mainly used today; those that were formerly used to hold bourbon, and those that once contained sherry.

Ex-bourbon casks fall into two categories:

After-bourbon barrels, or "American Standard Barrels" (ASBs), with a capacity of between 180 and 200 litres, usually transported whole.

Re-made hogsheads, also called "dump hogsheads", with a capacity of 250 litres. For these, the ASBs are transported as staves in bundles known as "shooks" then re-assembled in Scotland with new heads, five ASBs creating three hogsheads. Both barrels and hogsheads will have held bourbon for at least two years.

Ex-sherry casks are **butts or puncheons** (both with a 500 litre capacity, although the former is taller and narrower than the latter). These will have been "seasoned" with sherry (usually oloroso, sometimes fino) for between one and four years; very occasionally they are ex-solera (ie. used for maturing sherry), and will have held sherry for much longer.

The volume to surface area ratio dictates the speed at which the contents will mature: the smaller the cask, the faster the rate. Ex-bourbon wood accounts for 93 per cent of current cask imports, but since sherry-wood can be used beneficially many more times, the number of sherry casks in use is much higher than seven per cent. Sherry casks cost considerably more than bourbon barrels – about £650, compared with £75.80 – but the price of both rises continually. The current stock of casks in Scotland is about 20 million. In the seminal investigation, *Specification of American Oak Wood for Use by the Scotch Whisky Industry,* undertaken by Swan and Gray, chemical analysts, during the late 1980s, it was discovered that the rate of maturation of Scotch whisky is adversely affected unless the oak is slow-grown and air-dried rather than kiln-dried.

ABOVE A cask cools off after firing at Speyside Cooperage.

CASKS SIZES AND TERMS

Name	Description
GORDA	also called a "bodega butt"; 130 gallons (600 litres)
PIPE	formerly used for maturing port; 110 gallons (500 litres)
HOGSHEAD "re-made hogshead"' or "dump hogshead"	the most common cask for whisky; 55 gallons (250 litres)
PUNCHEON	120 gallons (545 litres)
BUTT	formerly used for maturing sherry; 110 gallons (500 litres)
DUMP PUNCHEON	100 gallons (460 litres)
BARREL	usually referred to as an "American Barrel"; 40 gallons (180 litres)
KILDERKIN	in Old Scots "kinken"; 18 gallons (82 litres)
QUARTER	also called a "Firkin"; nine to ten gallons (approximately 45 litres)
ANKER	eight to ten gallons (approximately 40 litres)
OCTAVE	five gallons (22.5 litres)

The original source of American oak was the Ozark Mountain district of Missouri, a remote region with poor soils that grows trees that are too small for most purposes other than for making barrels. However, in recent times the bourbon industry has been sourcing timber from more accessible regions further east, where the soil is better and where the trees grow faster and provide a greater yield. Also many cooperages now kiln-dry their timber in a mere 23 days, rather than leaving it out to season in the open air for 18 months, as was the traditional way.

Swan and Gray found that while kiln-drying makes no difference to the maturation and flavour of bourbon, it does have a drastic effect on the second incumbent – Scotch, Canadian or Irish whisk(e)y. The report suggested that to achieve the desired rate of maturation in all three, at least a quarter of the cask should be made from slow-grown, air-dried oak.

The cask performs three vital functions during maturation: it adds desirable flavours to the spirit, it removes unwanted flavours and it allows the spirit to interact with its environment, losing harsh alcohols and developing complexity through oxidation. This last mechanism is not fully understood.

In order to be bent into shape, the new oak staves must be heated, "toasted". Toasting performs the vital function of altering the chemical structure of the cask's inside surfaces – for example hemicellulose and lignin in the wood degrade to produce caramel, vanilla and coconut flavours that leech into the spirit along with colour and wine residues (if the cask is ex-sherry). Without toasting the cask will not add these and other desirable flavours to the spirit; indeed, if the staves were to be bent with steam, the resulting cask would not mature its contents at all.

Following toasting, the insides of American barrels are set on fire and "charred". The carbon char forms a useful "purifier", removing immature characteristics and unwanted compounds (mainly sulphur molecules), which is why many vodka and bourbon makers filter their spirits through beds of carbon to increase their purity. This does not happen with ex-sherry casks, which may account for the sulphury flavours sometimes found in whiskies matured in such casks.

As might be expected, a brand-new cask is much more active than one that has been filled before, and quickly dominates the flavours coming from the spirit, the "distillery character". So much so that Scotch spirit is almost never filled into new wood. Likewise, the cask's ability to mature its contents reduces over time. After three or four fills (depending how long the first and second fills were, and upon the chemistry of the individual staves) they lose their activity and become mere vessels. Now they are deemed to be "exhausted" or "spent". They can be "rejuvenated", however, by being reamed out and re-toasted/burnt – a process called "de-char, re-char". This re-activates the layer of wood beneath the char, but it does not make the cask as good as new, and a rejuvenated cask will not mature its contents in the same way as a first-fill cask.

The cask performs three vital functions during maturation: it adds desirable flavours to the spirit, it removes unwanted flavours and it allows the spirit to interact with its environment, losing harsh alcohols and developing complexity through oxidation.

WAREHOUSES

Traditional bonded warehouses – called "dunnage" warehouses – are low, stone-built and earth-floored with casks racked three high. Modern "racked" warehouses are much larger, temperatures are mechanically controlled and the casks are stacked up to 12 high. The largest modern warehouse is Macallan's at Craigellachie which covers half an acre and holds over 70,000 casks.

The way in which whisky matures is influenced by the style and location of the warehouse. Wherever it matures the whisky "breathes" through the cask, losing two per cent of its volume each year, and this is known as "The Angel's Share".

In dunnage warehouses, which are more humid and where there is more air circulation, the volume of whisky in the cask remains high, but its strength declines (by about 4% to 5% ABV in ten years). In racked warehouses, the opposite is true – strength remains high but volume declines. Traditional warehouses will impart a greater mellowness, over the same period of time, than racked warehouses but state-of-the-art modern warehouses, like Macallan's, seek to combine the virtues of both.

The physical location of the warehouse also imparts character to the maturing spirit. Whisky matured on one site will be different from the same spirit matured at another geographical area. Coastal bonds lashed by winter gales and permeated by damp salty air produce whiskies with different characteristics (mainly salty) than those matured far inland. Summer and winter temperatures vary more widely inland than on the coast (-3°C to 20°C/30°F to 68°F in Orkney; -25°C to 25°C/18°F to 77°F on Speyside); it is claimed that steady maturation is upset by wide temperature fluctuations. It is instructive to taste Bowmore that has been matured on Islay against the same whisky matured in the bond at Bowling, on the banks of the River Clyde, or Highland Park matured in Orkney, against the same matured at the bonded warehouse in Glasgow.

TIME

Although by law, whisky cannot be called Scotch until it has matured for at least three years, just how long it should be left in the cask depends on the individual whisky and on the individual cask. Unlike wine, it does not continue to mature in the bottle, although it might change. Lighter alcohols and esters may find their way through the stopper in time, and some oxidation occurs, so the overall impression may be of a heavier whisky.

OPPOSITE Applying a stencil to the head of a cask at Glenrothes distillery.

Generally speaking, lighter whiskies (Lowlands, for example) mature more quickly than heavier malts (like some Islays or Campbeltowns), but everything depends on the character of the wood. No two casks are the same. Even consecutively numbered casks filled with whisky from the same still-run can, after the same period of time, produce very different whiskies, one fully mature, the other nowhere like it. It is also important to understand that maturation is not a simple linear improvement. The spirit matures in fits and starts, influenced by the specific microclimate of the warehouse and seasonal changes that might carry over from one summer to the next.

Some commentators believe that whisky might have more than one peak in maturation which would include dull periods where the spirit flavours lie dormant. This seems to me to be unlikely. Personal taste, and the occasion of drinking, also come into the equation. There seems to be a difference in how whiskies taste according to where they are drunk. The Italian market, for example, drinks malt younger than the home market. Some whiskies will continue to improve greatly for 30 years or more; others become spoiled by an excess of woody flavours after only half that period.

From this we can see how much of the final character of the whisky we drink depends on the cask; only now is it recognised just how much truth there is in the saying, "The Wood Makes the Whisky".

WHISKY TASTING

"Let us number their sins. Foremost among these is that they drink not for the pleasure of drinking nor for any merits of flavour or bouquet which the whisky may possess but simply in order to obtain a certain physical effect. They regard whisky not as a beverage but as a drug, not as an end but as a means to an end... Whisky suffers its worst insults at the hands of the swillers, the drinkers-to-get-drunk who have not organs of taste and smell in them but only gauges of alcoholic content, the boozers, the 'let's-have-a-spot' and 'make-it-a-quick-one' gentry, and all the rest who dwell in a darkness where there are no whiskies but only whisky – and, of course, soda."

Writing in the 1930s, Aeneas Macdonald bemoaned the lack of appreciation shown to malt whisky. He would have rejoiced at the situation today. When it comes to appreciation, I believe he would have agreed that you should enjoy your dram as you choose, without pomposity, for the conviviality that is inherent in drinking whisky, for the effect as well as for the flavour. Having said this, properly shaped glasses, the right amount and quality of water, serving at the correct temperature and observing a simple procedure enhances appreciation greatly. This is what we shall look at in this chapter.

ABOVE Tasting in uncontrolled conditions in an Edinburgh bar.

LEFT Samples of malt whisky ready for tasting in controlled conditions.

SENSORY EVALUATION

Whisky "tasting" is something of a misnomer, since most of the work of evaluation is done by the nose not the palate. Professional whisky tasters are themselves called "Noses". We should really be talking, more correctly, about "sensory evaluation", for the proper assessment of a glass of whisky employs four of our five senses – sight, smell, taste and touch. Flavour is a combination of the last three. It might even be claimed that our fifth sense – hearing – comes into play when the cork is drawn and the first measure glugs into the glass. Indeed, we should not forget the clink of glass against glass to the words *slainte* – health – or *slainte mhath* – good health. To which the proper reply is *slainte mhor* – great health!

SMELL

Although it is under-used in daily life, smell is our most acute sense, and can have a powerful subliminal influence upon our reaction to a place or a person. The acuteness of our sense of smell is demonstrated by the fact that scientists have identified 32 primary aromas, while there are only three primary colours and four primary tastes. Smell is also the most evocative trigger for memory – think how scenes of childhood can be instantly conjured by certain smells – and professional whisky noses and wine tasters consciously store their memories with key aromas, standard norms and exceptions to the rules. Upon these they are able to base their judgement of a particular sample, to identify its age and provenance, and if they are experienced, to name the distillery, château or domaine where the sample was created.

The nose is our most sensitive organ, able to identify aromas diluted to one part per million (even in a few parts per trillion in certain chemicals) and capable of isolating individual scents from a confusion of aromatic information. The information is conveyed by volatile molecules, either via the nostrils or through the back nasal passage, when the liquid is tasted and swallowed. It is picked up by myriad complex receptors located in the olfactory epithelium in the base of the skull, and thence direct to the brain via the olfactory tracts.

However, repeated sniffing can tend to cause a dulling of the olfactory nerves towards that particular group of aromas which means that:

a) first impressions are the most important ones;

OPPOSITE The author noses a new batch sample for the Scotch Malt Whisky Society.

BELOW The spirits nosing glasses used by professionals are made of crystal and calibrated in fluid ounces.

b) if the first impression is vague or difficult to pin down, there is not much point in continuing to sniff. Move on to another sample or rest your nose.

By and large, one person's ability to identify aromas is much the same as the next – most people will score between 70 and 80 per cent in simple odour recognition tests – although some people suffer from anosmia (ie. "odour blindness"), or particular sensitivity to certain groups of smells at the expense of others. Obviously, a blocked nose or a heavy cold impairs one's ability to smell. Also, as with our other faculties, one's sense of smell can deteriorate with age.

Despite what one might assume, our sense of smell is not affected by smoking – although you should not smoke during, or half an hour before a tasting, since this tends to anaesthetise your sensory receptors. Some of the greatest noses and wine tasters are enthusiastic smokers.

BELOW An immemorial custom of Scotland, a "hauf-an-a-hauf", comprises a glass of beer and a glass of Scotch whisky.

TASTE

Taste is identified by receptors (tastebuds) on the tongue and soft palate; these are connected to the medulla (situated at the top of the spinal cord) and thence to the areas of the brain that interpret taste. There are only four primary tastes – sweet, sour, salty and bitter – and the distribution of the receptors sensitive to each varies from person to person. Generally however, it tends to be: sweet on the tip of the tongue, sour/acidic on the upper edges, salty at the sides and bitter/dry at the back. Because of this distribution, it is essential to take a decent sip of liquid and swirl it about your mouth if you are properly to assess its primary taste.

In the eighteenth century people went in for "tongue scraping" to keep their tastebuds fresh. This involved drawing a little whalebone strip, often mounted with silver handles, across the surface of the tongue. I have not tried it but it is possible that it might revive a jaded palate.

Tastebuds take a moment or two to return to normal after having been stimulated, although the time varies from receptor to receptor, with those on the back of the tongue taking longest, thus sometimes leaving a lingering bitterness in the aftertaste. Physiologically, the tongue only collects primary data but the volatiles within the mouthful have an effect on the olfactory epithelium via the back nasal passage. So tasting is a combination of primary tastes and aromatics, and it becomes possible to use a more accurate and wider vocabulary than sweet, sour, salty and bitter to describe how whisky tastes.

Sensory scientists have identified some 300 constituent flavours in malt whisky, and estimate that there are as many more which have yet to be isolated and described. Yet the flavour elements, called "congeners", in a bottle of whisky at 40% ABV must be sought in a mere 0.2 per cent of its contents. The remaining 59.8 per cent is water, and both it and the 40 per cent alcohol are neutral in smell and taste.

TOUCH

The final component of flavour is how it feels in the mouth or on the nose. Feeling factors come into play most obviously when assessing the texture or temperature of food.

In relation to whisky, nose-feel effects are often associated with pungency – prickly, sharp, even painful – but may also be acrid, warming or cooling. Mouth-feel effects cover a range of sensations, collected by the tongue, palate, cheeks, throat, and even teeth; such feelings as astringent, drying, viscous, mouth-filling, mouth-coating, cloying, warming, metallic, mouth-watering/salivating, tingly, fizzy and so on. Physiologically, we must add another mechanism to the tastebuds and olfactory epithelium. This is termed trigeminal stimulation – the detection of pungency by the free nerve endings of the trigeminal nerve.

Basically these are pain sensors which register the presence of feeling factors such as irritation, pungency and nose warming. Whisky is usually diluted to a point where trigeminal stimulation ceases to be important; however, it is useful to remember that whilst the sense of smell adapts rapidly (one quickly becomes used to a smell as its intensity falls away), the sense of pungency increases equally rapidly until it eventually becomes painful.

ABOVE The nosing
room at Strathisla
distillery.

PREPARING FOR A TASTING

THE NOSING ROOM
This should be free of extraneous smells, like fresh paint, cooking, smoke or floor polish. It should also be well enough lit for you to be able to consider the appearance of the samples presented. I prefer to be seated at a table but many expert blenders, who have to nose large numbers of samples, and who know what they are looking for, do it standing – even "on the run".

THE TASTING PANEL

Tasting in company and comparing notes is much more useful than nosing alone, as well as being more fun. Alone, it is easy to become trapped in one train of thought or to become manacled by related descriptors. The comments of other members of the panel can break this pattern and set you off into new areas of exploration. Recently, I was nosing a range of whiskies and for some reason found myself stuck in cereals – maize flour, cornflakes, Weetabix, chicken mash, etc. Someone else on the panel was focused on puddings, so we were able to open each other's minds to further possibilities!

For serious tastings, the room should be quiet and well ventilated. Panel members should not wear perfume and should not wash their hands with strong-smelling soap immediately prior to a tasting. They should not have eaten a large meal before the tasting – the senses are sharpened by hunger. Most people are at their best from a sensory point of view in the morning, before lunch. At important tastings, the glasses should be washed with odour-free detergent and allowed to drain dry before use, since even polishing with a cloth might leave a trace of scent.

GLASSES

The right size and shape of glass is vital, and makes a huge difference to one's ability to nose effectively. Traditional whisky tumblers are hopeless. They were designed for drinking whisky and soda – for which they are fine. What is required is a "snifter" that allows you to swirl the spirit and gathers the aromas around the rim. A sherry *copita* or small brandy balloon are ideal. The trade uses a "spirits nosing glass", made of crystal, for sharpness and clarity, often calibrated in fluid ounces so you can tell at what strength you are nosing – eg. if the sample is at 60% ABV and you pour one ounce, then dilute up to the two ounce mark, the drink is now at 30% ABV. "Black" glasses (they are really dark blue) of a similar style are useful for blind tastings, where you want to hide the colour of the spirit.

DILUTION

Whisky at high strength anaesthetises the nose and sears the tongue, rendering you incapable of evaluating the sample. Almost all whiskies benefit from the addition of water, which with most whiskies "opens up" the spirit by breaking down the ester chains and freeing the volatile aromatics. Very occasionally one encounters a whisky whose virtues are better displayed neat.

Panel members should not wear perfume and should not wash their hands with strong-smelling soap immediately prior to a tasting.

Outside the tasting room, many people prefer to drink their after-dinner malts straight – with sound medical justification. In these cases your own saliva acts as the dilutant, and they should be sipped in very small amounts.

Blenders nose at 20% ABV, but this can drown some whiskies, especially old, delicate malts, and heavily sherried whiskies, which tend to "break up" with too much water. I once tasted a very special blend called "The 500" made to celebrate the 500th anniversary of the first recorded mention of Scotch, and selling for £500 a bottle. Although I added only a small amount of water, it was too much and the expensive dram in my glass was rendered worthless. It is always best to add water a little at a time until any nose prickle has disappeared and the sample has fully opened up.

WATER

The water you use to reduce the strength of your dram should be still and not too high in minerals. True aficionados will use the water used in the production of the individual whisky they are tasting. This is often difficult to come by, although I know of a man who regularly exchanges a litre of Glenlivet spring water for a half bottle of whisky, so much is it esteemed. Scottish water is predominantly soft, so if your local tap water has a suspicious taste, is heavily recycled or chlorinated, your best bet is to use plain bottled water from Scotland. The important thing is that the water is odourless and tasteless.

TEMPERATURE

The ideal temperature at which whisky should be drunk varies according to the climate of the country in which you are drinking it. However for the purposes of tasting malt whisky it is best appreciated at the equivalent room temperature of an old-fashioned Scottish parlour (however it's difficult to recreate in these days of central heating, and hermetic glazing). In other words, you should nose at about 15°C (59 °F). Chilled whisky does not readily yield up its aromas and the addition of ice will close them down altogether. On the other hand, warming the glass in the hand – as one does with brandy – helps to release the volatiles in the spirit, especially when the sample you are tasting is neat.

THE TASTING PROCEDURE

ABOVE Standard whisky sample bottles, showing the range of colours between malts, from lightest straw to deepest copper.

We have seen that the evaluation of Scotch whisky, and other spirits, employs our senses of sight, smell and taste. This logically gives rise to three main stages in the tasting procedure, during which one assesses appearance, aroma and taste.

APPEARANCE
You are evaluating colour and clarity (brightness), beading and body.

Colour – This ranges from gin-clear to deep liquorice, with every imaginable bronze-gold hue in-between. When it is filled into the barrel, whisky is clear and draws its colour from the cask during maturation. So considering the colour of the sample should tell you something about the cask in which it has been matured and the length of time it has been in it; the longer the maturation, the deeper the colour. But beware. Oft-filled casks, especially bourbon-wood, impart little colour, even over a lengthy period, while a first-fill oloroso might be the colour of treacle after five years. In general, American oak imparts a golden colour and European oak an umber hue. So if a ten-year-old malt is pale straw in colour, it would indicate that it has come from a much-refilled cask. If it is the colour of polished mahogony, it would suggest a first-fill European cask. Beware, however, since the colour is often enhanced by the addition of spirit caramel, generally used to ensure uniformity from batch to batch.

Clarity/brightness – Most whisky undergoes chill-filtering prior to bottling. During this process, the temperature of the spirit is reduced to between 4°C and -10°C (39.2°F to 14°F), while it is squeezed through a series of paper filters. The effect is of "polishing" and clarifying the whisky, by using either a few or multiple filter-pads. However, the latter can take some of the flavour and colour out of the whisky.

The technique was developed in the 1970s when distillers wanted to find a way to extract the elements in the spirit that cause the whisky to become hazy if served chilled or with ice. Pentlands Scotch Whisky Research, chemical analysts to the industry, developed this process at the request of Teacher's, which had a shipment of Scotch returned from Chicago on account of its being "cloudy". It transpired that the consignment had lain on the dock for some weeks in sub-zero temperatures, because of a stevedores' strike. Although there was nothing wrong with the flavour, the contents looked strange. The technique was used in the wine trade prior to the 1970s; before this whisky was merely hand-filtered to remove the physical particles present.

Chill-filtering makes for a brighter dram, certainly, but there is no doubt that it also reduces flavour and mouth-feel. So if your sample looks a bit dull, and goes slightly opaque when you add water, it has probably not been chill-filtered, a good sign.

Beading – If you shake the bottle vigorously, the whisky foams up then dissipates. Whisky at below 50% ABV dissipates much more quickly than high strength spirit, and the bubbles are smaller. In full-bodied whiskies, the beads lie like pearls on the surface of the liquid for some time after it has settled.

So a consideration of beading tells you something about the strength and weight, or "body", of the sample. I remember an occasion when I was out stalking being handed an unlabelled bottle by Brian Hamilton, head stalker on Dorback Estate, Speyside. He asked me what it was. While I was nosing it the bottle was passed to Willie Grant, the ancient assistant stalker. Willie shook the bottle vigorously, considered the beading and guessed, correctly, that it was a cask strength Glenfarclas from a sherry butt, at about 15 Years Old!

Body – The body of a whisky is judged "light", "medium" or "full" by mouth-feel and appearance. Swirl the neat spirit in the glass. As it slides back down to the surface again, globules with tails are visible against the sides of the glass. These are called "legs". Long legs indicate high alcohol and legs that are slow to disappear indicate the presence of oils that give the spirit a fuller body, implying richness.

AROMA

You are assessing first the "nose-feel" of the undiluted (unreduced strength) whisky, then its aroma and then the aroma of the diluted (reduced) whisky.

Nose-feel – The tingle you get at the back of your nose when sniffing high-alcohol spirit. It is a register of pungency and ranges from "prickle" to "pain", through "nose-warming", "nose-drying", even "nose-burn". When it comes to diluting the spirit, it is best to reduce the strength to the point that nose-feel disappears. Sniff gingerly at the outset if you are not sure of the strength of the whisky and want to avoid an unpleasant surprise. A deep sniff can anaesthetise your nose for a while; this is known as "palate fade".

Aroma (unreduced) – First impressions are most important. Swirl the sample in the glass and sniff it carefully, bearing in mind the nose-feel you have already identified. The cardinal characteristics of the whisky should be identifiable, but in many cases the aromatics will be spirity, vaporous or "closed" until water is added. Ask yourself how "forward" or "shy" the spirit is. Evaluate its intensity and complexity. If the sample presents you with an intriguing and delightful complex of aromas at this stage, beware how much water you add at the next. Note your impressions.

Aroma (reduced) – Add a little water and watch the threads and eddies of the scent-bearing ester chains as they are released. These are called "viscimetric whorls", appear similar to a viscous substance added to water. Sniff again and then add a little more water until any nose prickle has vanished. Nose first over the top of the glass to catch the "bouquet" of the whisky and then within to penetrate the deeper secrets. Again, first impressions are most important. Note the first descriptors that come to mind. Always take a good sniff of fresh air from time to time and beware of repeated nosing and deep sniffing in the attempt to identify a single elusive smell: your olfactory equipment becomes bored and will close it off. Go to another sample or rest for a while.

Professional noses and whisky blenders learn all they need to about a sample when they have reached this point, but we enthusiasts continue to the final reward.

TASTE

By definition, "flavour" is a combination of "smell" and "taste". Taste itself breaks down into mouth-feel (texture), primary tastes, overall flavour and finish.

Always take a good sniff of fresh air from time to time and beware of repeated nosing and deep sniffing in the attempt to identify a single elusive smell: your olfactory equipment becomes bored and will close it off.

RIGHT By adding a little water at a time, the spirit will relax and open up.

Mouth-feel – Take a large enough sip to coat the entire tongue. Hold it in the mouth for a moment, then either spit it out or swallow. What is the whisky's intensity and texture? Malts can usually be divided into those which are "mouth-coating" (creamy, viscous, smooth, etc.), "mouth-warming" (spirity) or "mouth-furring" (astringent, puckering). Some also have an intriguing "fizz" about them, like Space Dust or sherbet.

Primary taste – Take another sip. Chew it a bit, and squelch it around your mouth. Feel it sliding over your tongue and activating your tastebuds. What is the balance of sweetness (this is picked up by the tip of the tongue), saltiness (identified by the sides of the tongue), acidity or sourness (on the tongue's upper edges) and bitterness or dryness as it slides over the back of your tongue?

Most whiskies will present all the primary tastes, but in different proportions; some have a centre palate directness, some stimulate one area more than the others. For your own tasting notes you may like to mark each taste on a one to five scale.

Overall flavour – The first question sensory analysts ask is whether the sample tastes like whisky. The sample loses points if there is any doubt, although you and I might be curious and entertained by a sample with odd characteristics, so long as they were pleasant. I remember drinking some independently bottled Glen Garioch that tasted deliciously like green ginger wine. On another occasion I tasted some Glenlivet that had spent 60 years in a sherry butt and was disappointed to discover that it smelled and tasted like over-strength dry oloroso.

As with wine, a whisky can be judged as being good if it is well balanced. That is, if all the aromatic and taste elements within it are in pleasing harmony. It is important that the taste matches or surpasses the expectation set up by the aroma.

Whiskies that smell sweet and taste as dry as a bone are unsettling; whiskies that promise to be full-flavoured but turn out to be thin and fade quickly, cannot help but disappoint. However, whiskies with limited scent that are discovered to be wonderfully mouth-filling and flavourful bring satisfaction all round.

Finish – Finish is the length of time the flavour of the whisky lingers in the mouth after swallowing, the pleasantness of this flavour and its aftertaste. A medium to long finish is desirable, although a short finish lends a crispness to certain malts.

Occasionally a perfectly good sample is spoiled by an unpleasant aftertaste. The flavour of very old, very rich whiskies can linger for hours. Richard Paterson, the master blender at Whyte & Mackay, once gave me a glass of Dalmore that had been distilled in 1893. It was dark as molasses and miraculously intense – the very quintessence of malt whisky. We did not add water, rather allowing the delicious complexities of flavour in the spirit to unravel in our mouths; enjoying the sensation as it rolled down our throats. The finish was the longest I have ever encountered and he added to the mystery of the occasion by telling me that I would still taste it in the morning. Indeed I did, and the next day awoke with a deep, resonant, glorious memory.

Exposed to the air, the flavour of whisky changes in the glass. This can be checked (although not eliminated) by placing a watch glass over the top. However, when you are doing a serious evaluation, it is well to leave the samples uncovered for a time, and nose them again after 30 minutes and 60 minutes to see whether any off-notes have developed. Many blenders leave their samples uncovered for 30 minutes before nosing.

It is continually brought home to me how the flavours of whiskies can change according to the time of day and the circumstances in which you taste them. Both objective and subjective factors play a role here. In the morning, with a clean palate and a clear head, one's senses are sharper than late at night, after a good meal. Aromas and flavours are registered differently; lighter whiskies, of subtle bouquet before lunch, may seem nondescript in the evening, just as pungent whiskies can reveal layers of floral and fruity scents in the evening. So in order to register these variations it is rewarding to evaluate individual whiskies at different times of day.

It is continually brought home to me how the flavours of whiskies can change according to the time of day and the circumstances in which you taste them. Both objective and subjective factors play a role here.

THE LANGUAGE OF
WHISKY TASTING

ABOVE A rare nineteenth-century nosing glass at Tamdhu distillery.

It is difficult to put words to smells, and the language used is hotly debated. Just how effusive and allusive should one be? How many similes are permissible? There are two broad camps: the "Traditionalists" who are tight-lipped and the "Modernists" who are florid. Both styles of notes are justifiable and much depends upon the purposes to which they will be put. Are they for personal use, as an aide-memoire, or purely for the pleasure of exploring a whisky? Are they to be used for describing a whisky to others, in a newspaper, say? Will they form the basis for purchasing a cask, or a bottle? Are they to be used as advertising copy, for selling the whisky? And so on. Clearly, some uses demand greater objectivity and linguistic control than others.

OBJECTIVE AND SUBJECTIVE TASTINGS

Sensory analysts draw a distinction between "objective" and "subjective" tastings. In the first (also termed "analytical tastings") everything is arranged to encourage the members of the tasting panel to describe only "what is there". The situation in which the tasting takes place is controlled and tasters are carefully screened to identify bias or anosmia (*see* page 92) in their aromatic spectrum. As with a scientific experiment, procedures are controlled so that the results can be verified by repetition. The language used tends to relate to the chemistry of the product being evaluated. Below is one distiller's check-list of aromas and off-notes in new-make spirit. Subjective tastings – also termed "hedonic tastings" (as in "hedonism", the pursuit of pleasure) – are not as rigorous. Tasters receive no formal training, personal biases are not suppressed and descriptors might be more colourful. These are the commonest form of tastings outside a blender's nosing room and are no less valuable than analytical tastings.

Anyone who has had the chance to sit on a tasting panel will be aware that consensus of opinion is the rule, not the exception. There is no sounder test of the accuracy of a descriptor than the enthusiastic nodding of heads around the table, and where required, the chemical compounds, congeners and aromatic groups can be identified from even the most personal and colourful of similes. In other words, the two approaches are not mutually exclusive.

TASTING NOTES
Until the late 1970s the whisky industry relied upon the flavour terminology and aromatic classifications used to describe wine

STANDARD REFERENCE ODOURS IN GRAIN SPIRIT

Name	Description
ACROLEIN	sharp, acid, pungent
B	meaty, Marmite, burnt rubber
DI-METHYL TRI-SULPHIDE	cooked cabbage, water, drains, spent matches
FEINTS	amyl alcohol, plastic, cheesy
ACETAL	green apples
DIACETYL	buttery, sweet, heavy
RIBES	cats, tomato leaves, redcurrant leaves
PHENOLS	iodine, carbolic, peat, smoke, bonfires

and beer. These were found to be inadequate in many respects, as they did not include the principal aromatic groups or the key terms needed to describe whisky. What is more, the words used to describe wine or beer were ambiguous or inaccurate when applied to whisky. For example, when a beer is described as malty or grainy this is a plus point; in whisky it is likely to be the opposite. Wine derives "fruitiness" from grapes, which – although they impart a wide range of scents – smell very different from the fruity aromas discovered in whisky.

The task of systematising and expanding upon the language of whisky was eloquently undertaken by Shortreed, Rickards, Swan and Birtles of Pentlands Scotch Whisky Research in 1979. They adopted a tasting wheel that could be used by the industry, not the consumer, for assessing "new-make" and mature spirit. In 1996/97, I collaborated with Dr Jim Swan and Dr Jennifer Newton of RR Tatlock & Thomson (Analytical and Consulting Chemists) to redraw the "Whisky Wheel", with a view to making it less confusing for the non-specialist consumer. Our new wheel (see pages 108–9) has three tiers. The inner hub comprises the cardinal aromatic groups to be found in Scotch whisky. The middle tier breaks these down into secondary aromatic groups. And the outer rim supplies loose, hedonic descriptors. So if a particular scent is discovered in a sample, it can be identified on the outer rim and then attributed to its aromatic group on the first tier. Not all the aromas (even aromatic groups) will be found in every malt whisky. Taste (ie. mouth-feel and primary tastes) is measured on the smaller wheel. "Complexity", "Intensity" and "Pungency" might also be scored.

THE CHEMICAL DERIVATION OF FLAVOUR

WHERE DO FLAVOURS COME FROM?
Aromas and flavours in malt whisky come either from the production process (including the raw materials) or from maturation. Reading the wheel clockwise, the first five (Cereal, Estery, Floral, Peaty and Feinty) derive from production. They also emerge in the spirit in that order, during distillation. Sulphury comes from both production and maturation. Woody and Winey flavours are communicated during maturation.

The aromatic groups have their roots in organic chemistry. A list of some of the chemicals within each group is supplied below. It provides an indication only and is not exhaustive.

CEREAL Organo-nitrogen compounds. Found in all malt whiskies, especially immature samples. To have too many cereal notes is not good.

FRUITY Ethyl acetate, isoamyl acetate, hexyl acetate, pear-drops, nail-varnish remover etc. These scents are highly desirable and often found in Speysides.

FLORAL Acetal, acetaldehyde, beta ionone, phenlyethanol. Fragrant, perfumed, green grassy aromas often found in Lowland malts.

PEATY Phenols. Phenolic notes are either smoky or medicinal and typical of the more pungent Islay whiskies.

FEINTY Volatile acids, organo-nitrogen compounds, amines. The most difficult aromatic group to describe. They give whisky its essential character, yet they are generally unpleasant on their own. They begin to emerge about halfway through the spirit run and increase in pungency and noxiousness.

WOODY Hemicellulose, lignin, vanillin. The chemicals in oakwood react with the spirit, adding vanilla and caramel flavours, colour and complexity.

SULPHURY Organo-sulphur compounds, di-methyl sulphide, mercaptans. These come from both malt and maturation and while a little is fine, too much "brimstone" is a minus point.

WINEY Extractives. From a leeching of the previous contents of the cask, such as sherry.

BLAND Recognisable as whisky but lacking in distinguishable characteristics, or personality.

ABSTRACT TERMS USED TO DESCRIBE SCOTCH WHISKY
Many descriptive terms, commonly used in whisky assessment
– especially in assessing mature samples – cannot be defined by
reference to a standard. They are abstract, comparative terms,
describing an overall impression, rather than a specific aroma.
Pentlands Scotch Whisky Research has produced a list, as follows,
in alphabetical order.

BODY Essentially related to
the mouth-feel of the product,
and indicative of the amount of
product character.

CLEAN Free from off-notes
from any source. Used primarily
as an indicator of acceptance of
new distillates.

COARSE Implies a product
of indifferent quality, often
associated with a high intensity
of certain flavour characteristics
imparting pungency.

DRY Overall impression of
astringency at an acceptable
level.

FLAT Dull and flavourless
effect, often related to low
intensity or staleness.

FRESH The opposite of
flat; bottled whisky in good
condition.

GREEN Usually denotes a
preponderance of aldehydic
notes.

HARD Where metallic, flinty
and nasal astringency effects
dominate the product.

HEAVY Possessing a high total
intensity of detectable aroma
and flavour characteristics. May
or may not be desirable.

LIGHT Possessing an adequate
intensity of aroma and flavour
characteristics in good balance,
but tending to be delicate.

MELLOW Associated with
good maturation, whereby
alcoholic pungency is suppressed
and the effect of hotness
reduced to a pleasing warmth.

NEUTRAL Implying a plain,
silent spirit, thereby tending
to present only the aroma of
ethyl alcohol.

RICH Implies a high total
intensity of character in relation
to an appropriate standard for
the product. This term should be
used with caution,

however, since it may
also be used to indicate a
preponderance of sweet-
associated aromatics (like sherry
or Christmas cake).

ROBUST A whisky with a high
intensity of aroma and flavour.

ROUND Implying a good
balance and intensity of
aroma and flavour, all of them
appropriate to the product.

SHARP Imparting nose-prickle
or mouth-prickle.

SOFT Implying suppression of
alcoholic and aromatic pungency.

THIN Lacking in aroma
and flavour that should be a
characteristic of the product.
"Diluted" and "watery" might
come to mind (but not "bland").

YOUNG Generally used to
imply that a whisky has not
reached its optimum stage of
development.

WHISKY WHEELS

AROMA

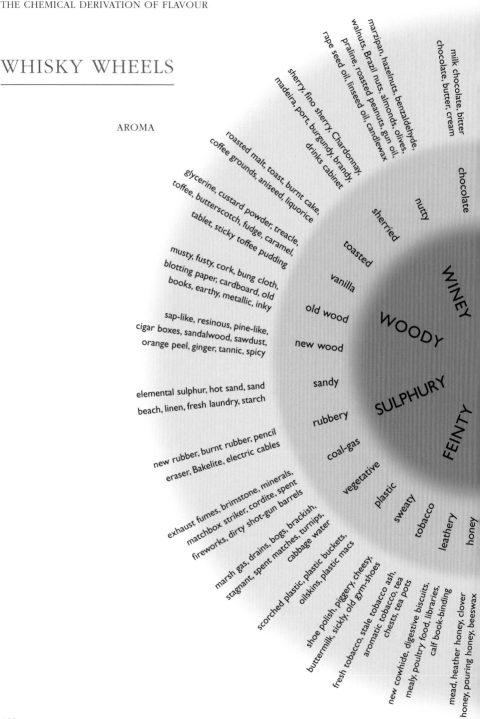

milk chocolate, bitter
chocolate, butter, cream

marzipan, hazelnuts, almonds, olives,
walnuts, Brazil nuts, benzaldehyde,
praline, roasted peanuts, gun oil,
rape seed oil, linseed oil, candlewax

sherry, fino sherry, Chardonnay,
madeira, port, burgundy, brandy,
drinks cabinet

roasted malt, toast, burnt cake,
coffee grounds, aniseed, liquorice

glycerine, custard powder, treacle,
toffee, butterscotch, fudge, caramel,
tablet, sticky toffee pudding

musty, fusty, cork, bung cloth,
blotting paper, cardboard, old
books, earthy, metallic, inky

sap-like, resinous, pine-like,
cigar boxes, sandalwood, sawdust,
orange peel, ginger, tannic, spicy

elemental sulphur, hot sand, sand
beach, linen, fresh laundry, starch

new rubber, burnt rubber, pencil
eraser, Bakelite, electric cables

exhaust fumes, brimstone, minerals,
matchbox striker, cordite, spent
fireworks, dirty shot-gun barrels

marsh gas, drains, bogs, brackish,
stagnant, spent matches, turnips,
cabbage water

scorched plastic, plastic buckets,
oilskins, plastic macs

shoe polish, piggery, cheesy,
buttermilk, sickly, old gym-shoes

fresh tobacco, stale tobacco ash,
aromatic tobacco, tea
chests, tea pots

new cowhide, digestive biscuits,
mealy, poultry food, libraries,
calf book-binding

mead, heather honey, clover
honey, pouring honey, beeswax

chocolate

nutty

sherried

toasted

vanilla

old wood

new wood

sandy

rubbery

coal-gas

vegetative

plastic

sweaty

tobacco

leathery

honey

WINEY

WOODY

SULPHURY

FEINTY

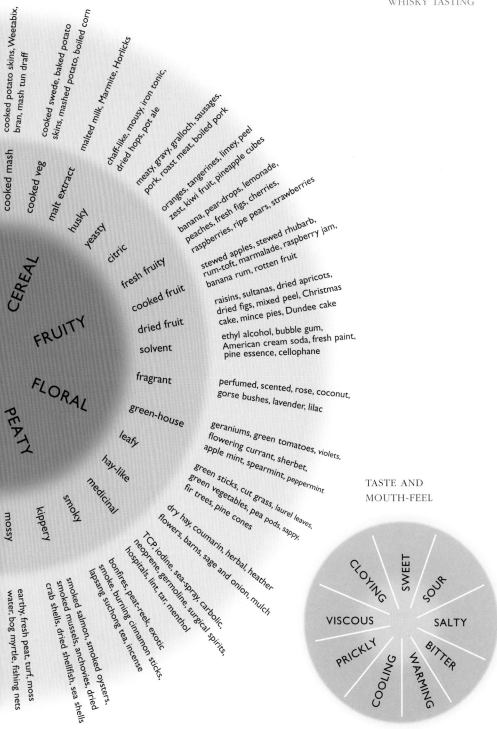

cooked potato skins, Weetabix, bran, mash tun draff

cooked swede, baked potato skins, mashed potato, boiled corn

malted milk, Marmite, Horlicks

chaff-like, mousy, iron tonic, dried hops, pot ale

meaty, gravy, gralloch, sausages, pork, roast meat, boiled pork

oranges, tangerines, limey, peel zest, kiwi fruit, pineapple cubes

banana, pear-drops, lemonade, peaches, fresh figs, cherries, raspberries, ripe pears, strawberries

stewed apples, stewed rhubarb, rum-toft, marmalade, raspberry jam, banana rum, rotten fruit

raisins, sultanas, dried apricots, dried figs, mixed peel, Christmas cake, mince pies, Dundee cake

ethyl alcohol, bubble gum, American cream soda, fresh paint, pine essence, cellophane

perfumed, scented, rose, coconut, gorse bushes, lavender, lilac

geraniums, green tomatoes, violets, flowering currant, sherbet, apple mint, spearmint, peppermint

green sticks, cut grass, laurel leaves, green vegetables, pea pods, sappy, fir trees, pine cones

dry hay, coumarin, herbal, heather flowers, barns sage and onion, mulch

TCP, iodine, sea-spray, carbolic, neoprene, germoline surgical spirits, hospitals, lint, tar, menthol

bonfires, peat-reek, exotic smoke, burning cinnamon sticks, lapsang suchong tea, incense

smoked salmon, smoked oysters-smoked mussels, anchovies, dried crab shells, dried shellfish, sea shells

earthy, fresh peat, turf, moss water, bog myrtle, fishing nets

cooked mash
cooked veg
malt extract
husky
yeasty
citric
fresh fruity
cooked fruit
dried fruit
solvent
fragrant
green-house
leafy
hay-like
medicinal
smoky
kippery
mossy

CEREAL
FRUITY
FLORAL
PEATY

TASTE AND MOUTH-FEEL

CLOYING
SWEET
SOUR
VISCOUS
SALTY
PRICKLY
BITTER
COOLING
WARMING

THE WHISKY REGIONS

During the 1980s, with the growing interest in malt whisky, these regions were subdivided, and stress was laid upon the characteristics of whiskies coming from each region. This appealed to consumers familiar with wine regions and terroir; it appealed to producers, since it encouraged exploration across the whole range of malts; and it appealed to publishers as a convenient way of breaking up the subject into manageable topics!

However we must be cautious. Regional distinctions have been reduced in recent years, as increasing technological advances in the production process have allowed distillers far greater control over the final flavour of their whiskies. Also, such considerations as the origins of the cask, where the whisky was matured, and for how long, will all influence the flavour and make regional judgements difficult.

Here I use the division of Highland, Island and Lowland, and subdivide Highland into "North", "Speyside", "Central", "East", "West" and "Campbeltown", and the Islands into "Islands" and "Islay".

LEFT The first harbour at Portsoy, on the Moray Firth, was built in the sixteenth century. Ships carried whisky from here to the ports of Northern Europe.

THE HIGHLANDS

Defining the whisky regions has been an everchanging process. For excise tax purposes the 1784 Wash Act drew a line across Scotland loosely following the lie of the land between Dunoon in the west and Dundee in the east, dividing the country into "Highland" and "Lowland". Highland distillers were permitted to work smaller stills with weaker washes more slowly than their Lowland counterparts, so producing higher quality whiskies of more complex character. Then in 1797 an intermediate area was defined, and although this lasted only two years, it shifted the Highland Line so that it ran from Lochgilphead to Findhorn, excluding the low ground of Angus and Aberdeenshire.

It was at this point in the history of whisky production that certain districts began to be recognised by connoisseurs as producing especially fine and distinctive styles of whisky. "Glenlivet" is the leading example: it is a name that began by describing a small parish deep in the heart of the Cairngorm Mountains and ended up becoming the generic term describing the style of whisky that we know today, under the regional appellation of "Speyside".

During the nineteenth century, blenders were sub-classifying the Highland region into the "Northern Malts", the "West Highlands", the "whiskies of Aberdeenshire" and those of "Perthshire". Although the terms were more or less synonymous, "Speyside" and "Strathspey" whiskies were also recognised as having distinct characteristics. Until at least the 1970s Highland whiskies were rated by blenders into "Top", "First", "Second" and "Third" Class, according to how desirable a particular whisky was for blending. Several malts which have long been highly rated are termed "Second Class" and all the "Top Class" whiskies are Speysides, which is the style of malt that blenders find most useful. For interest, I include the rating of one blender in 1974 in the distillery directory that follows this chapter.

BELOW The Scottish Highlands have a timeless quality. In French they are named, accurately, *"le pays sauvage"*.

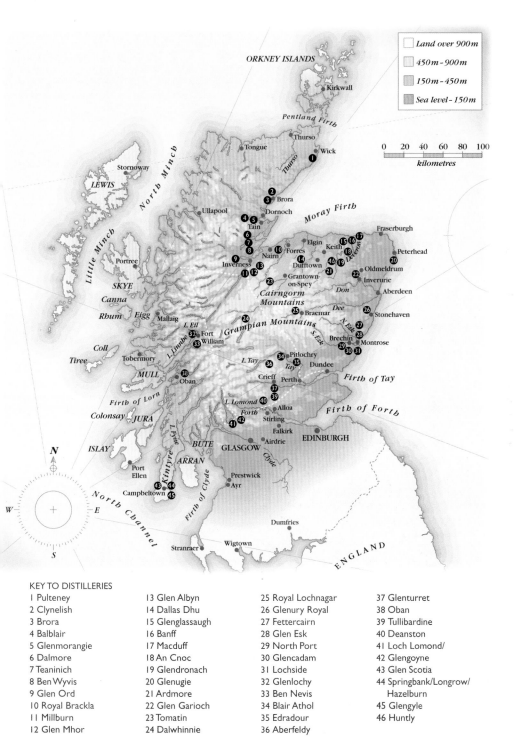

KEY TO DISTILLERIES

1 Pulteney	13 Glen Albyn	25 Royal Lochnagar	37 Glenturret
2 Clynelish	14 Dallas Dhu	26 Glenury Royal	38 Oban
3 Brora	15 Glenglassaugh	27 Fettercairn	39 Tullibardine
4 Balblair	16 Banff	28 Glen Esk	40 Deanston
5 Glenmorangie	17 Macduff	29 North Port	41 Loch Lomond/
6 Dalmore	18 An Cnoc	30 Glencadam	42 Glengoyne
7 Teaninich	19 Glendronach	31 Lochside	43 Glen Scotia
8 Ben Wyvis	20 Glenugie	32 Glenlochy	44 Springbank/Longrow/
9 Glen Ord	21 Ardmore	33 Ben Nevis	Hazelburn
10 Royal Brackla	22 Glen Garioch	34 Blair Athol	45 Glengyle
11 Millburn	23 Tomatin	35 Edradour	46 Huntly
12 Glen Mhor	24 Dalwhinnie	36 Aberfeldy	

NORTH HIGHLANDS

The North Highland distilleries are all coastal, except for Glen Ord, and that is a mere three kilometres (1.6 miles) from the sea. This proximity influences the flavour of the whiskies they produce, many of them having a noticeable saltiness. In general they are complex, medium-bodied and sometimes spicy. The most northerly (Pulteney, Balblair and Clynelish) are faintly smoky, especially the last, which can sometimes be mistaken for an Islay. They are mostly too delicate to benefit from complete maturation in sherry-wood, but "sherry-finishing" (ie. re-racking into sherry-wood for the last year or so of maturation) suits them well. This technique was first developed at the Glenmorangie distillery near Tain.

Beginning in the south, we should look briefly at the distilleries of Inverness – now all defunct although three malts, Glen Albyn, Glen Mhor and Millburn are still occasionally available, all of them classic examples of the Highland style. Other, earlier distilleries in the town had colourful names like Ballackarse and Phopochy, Polnach and Torrich. The capital of the Highlands, Inverness is an untidy, sprawling place that nevertheless has some pretty streets around the city centre and attractive boulevards along banks of the River Ness. It is a town of great antiquity, dating back to at least the sixth century, when St Columba met King Brude of the

BELOW Mountains, lochs and vast tracts of empty marshland characterise the North Highlands.

Picts at a castle "near the Ness", which has since been identified as Auld Castle Hill. There have been several castles on this site. King Macbeth built a stronghold there in the eleventh century, which was the scene of Duncan's murder in Shakespeare's play. This was razed by Macbeth's successor, Malcolm Canmore, and either he or David I built a new castle and made Inverness a Royal Burgh. This was destroyed by Robert the Bruce in 1307, but was again rebuilt, only to be finally destroyed by Bonnie Prince Charlie in 1745. The present castle, which looks like a child's toy fort, was built in 1834. Today it houses the county law courts and local government offices. Whisky distilling was a common practice in and around Inverness from an early period. Official tasters were appointed by the burgh's magistrates to test quality and fix prices from the 1550s. Prices rose and fell according to the price of malt, but in 1557 were set at 12/- per Scots quart, which was four English shillings (20 pence today) per six imperial pints (3.4 litres).

Across the Moray Firth, on the fertile Black Isle, once stood the famous Ferintosh distillery owned by the Forbes of Culloden. The distillery was sacked by Jacobite troops in 1689 and Duncan Forbes, a prominent Whig, was granted the right to distil free of duty from grain grown on his own lands. The Forbes' operation might have comprised more than one distillery and by the time this duty-free right was revoked in 1784, the family was producing almost two thirds of the legally produced whisky in Scotland. This amounted to some 90,000 gallons (400,000 litres) bringing an annual profit of £18,000 (about £700,000 a year in today's money). The precise position of the distillery is unknown, but was probably in the parish of Ryefield. Later another distillery near Dingwall, formerly called Ben Wyvis, took the name of Ferintosh in 1893 and operated until 1926 (not to be confused with Ben Wyvis [2] at the Invergordon complex from 1965 to 1977).

If the *Report of the Select Committee on The Distillery in The Different Parts of Scotland* (1798 to 1799) is anything to go by, the high point for distilling in the north of Scotland would seem to have been the late eighteenth century. The report lists 33 distilleries and a further 31 are recorded as having been established before 1824. Following the Excise Act of that year, an additional 16 were added. Many of these lasted only a short time, although some may have been absorbed into other concerns. After this, fewer new malt whisky distilleries were built in the north; six since 1880, only one of which (Clynelish) is still in operation. A large grain whisky production plant was opened at Invergordon in 1961.

The most northerly [distilleries] (Pulteney, Balbair, Clynelish) are faintly smoky, especially the last, which can sometimes be mistaken for an Islay.

SPEYSIDE

Speyside is the acknowledged heartland of whisky production. Today, it contains two-thirds of the malt whisky distilleries in Scotland. Forty-nine are operational and three have closed (Dallas Dhu, Convalmore and Coleburn), although their malts are still available. "It would be no true – or, at least, no very discerning – lover of whisky who could enter this almost sacred zone without awe." These words, written by Aeneas Macdonald in 1930, are as accurate today as they were then.

Speysides are generally sweet and high in estery notes, which makes them redolent of pear-drops and acetone (nail varnish remover), even of carnations, Parma violets, roses, apples, bananas, cream soda and lemonade. They have great finesse and are the most complex and sophisticated of malt whiskies. They are generally made from unpeated malt, although delicate whiffs of smoke can come from the barley itself. They tend to be lighter than other Highland and Island whiskies, although those that are

BELOW Stones were quarried from the Rothes Burn to build Glen Spey distillery.

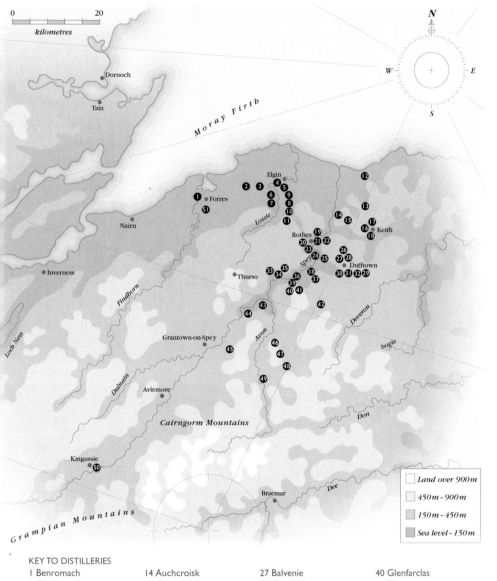

KEY TO DISTILLERIES

1 Benromach	14 Auchcroisk	27 Balvenie	40 Glenfarclas
2 Glenburgie	15 Glentauchers	28 Glenfiddich	41 Benrinnes
3 Miltonduff	16 Strathmill	29 Dufftown	42 Allt-á-Bhainne
4 Glen Moray	17 Strathisla	30 Pittyvaich	43 Cragganmore
5 Linkwood	18 Glen Keith	31 Mortlach	44 Tormore
6 Glenlossie	19 Speyburn	32 Glendullan	45 Balmenach
7 Mannochmore	20 Glenrothes	33 Knockando	46 The Glenlivet
8 Benriach	21 Glen Grant	34 Tamdhu	47 Tamnavulin
9 Longmorn	22 Caperdonich	35 Cardhu	48 Braeval
10 Glen Elgin	23 Glen Spey	36 Imperial	49 Tomintoul
11 Coleburn	24 The Macallan	37 Glenallachie	50 Speyside
12 Inchgower	25 Craigellachie	38 Aberlour	51 Dallas Dhu
13 Aultmore	26 Convalmore	39 Dailuaine	

117

RIGHT Although Speyside itself is gentle and pastoral, this fertile region is surrounded by high, rugged mountains.

matured in European oak (such as Macallan, Mortlach, Balvenie, Benrinnes and Glenfarclas) achieve a chocolatey richness. Some claim that the Keith whiskies often have a delicate woody aroma.

Prior to 1824, there were only two licensed distilleries on Speyside – Strathisla at Keith, which was founded in 1786, and Dalvey near Grantown-on-Spey, founded in 1798 and closed in 1828. The many hundreds of other distillers saw no need to register themselves, and cocked a snook at the authorities. As the Rev. John Grant, minister at Tomintoul, wrote succinctly in his entry for the *Statistical Account of Scotland* (1790): "Tammtoul [*sic*] is inhabited by 37 families... all of them sell whisky and all of them drink it".

Historians know of only 16 farmer-distillers who took advantage of the 1823 Excise Act. Although seven of them survived only a few years, nine are still in operation today. They are Aberlour, Cardhu, The Glenlivet, Longmorn, Macallan, Miltonduff, Mortlach, Glenburgie and Balmenach.

The next phase of building came in the 1840s and 1850s, with Glen Grant and Glenfarclas, Dufftown and Dailuaine. The laying down of a branch line of the Great North of Scotland Railway between Dufftown and Keith in the late 1850s, and the Speyside Railway from Keith to Boat of Garten in 1867, encouraged further development. Mortlach distilleries and Cragganmore both took advantage of this. But it was not until the mid-1880s that Speyside really took off. Some 23 distilleries, all of them in production today, were built between 1886 and 1899. These were the decades of the "whisky boom" when blenders could not get enough of the sweet, fragrant, sophisticated malts of Speyside.

When this period of expansion ended in 1900, many distilleries were mothballed, but they were revived and refurbished in the 1960s when demand picked up again. A further ten distilleries were built on Speyside between 1958 and 1975, all but one of which (Pittyvaich) are currently in production.

The district which lends the appellation "Speyside" is a blunt wedge-shape, with its apex deep in the northern foothills of the Cairngorm Mountains, its base the Moray Firth, its western boundary the River Findhorn and its eastern march the River Deveron. It is an area about 32 kilometres (17 miles) deep by 50 kilometres (27 miles) broad, bisected by the River Spey – the fastest flowing of all Scottish rivers (although none of the distilleries draw their production water from it) – and watered by its tributaries, the Rivers Avon, Livet, Fiddich and Dullan, and the River Lossie.

It is no historical accident that the region has gained pre-eminence. The low country that lies between the mountains and the sea, called the Laich o'Moray and known as "The Garden of Scotland", has wonderfully rich and fertile soils running some 1.8 metres (6 feet) deep in the Spey's alluvial plain. Its climate is equable, owing to the influence of the Gulf Stream, and its northern latitude makes for long hours of daylight during the summer months. In other words, perfect barley-growing country.

At the same time, the upland moors that gird the Laich in the south provide an ample supply of peat, while the relative inaccessibility of the mountains that form the region's southern boundary were an ideal sanctuary for illicit distillers. Generations of small farmers learned their craft in these hills. In Glenlivet parish alone there were over 200 private stills in the early 1800s.

GLENLIVET

The only drove road connecting Speyside with Deeside ran through this parish, and there are extensive deposits of high-quality metamorphic limestone under almost every field, which increases the water's alkalinity and hardness. In days gone by the country all about was wild and remote, especially its southern part, known as the Braes o'Glenlivet. It has an undulating topography of countless hidden glens watered by tumbling

BELOW In 1689, a band of Jacobites held a council of war at Auchindoun Castle, following the death of their leader " Bonnie Dundee".

burns fed by tiny lochans (lakes) high among the rolling hills above. The Seminary of Scalan, tucked away in these hills, was the only place in post-Reformation Scotland where young men could study for the Roman Catholic priesthood. A fierce battle was fought here in October 1594, when the Catholic Earl of Huntly, chief of the Gordons and baron of Glenlivet itself, drove a sizeable army of Campbells, Macleans and Mackintoshes, commanded by the Protestant Earl of Argyll, down the glen and back whence they had come.

After the failure of the Jacobite Rising of 1745, a military road replaced the old drove road, and Government troops were billeted in the glen itself. This did not prevent one John Gow, who had fought for Bonnie Prince Charlie, settling in the parish. He changed his name to Smith and began to farm a stretch of land there. His grandson, George Smith, like most farmers, was distilling whisky illegally but was later the first person in the area to take out a licence to distil under the 1823 Excise Act. This roused the wrath of many local smugglers.

Such was the fame of the whiskies of Glenlivet that by the 1860s many distilleries were adopting the name, some of them over 50 kilometres (27 miles) from the glen itself, which gave rise to Glenlivet being described as the longest glen in Scotland. George and his son, John Gordon Smith, made the journey to

ABOVE The Macallan
maturation warehouse
at Craigellachie is the
largest and the most
modern in the world.

register the name "Glenlivet" at the Stationers' Hall, London, in 1870, and later a court ruling ordered that only their whisky could call itself "The Glenlivet". Nevertheless 25 distilleries continued to use, or adopted, the appellation as a suffix for their products.

STRATHSPEY

The River Livet joins the River Avon, and together they meet the Spey at Ballindalloch, in Strathspey. The river valley or "strath" begins below Aviemore and follows the river northeast for some 56 kilometres (30 miles) until it debouches into the Laich o'Moray beyond the township of Rothes. Even in the late nineteenth century, Strathspey was cultivated only in pockets, and today large tracts of it, such as the Forest of Abernethy, are still protected as primal woodland.

The quality of the scenery is quintessentially Highland, with the craggy foothills of the Monadhliath Mountains on one hand and the snowy peaks of the Cairngorms on the other. After the Strathspey Railway opened, hundreds of tourists joined the many sportsmen who came to Speyside to stalk, shoot and fish. Until the 1950s, tenants of the Earl of Seafield, Speyside's principal landowner, were required to plant their gardens so that they were looking at their best for the start of the shooting season. In the 1960s, developments began at Aviemore for Scotland's first winter sports resort.

Grantown-on-Spey is the district's main town but it has never been a distilling centre. It was laid out in 1776 by Sir James Grant of Grant and is spacious and elegant. The Strathspey distilleries lie between here and Craigellachie, 27 kilometres (14.5 miles) downstream. To the north of the river is the parish of Knockando, which rises from the lush, low grounds of the Spey, into the mountainous, heathery wilds of Morayshire. The springs in this high ground flow over granite, schist and sedimentary rocks, which give the water a high mineral content: perfect conditions for distilling whisky and for smugglers' lairs. The springs and burns that supplied them years ago provide production water for five distilleries today.

On the other side of the river rises the rounded mass of Ben Rinnes, which at 2,759 metres (9,050 feet) is the dominant feature of the landscape in these parts. Its springs and burns supply sweet, soft water to a handful of distilleries around its broad base, as well as to the sizeable village of Charlestown of Aberlour. Five miles from here is Dufftown, the first of the whisky towns. "Rome was built on seven hills," runs the rhyme, "Dufftown stands on seven stills".

"Rome was built on seven hills," runs the rhyme, "Dufftown stands on seven stills".

DUFFTOWN

The town was founded in 1817 by James Duff, Fourth Earl of Fife, to provide employment after the Napoleonic Wars. Dufftown has excellent water as it stands at the confluence of the Rivers Fiddich and Dullan, and the geology of the district is largely granite, with substantial deposits of limestone and other minerals. In spite of this, only one of the town's six distilleries was established before 1886.

KEITH

North and west of Dufftown, the country becomes gentler and more pastoral. Indeed Keith, the second whisky town, was once a burgh of considerable importance on account of the fine tracts of corn-land along the River Isla. As early as the sixteenth century, even when it was very poorly cultivated, this land yielded its owners, the abbots of Kinloss, considerable income. By the following century it excelled most parishes in the north of Scotland in its expanse of fertile farming land.

Keith has long ecclesiastical traditions and its associations with making alcohol are recorded as early as 1208. The site chosen for the first legal distillery here was described in a charter of 1545 as having had a *brassina*, or warehouse, built upon it. This distillery opened in 1786, and is thus one of the oldest in Scotland. It was first called Milton, and was later renamed Strathisla. There are now four distilleries situated in and around Keith.

ROTHES

Fifteen kilometres (nine miles) due east of Keith stands the smaller and more compact township of Rothes, which was established in 1766. The low ground towards the Spey around Rothes is deeply covered with rich alluvial soils. The uplands are clad with peat and watered by numerous springs and burns flowing over granite, sandstone and mica. So it is not surprising that there were many illicit operations in the parish, including those of John and James Grant, who built the first legal distillery here in 1840. They named it Glen Grant. There are now five distilleries in the village, although so discreetly are they situated, that a visitor might pass through without noticing them.

ELGIN

The Royal Burgh of Elgin is the acknowledged whisky capital. It stands in the heart of the Laich o'Moray, 13 kilometres (seven miles) north of Rothes, and was once the historical seat of the ancient kings, the Earls or "*Mormaers*" of Moray. Elgin is the county-town of Morayshire and has long been an important market centre. Standing on the main road between Inverness and Aberdeen, communications were always good. By 1845 there was a railway connection to Lossiemouth, eight kilometres (four miles) to the north, which, as one enthusiastic contemporary put it, "makes Elgin virtually a sea-port". In spite of the link to the Great North of Scotland Railway built in the 1850s, the Elgin distilleries all date from the 1890s.

BANFF

On the eastern boundary of Speyside region is the ancient Royal Burgh of Banff. Until the the River Deveron changed its course and the harbour silted up in the nineteenth century, an active trade was carried on from here with the Baltic and the Low Countries, and the carrying of contraband whisky was widespread. Although the distilleries around Banff, sometimes called the "Deveron Malts", are a long way to the east of Speyside, and might more logically be placed in the East Highland region, they share the characteristics of Speyside malts as do their much distant cousins in the vale of Glenlivet.

OPPOSITE There was once a ghost in the still house at Glenrothes distillery, which overlooks the ancient cemetry of Rothes.

CENTRAL HIGHLANDS

This region encompasses Perthshire, part of Dumbartonshire and Stirlingshire in the south, and part of Inverness-shire to the north. The landscape is intensely romantic and often very dramatic. The terrain is mainly mountainous, but the hills are divided by deep glens, lochs and broad straths (valleys). Most distilleries in the region, both historical and contemporary, were built along the fertile alluvial glens carved by the mighty River Tay, the largest river in Scotland, and its tributaries the Earn and the Tummel. Barley grew well in the lush valley bottoms and water and peat were in abundant supply. In the past the whiskies of the region

RIGHT Ripe, bearded barley.

were often referred to as "The Perthshire Malts". In terms of flavour they tend to be lighter bodied and sweeter than other Highland malts, apart from the Speysides. Like the latter, they can be fragrant with blossom, elderflowers, heather, honey and spice. Unlike Speysides, they have the dry finish typical of other Highland districts.

In the southwest of the region are Loch Lomond and the Trossachs, literally "The Bristly Country", on account of its many rocky hummocks and hillocks covered with oak, birch, hazel and rowan – made famous by Sir Walter Scott and the tales of the Rob Roy.

Travelling north and east one enters the Stirling Plain, the rich alluvial strath of the River Forth, that once supplied grain

to the grain distilleries of Clackmannanshire: Cambus, Carsebridge, Glenochil, Grange, Kennetpans, Kilbagie and Strathmore. Deanston malt whisky distillery is situated in the historic town of Doune, on the northern edge of the plain.

To the north the mountains beckon. First the Ochils, which serve as a barbican to the mighty ramparts of the Grampians rising beyond Perth. Strathearn nestles here and Glenturret and Tullibardine distilleries are at Crieff and Blackford respectively; both of which are ancient sites of brewing and distilling. Then the scenery becomes increasingly wild and dramatic as we enter the rugged mountains.

The records list 128 distilleries as having been established within the Central Highland region, over 30 more than any other part of Scotland. All except nine of these were founded prior to 1840, and only five of the early establishments still exist: Glenturret, Blair Athol, Tullibardine, Glengoyne and Edradour. They were all farm distilleries, the leading surviving example of which is Edradour, near Pitlochry. In the mid-eighteenth century there were 30 small stills around here. Alfred Barnard visited Auchnagie Distillery at Ballinluig in 1887, that had a potential annual output of 24,000 gallons (109,000 litres), Ballechin distillery, also at Ballinluig, that had an annual output of 18,000 gallons (82,000 litres) and the tiny Grandtully distillery on the road to Aberfeldy that produced 5,000 gallons (23,000 litres) a year. Today all three are long silent.

During the nineteenth century the city of Perth emerged as the "Blending Capital" of Scotland. Situated on the banks of the River Tay, it had easy access to the Highlands for malt whisky fillings and the Lowlands for its markets. It was the birthplace of many of the great blending houses like Dewar's, Bell's and Gloag's, and lesser concerns like RB Smith & Co, Peter Thomson and CC Stuart Ltd.

Characteristic of the distilleries of this region in recent years are well-developed visitor facilities, with restaurants, exhibitions and guided tours. This is a sensible move on the part of their owners, since all are close to popular tourist destinations or travel routes – to the Trossachs in the case of Glengoyne, Crieff in the case of Glenturret and the A9, the main trunk road to the north, in the case of the others. Throughout the rest of Scotland many distilleries have followed their example, and today whisky distilleries are second only to castles as favourite tourist attractions.

Characteristic of the distilleries of this region in recent years are well-developed visitor facilities, with restaurants, exhibitions and guided tours... today whisky distilleries are second only to castles as favourite tourist attractions.

EAST HIGHLANDS

The East Highlands region falls almost entirely below the
Highland Line, as defined in the Act of 1797, although above the
original line drawn by the Wash Act of 1784. It embraces the old
counties of Forfarshire and Aberdeenshire, and the whiskies of
the region fall naturally into two groups, roughly corresponding
to the old county boundaries. Eastern malts tend to be medium-
to full-bodied, smooth and sweetish, but with the recognisably
dry Highland finish. They are malty and often slightly smoky;
sometimes fudge- or toffee-like, with citrus notes, ginger and
spice. They benefit from maturation in sherry-wood.

The countryside in the northeast of Scotland is bountiful. The
traveller passes from the lush berry fields of Angus, through the
rich red earth of the Mearns, into the rolling, pastoral scenery of
Aberdeenshire, Buchan and Banff; the most desirable arable land
in Scotland. It is also castle country. There are more castles and
tower houses per square kilometre in the northeast than anywhere
else in the world. This is an evocative reminder not only of the
former wealth and success of merchants and landowners in these
parts, but also of the troubled times they had to endure in the
past. Indeed they were building fully defensible castles here later
than might be expected; the last true castle in Scotland having
been built at Leslie near Insch in Aberdeenshire as late as 1661.
These castles would have had still-rooms, as would many of the
farms that populate the region. In total 76 distilleries are known
to have existed in the east. The hey-day was immediately after the
1823 Excise Act. Some 36 distilleries were established in the region
between 1825 and 1830

In the words of the whisky enthusiast, Aeneas Macdonald,
"With Forfarshire we have reached the southern edge of the range
of North country malts that extends to Peterhead. The beautiful
glens and uplands of the Sidlaws are the cradle of Glencoull,
Glencadam, and North Port, the Brechin whisky. Kincardine
adds two Mearns whiskies, Auchenblae and Glenurie, distilled at
Stonehaven."

Alas, today the East Highlands region has been hard hit by
closures. Glencadam is the only one of those mentioned above
still in operation, Glencoull was converted to a grain mill following
its closure in 1929 and North Port closed in 1983 and has been
demolished. Auchenblae closed in 1926, although its buildings are
largely intact, partly used as a garage, and Glenurie, more usually

known as Glenury Royal, ceased production in 1985 and was sold for residential development. Malts from Glencadam (not bottled as a single), North Port and Glenury are still around, but rare. Three other Mearns whiskies are still occasionally found: Glenesk and Lochside from Montrose, and Old Fettercairn from Laurencekirk, in the heart of the Mearns itself. The first two distilleries are closed, but Fettercairn distillery is operational.

OPPOSITE The breathtaking quality of light in the north never ceases to amaze.

The Aberdeenshire distilleries have fared slightly better this century than those of Forfarshire. The most southerly is Royal Lochnagar, a small, historic distillery built on the edge of the Balmoral Estate, and favoured with its first Royal Warrant in 1848, following a visit by Queen Victoria and Prince Albert, who had taken up residence nearby in Balmoral Castle only three days before. Glen Garioch (pronounced "Glen Geerie"), near Old Meldrum, was founded in 1797 but has had a patchy history owing to an unreliable water source. Ardmore stands deep in the rolling farmlands of "The Garioch", some 30 kilometres (16 miles) east of Old Meldrum, close to the River Bogie at the village of Kennethmont. It has been producing fillings for the Teacher's blends since 1898, and is rarely seen as a single. Teacher's also owned Glendronach distillery at nearby Huntly between 1960 and 2008. Its foundation was as early as 1826 and its malt was much favoured by the Fifth Duke of Gordon, the landowner responsible for bringing in the 1823 Excise Act which went so far to encourage the practice of licensed distilling in the Highlands.

The city of Aberdeen itself has been home to a dozen distilleries, the most long-lived of which were Bon Accord (1855 to 1910) and Strathdee (1821 to 1938). A less successful venture, Banks o'Dee distillery, was burnt down by smugglers in 1825. Aberdeen was also the birth-place of Chivas Bros, creator of the world famous blended whisky, Chivas Regal. James Chivas became a partner in an existing wine merchant and grocer's business on Union Street in 1838, and was producing his own blended whisky by the 1870s. The company is now part of The Chivas and Glenlivet Group, which is itself owned by the French company, Pernod Ricard.

WEST HIGHLANDS

Apart from at Campbeltown, which is classified as a separate whisky region, there have been surprisingly few licensed distilleries in the West Highlands. *The Scotch Whisky Industry Record* lists only 28, most of them early operations established before 1830, and many of them of unknown location.

Yet early travellers and commentators remark on the widespread availability of whisky. The ministers who contributed reports on their parishes to Sir John Sinclair's *Statistical Account of Scotland* of 1794 often bemoaned the endemic habit of "dram-taking". Whisky was clearly made on many, indeed most, farms. Why did the owners choose not to register their activities as did their fellow distillers in the east? The answer is, first, they did not need to. Policing such a remote and diverse territory was nearly impossible, and magistrates tended to show favour to illicit distillers, from whom they no doubt received supplies for their cellars. Second, the smallness of the barley crops in the West Highlands, owing to high rainfall and lack of fertile areas of any size, meant that barley had to be imported by distillers who chose to go into large-scale production. They also had to import fuel and export their product to the centres of population, and although sea transport had been highly developed in the west since the time of the Vikings, this added considerably to costs. Significantly, nine of the known distilleries in the West Highlands were on the Firth of Clyde; another three were at Ardrishaig near Lochgilphead; three were close to Tarbert, and there was one each at Dunoon, Sandbank and Ardincaple where transport to Glasgow and the Lowland markets was easier.

OPPOSITE AND RIGHT The west coast of Scotland is riven with sea lochs and until recently the principal mode of communication was by sea.

Equally significantly, the two surviving distilleries on the west coast today, excluding those in Campbeltown, are both at rail-heads. The first is Ben Nevis distillery at Fort William, established by the much respected "Long" John Macdonald of Torgulbin in 1824 and the second is Oban, founded as early as 1794 by the entrepreneur Hugh Stevenson.

CAMPBELTOWN

Founded by Archibald Campbell, Seventh Earl of Argyll, in 1609, the Royal Burgh of Campbeltown today has around 6,000 inhabitants and lies at the southern tip of the Kintyre peninsula in Argyll. The district was well suited to the production of whisky, being remote from centres of government and having abundant supplies of barley and peat. When Thomas Pennant, the English traveller, visited the town in 1772 he remarked that "the inhabitants [were] mad enough to convert their bread into poison, distilling annually 6,000 bolls of grain into whisky" (ie. nearly 400 tonnes). By 1794, when the *Statistical Account of Scotland* was compiled, there were 22 illicit distilleries known to be operating in the town, and a further ten in the surrounding countryside.

Before 1823 there were only three legal distilleries at Campbeltown, yet Kintyre whisky was in great demand in Glasgow. Between 1823 and 1834 a further 27 Campbeltown distilleries are known to have registered for distilling licences. In 1824 some 25 distilleries were cheerfully producing 748,000 gallons (3.5 million litres) of spirit according to *The Imperial Gazetteer of Scotland.* Most of this was exported to the Scottish Lowlands, to England, Ireland and abroad. When Alfred Barnard visited in 1887, there were 21 distilleries in operation, directly employing over 250 men and producing nearly two million gallons

BELOW Rolling empty casks at Springbank.

(approximately nine million litres) of whisky. He was able to describe Campbeltown as "The Whisky City".

This was the high point of the region's fortunes. During the latter decades of the nineteenth century, blenders favoured the lighter, more fragrant malts of Speyside over the heavier product of Campbeltown, and although many distilleries seem to have survived the slump at the turn of the century, the Depression of the 1920s swept all but three away.

This was in spite of a reprieve from across the Atlantic, for the whisky of Campbeltown enjoyed a high reputation among bootleggers during the years of Prohibition, and several Campbeltown distilleries arranged for ship-loads of their product to be exported directly to the Caribbean whence the whisky was smuggled into the USA. Some whisky commentators, notably Professor McDowall, believe that it was this very demand that caused the demise of the Campbeltown distilleries. "Success, however, contained the seeds of destruction," he wrote, "for some distilleries, in order to satisfy demand, began to pour poor spirit into poor casks." It was even believed that old herring barrels had been pressed into service, and Campbeltown whisky was derogatively referred to as "stinking fish"!

In 1930 Aeneas Macdonald noted the existence of Benmore, Scotia, Rieclachan, Kinloch, Springside, Hazelburn, Glenside, Springbank, Lochruan, Lochead and Dalintober distilleries. However in truth, all except Springbank, Scotia and Rieclachan had already gone out of production by then, and the latter was to follow only four years later.

What were the characteristics of the Campbeltown malts that made them so popular in the decades before the whisky boom? Although historical commentators are agreed that they had a character distinct from other regions, they differ in their accounts of what that was. Barnard dismissed them as "generally thin, useful at the price"; Aeneas Macdonald called them "the double basses of the whisky orchestra... potent, full-bodied, pungent whiskies". In 1967 Professor McDowall referred to the "full-flavoured, pleasant lightness" of Springbank, "somewhat reminiscent of Rosebank" (a Lowland whisky) and the "oily, Irish" character of Glen Scotia, while in 1969 David Daiches supported Macdonald's view that "Campbeltowns have in the past had something of the strength and body of Islays, and are indeed traditionally regarded as the most manly of whiskies". Present day Glen Scotia can be variable, but old Springbank is majestic in its resonant complexity, its subtlety and weight.

THE ISLANDS

For many, the wind-swept islands lying off Scotland's west and north coasts sum up the wild beauty of the whole country. For centuries these islands were separate kingdoms, ruled respectively from Islay (the South Isles and the Isle of Man) and Norway (Orkney, Shetland and the Northern Isles).

The Kings, later Lords, of the South Isles, founded the Royal House of Scotland in 843, but were themselves forfeited in 1492 when they refused to acknowledge the sovereignty of that same Royal House. Orkney became part of the Kingdom of Scotland as a princess's dowry in 1465.

Today, the Isles can almost be regarded as another country (or "countries", for each island is quite different from the next). The island climate is distinct from that of the mainland: maritime and wet, the winds are fierce, but the winters are rarely severe and palm trees flourish in several sheltered spots. The whiskies too have their own character. Typical Island malts are noticeably peaty, but less so than their cousins in Islay, and have a peppery "catch" in the finish, although this is not the case with Isle of Arran, situated between Ayrshire and Kintyre, whose product is sweeter and more floral than the rest.

BELOW Looking across the Sound of Sleat towards Kyle Rhea, from which a little ferry runs to Glenelg.

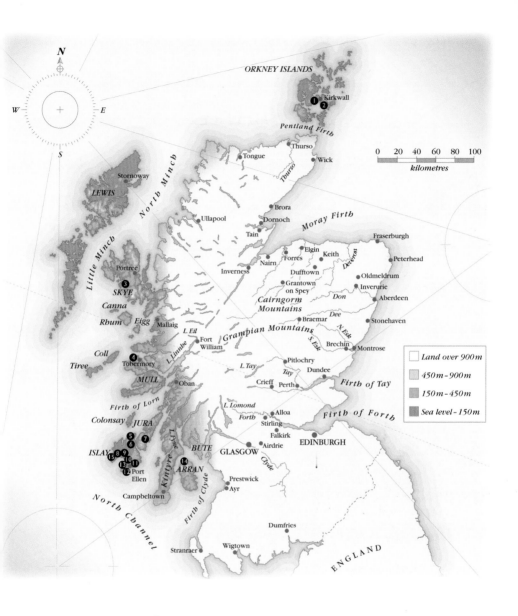

ORKNEY ISLANDS

① Kirkwall
②

Pentland Firth

● Thurso
● Tongue
Wick

0 20 40 60 80 100
kilometres

Stornoway

LEWIS

North Minch

● Brora
● Dornoch
Tain ●

Moray Firth

Ullapool ●

● Elgin
Keith ●
Forres ●
● Fraserburgh
Nairn ●
● Peterhead
Inverness ●
Dufftown ●
● Oldmeldrum
Grantown
on Spey ●
● Inverurie
Deveron

Little Minch

Portree ●

SKYE

Canna

Rhum *Eigg*

● Mallaig

Cairngorm
Mountains

Don

● Aberdeen

● Braemar
Dee
● Stonehaven

Coll

Tiree

④ Tobermory

MULL

L. Eil
Fort
William ●

Grampian Mountains

N Esk
Brechin ●
S Esk
● Montrose

● Oban

● Crieff

L. Tay
● Pitlochry
Tay
Dundee ●
Perth ●

Firth of Tay

Firth of Lorn

Colonsay *JURA*

L. Lomond
Forth
● Alloa

Stirling ●

Falkirk ●
● Airdrie

⑤
⑥
⑦

ISLAY ⑮⑧ ⑨
⑬ ⑩ ⑪
⑫ Port
Ellen

BUTE

⑭

ARRAN

GLASGOW ●

Clyde

EDINBURGH

Firth of Forth

	Land over 900m
	450m – 900m
	150m – 450m
	Sea level – 150m

Campbeltown ●

Kintyre

Firth of Clyde

Prestwick ●
● Ayr

North Channel

● Dumfries

Stranraer ●
● Wigtown

ENGLAND

KEY TO DISTILLERIES

1 Highland Park
2 Scapa
3 Talisker
4 Tobermory
5 Bunnahabhain
6 Caol Ila

7 Isle of Jura
8 Bruichladdich
9 Bowmore
10 Lagavulin
11 Ardbeg
12 Laphroaig

13 Port Ellen
14 Isle of Arran
15 Kilchoman

The earliest reference to distilling in the Islands is found in the Statutes of Iona of 1609, where it records the charter that allowed the islanders to distil but not import *aqua vitae*. Since then this tradition has continued – drinking in these parts is well attested during the following two centuries.

In 1775, for example, Dr Johnson recorded in his *Journey to the Western Isles of Scotland* that, "A man of the Hebrides as soon as he appears in the morning swallows a glass of whisky; yet they are not a drunken race, at least I was never present at much intemperance; but no man is so abstemious as to refuse the morning dram which they call a skalk."

He relates how guests were offered four kinds of this morning dram or *sgailc*, the first being the *sgailc-nide*, which was a full bumper of whisky taken while still lying down, followed by the *friochd-uilinn*, taken when propped up on the elbow, after which came the *deoch chasruisgte* drunk "while still barefoot" and *deoch bleth* while waiting for the breakfast porridge. After such

BELOW Built around 1500 BC as a lunar observatory, the Ring of Brodgar in Orkney had 60 stones originally, of which some 36 remain.

hospitality so early in the day one imagines that the inebriated guest would have been more than happy to return to his bed!

On their Scottish tour, Johnson and Boswell stayed in the house of Mackinnon of Corrie on Skye. Boswell tells of a splendid punch drinking session, from which he awoke at noon with a severe headache. He was afraid of Johnson's reproof and kept to his room. An hour later the doctor entered and affectionately upbraided his companion. When later in the afternoon Boswell's drinking companions returned with a bottle of brandy, Johnson laughed and said "Ay, fill him drunk again. Do it in the morning, that we may laugh at him all day. It is a poor thing for a fellow to get drunk at night, and skulk to bed, and let his friends have no sport!"

Johnson was a sober man himself who drank whisky only once as an experiment when at Inverary. He remarked that it was drinkable although he had no interest in the process by which it was made – "the art of making poison pleasant".

Interestingly the Mackinnons of Corrie are held locally to
have been the custodians of a secret recipe for a liqueur, given
to their kinsman Captain John Mackinnon of Elgol by Bonnie
Prince Charlie in gratitude for his help after the Battle of Culloden.
Shortly before the First World War the liqueur began to be made
in commercial quantities in Edinburgh by descendants of the Skye
Mackinnons. It was named Drambuie.

Distilling whisky throughout the Hebrides and other islands was
almost wholly illicit, even after 1823. *The Scotch Whisky Industry
Record* lists only 22 known legal distilleries in the Isles, including
those in Orkney. Among the short-lived and long-defunct are two
in Bute, one each in Arran and Jura, two in Tiree, seven in Skye
and nine in Orkney. Still in production are one each in Arran, Jura,
Mull and Skye, and two in Orkney. Yet there was a time when the
whiskies of Arran were mentioned in the same breath as those of
Glenlivet. An eighteenth-century commentator reported that a third
or fourth part of the barley crop in Mull was "distilled into whisky,
of which the natives are immoderately fond".

A friend of mine, whose family were prosperous tacksmen
(senior tenants and gentlemen farmers) in the north of Skye,
recently discovered by chance that his family fortunes had been
laid in the eighteenth century by smuggling. They made large
quantities of illicit whisky in Skye, transported it to Falkirk with
the cattle they were taking to the market and sold it there. As far
as my friend was concerned the family tradition had always been
that they had made their money solely from livestock.

In general, island distillers refused to register for licences
for the same reasons as their West Highland counterparts; the
difficulties of policing the areas and the favours of sympathetic
magistrates meant that they simply did not need to. Legal distilling
was also unattractive on the islands because of the inconvenience
and expense of sea transportation; poor soils and a wet climate
made it difficult to grow barley on all the islands except Tiree
and Orkney, so it had to be imported. And, although peat was
plentiful, the coal required to fire commercially viable stills had
to be brought in. Finally, the whisky had to be delivered to its
markets on the mainland.

Campbell of Shawfield once undertook to police Islay, until
two years later, so widespread was the illicit distilling, that he
was forced to hand over control to the excise officers who were
themselves soon begging for assistance from the army!

ISLAY

It is possible that the island of Islay was the cradle of whisky distilling in Scotland. Islay is the most southern of the Western Isles, only some 20 kilometres (11 miles) from the north coast of Ireland where the mysteries of distilling originated.

The first written record of whisky making in Scotland was in an Exchequer Roll of 1494 where it is recorded that King James IV ordered supplies of *aqua vitae* to be made. This was within a year of King James being on Islay where he had completed his third invasion into the Western Isles to subdue the power of the Lords of the Isles. The Lords of the Isles, styled "kings" by their own people, held parliaments, formed foreign treaties and considered themselves to be the equal of any prince in Europe. Their court at Finlaggan on Islay supported schools of harpers and bards, metal workers, stone masons and carvers. It is said that the zealots of the Reformation threw 360 Celtic High Crosses made there into the sea.

BELOW Casks waiting for their heads..

OPPOSITE The distinctive Paps of Jura, viewed from Caol Ila distillery.

Islay was the political and cultural hub of the dominion of these Scottish rulers. Their territories were the largest in Scotland, beyond those of the king himself, and embraced not only the western seaboard but the whole of Ross-shire and stretched east as far as Inverness. John, the last Lord of the Isles, was a scholar, interested in arts and sciences. He must have been familiar with the medical properties of *aqua vitae*, if not with its convivial uses.

Physically, Islay is 40 kilometres (21.6 miles) long from east to west, by 32 kilometres (17.3 miles) broad, almost divided southwest to northeast and north to south by two arms of the sea, Loch Indaal and Loch Gruinard. None of it is strictly Highland, and none strictly Lowland. The rocky, heather-covered hills in the north and east of the island rise only to 460 metres (1,508 feet) and the southern part is a combination of peat moss and fertile alluvial plain. Everywhere is battered by winter gales rolling in from the Atlantic, but the island also enjoys a higher than average amount of sunshine. It is the most fertile of the Western Isles; in the late 1500s the rich lands of Islay yielded nearly 4,000 bolls (245 tonnes) of malt per annum in rents. Fuel is also a plentiful commodity as at least a quarter of the island's surface is covered with peat.

Islay's principal villages are Bowmore, an attractive model village established in the 1760s, and Port Ellen, where the ferry lands. In 1727 the island was bought by Daniel Campbell of Shawfield, the MP for the Glasgow Burghs who had supported the Malt Tax of 1725 and had his house sacked by the Glasgow mob as a result. It is said that he paid for Islay out of the £9,000 compensation he received from the City of Glasgow. His descendants owned the island for over a century, and did much to encourage distilling, especially the last Shawfield laird, Walter Frederick Campbell, who inherited the island in 1816 and helped to establish or legalise a dozen distilleries during his lairdship. Illicit distilling was endemic, especially in the deep inland glens and caves of the Oa, the peninsula in the southern part of the island. The minister of Kildalton Parish, writing in the *Statistical Account* of 1794, lamented that "the quantity of whisky made here is very great; and the evil that follows drinking to excess of this liquor is very visible in this island". There was no excise presence on Islay until 1797, and in 1800 it was suggested that a body of militia be sent to Islay to police the distilling practices there. In any event, smuggling continued until at least 1850.

The Scotch Whisky Industry Record lists 21 distilleries known to have existed in Islay during the nineteenth century. All of the early legal operations were entirely farm based, some having only a short working life. Examples are Daill (1814 to 1830), Bridgend (1817 to 1822), Newton (1818 to 1937), Scarabuss (f.1817), Ballygrant (f.1821), Tallant (f.1821), Ardenistiel (1837 to 1848) and Kildalton (1849 to 1852). The last two were absorbed by Laphroaig and Lagavulin distilleries. Others lasted somewhat longer, like Octomore (1816 to 1852), Lochindaal (1829 to 1929) and Malt Mill (1908 to 1960). The last was established within Lagavulin distillery to produce a malt similar to that of its close neighbour, Laphroaig.

Islay whisky has long enjoyed a high reputation. As early as 1841, the Royal Household was ordering "a cask of your best Islay Mountain Dew", from Campbell of Shawfield, and the order was repeated two years later. Although the cask contained some legal Port Ellen, it also contained illicit whisky, including some 21 Year Old malt from Upper Cragabus, reputed to have been the finest whisky ever made in Islay.

The present day distilleries fall into two groups; northern and

BELOW The Lords of the Isles harboured their galleys of war at Dunyveg Castle, now overlooked by Lagavulin distillery.

southern, with Bowmore between the two, both geographically and aromatically. All but two of the surviving distilleries stand close to the sea and have their own piers. These were vital in days gone by for the delivery of grain and the shipping of casks. Islay malts are famous for their smokiness, attributable to the peat burned during kilning.

Three distilleries have their own floor maltings (Laphroaig, Bowmore and Kilchoman); most buy all or part of their malt from Port Ellen Maltings, specifying the degree of peating they require, from zero to 120 parts per million phenols. For not all the Islay malts are smoky. Bunnahabhain and traditional Bruichladdich have no smoke (although the latter also produces the smoky makes, Port Charlotte and Octomore). The others vary in intensity, with the malts made in Kildalton Parish (Ardbeg, Lagavulin, Laphroaig and Port Ellen) being the most smoky.

Although they must be used judiciously in order not to dominate a blend, a small amount of the smokier Islay malts will make a big difference to the overall flavour of the whisky; Lagavulin is a key filling in White Horse, and Caol Ila in Bell's.

Watching the world go
by is a popular pastime
in the islands. No
better place than the
pier-head for this!

THE LOWLANDS

The Highlands of Scotland finish suddenly, north of the Stirling Plain and west of the rich farmland of Aberdeenshire. In days gone by the inhabitants of the Lowlands looked askance at the mountain ramparts that defined the boundary. Beyond it were tribes that dressed differently, spoke a different language and had different customs, one of which was to regard the Lowlands as fair game for pillage. Intercourse there was, of course. Highlanders and Islesmen drove their shaggy ponies and black cattle out of the hills to the great market at Falkirk, just south of Stirling, to sell them to dealers who arrived from the south, and even from England. Highlanders there were a-plenty in Glasgow, Aberdeen and Edinburgh. But generally the attitude was one of mutual mistrust and misunderstanding.

Captain Edward Burt's *Letters From a Gentleman in the North* summed up the Lowland view in 1754, when he wrote: "Generations of an idle and predatory life had produced

BELOW The rolling countryside of southern Scotland provided safe retreats for illicit distillers in the eighteenth century.

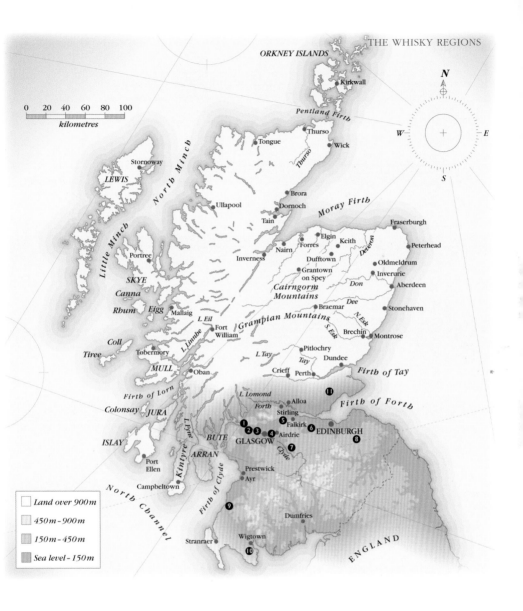

THE WHISKY REGIONS

0 20 40 60 80 100
kilometres

Land over 900m
450m – 900m
150m – 450m
Sea level – 150m

KEY TO DISTILLERIES
1 Inverleven
2 Littlemill
3 Auchentoshan
4 Glen Flagler
  and Killyloch
5 Rosebank
6 St Magdalene
7 Kinclaith
8 Glenkinchie
9 Ladyburn
10 Bladnoch
11 Daftmill

Grain for the Lowland
distilleries has long
been supplied from
the fertile valley of the
Forth in Stirlingshire.

LEFT East Lothian
is known as "The
Garden of Edinburgh".

LEFT East Lothian is known as "The Garden of Edinburgh".

throughout the Highlands the worst vices of barbarians... That
the Highlanders are for the most part cruel is beyond dispute."
After all, had not a Highland army put all London in a panic
when it advanced as far as Derby less than ten years before?

He omits to note that the advance and retreat of Prince Charles
Edward Stuart's army had been achieved without a single atrocity,
and that in the years following their defeat at Culloden, a Lowland
administration and a southern government had perpetrated horrors
against the people of the Highlands which bear comparison with
the worst savagery in Europe during the twentieth century.

But the division defined by the Wash Act of 1784 was ancient, cultural, sociological and economic. The Central Lowlands of Scotland, the alluvial plain of the Rivers Forth and Clyde; the coalfields of Stirlingshire, Lanarkshire, north Ayrshire and the Lothians, were the cradle of Scottish industry. In the late eighteenth century these districts supported the majority of the population – as they do today. The rich farmlands of Fife, Angus and Aberdeenshire were the backbone of the agricultural economy – as they are today. The Lowlands had the population and the markets – as they do today.

The key to the history of distilling in the Lowlands is found in the availability of grains – wheat and oats, as well as barley – and in developments in crop husbandry and harvesting. In the Highlands, distilling tended to be concentrated in, or close to, areas where there were grain surpluses. It was mostly a part-time pursuit, dependent upon agricultural production in a region where the farming was predominantly pastoral and based on livestock.

In the Lowlands, by contrast, the terrain lent itself better to arable farming. Indeed, in the eighteenth and nineteenth centuries there were dramatic developments in farming methods; improvements were made in land fertilisation and drainage, which made it possible to grow and crop more cereals. In the 1770s an innovative plough replaced the traditional one, making tilling the land far easier; in 1788 the first successful threshing mill was patented and in 1827 the scythe was replaced by the mechanical reaper. So it is not surprising that Lowland distilling became large-scale and industrialised long before this happened in the Highlands. The Wash Act of 1784, and other legislation that based excise duty on still capacity, encouraged and later enforced the use of large stills. Also, mixed mashes of grains other than malted barley were commonly used for distilling and many pot-still distilleries in the Lowlands produced grain whisky. Those that made malt whisky distilled a spirit with a much lighter and drier character than that from the Highlands.

The Scotch Whisky Industry Record lists 215 known distilleries in the Lowlands, the earliest founded in 1741. From the late eighteenth century to the 1850s, there were distilleries in every town of any size, most of them producing grain whisky for the local market, and after 1777 the larger ones began exporting their product to England for rectification into gin.

Following the invention of continuous distillation by Robert Stein and Aeneas Coffey in the late 1820s several of the larger operators installed patent stills. Some continued to use malt-only

The key to the history of distilling in the Lowlands is found in the availability of grains – wheat and oats, as well as barley – and in developments in crop husbandry and harvesting.

mashes; the Yoker distillery in Glasgow (1770 to 1927) made malt whisky in a Stein still until at least the 1880s, although it is reported to have had little flavour. Other distillers remained loyal to the pot still for grain whisky production; in the 1880s Dundashill had the largest pot stills in the industry. Some distilleries favoured the practice of triple distillation, which puts the low wines through an intermediate still before charging the spirit still.

In more recent times, other companies have produced malt whisky from pot stills situated within their grain whisky distilleries. Ladyburn malt was produced between 1966 and 1975 in William Grant & Sons' Girvan distillery; Inverleven (1938 to 1991) and Lomond (1956 to 1985) were produced within Hiram Walker's massive operation at Dumbarton; Kinclaith (1957 to 1976, demolished 1982) was made at Seager Evans/Long John International's Strathclyde grain distillery; Glen Flagler and Killyloch within Inver House's Moffat distillery at Airdrie (1965 to 1985). During the early 1960s, Hiram Walker & Company pioneered an adaptation to the head of a spirit still, replacing the tapering neck with a drum-shaped rectifying column. This made it possible to produce different styles of malt whisky from the same plant. By increasing or decreasing the number of rectifying plates, lighter or heavier whiskies could be made. The company named it the "Lomond still". The first one was installed in 1959 at Inverleven distillery, near Loch Lomond, within Hiram Walker's Dumbarton complex. Such was the success of the invention that the company went on to install the stills at its Highland distilleries, Glenburgie and Miltonduff, in 1960. The whiskies produced were Glen Craig and Mosstowie. The last Lomond still to be installed instead of a wash still, was at Scapa, Orkney.

Today the only operating malt whisky distilleries in the Lowlands are Auchentoshan (at Dalmuir, near Glasgow); Glenkinchie (at Pencaitland, near Edinburgh); Daftmill (near Ladybank, Fife; built in 2005); and Bladnoch (at Wigtown, Wigtownshire, the most southerly distillery in Scotland). The malts from the following closed distilleries are still encountered, though rare: Rosebank (at Falkirk); Littlemill (at Bowling, on the Clyde); Inverleven (at Dumbarton); and St Magdalene (at Linlithgow, West Lothian).

Not listed here, because it is doubtful whether they will ever be seen again, are four Lowland distilleries that closed in the 1920s – Auchtertool, at Kirkaldy (1845 to 1927), Bankier, in Stirling (1828 to 1928), Provanmill, Glasgow (1815 to 1929) and Stratheden, Auchtermuchty (1829 to 1927). Their products were available to blenders in the mid-1970s, so one never knows whether a long-lost cask from the 1920s might not one day be found in the deep recesses of a warehouse.

Lowland malts are generally light in colour and weight, and typically have a dry finish, qualities that make them excellent aperitifs. Their aromatic intensity is low, and tends to be grassy, green or herbal, with grainy and floral notes. On the whole they use unpeated malt, that lends a sweetness to the overall mouth-feel and flavour. Professor McDowall once observed that Lowland malts tend to give a slight brandy-like flavour to blends.

LEFT King Lot of Lothian had his capital on the summit of Trapain Law, seen in the far distance.

DIRECTORY

The high point of malt whisky production was in 1899, when there were 148 operating malt whisky distilleries. In 2010 there are around 100 distilleries operating full- or part-time. The following directory lists all the malt whisky distilleries in Scotland that are either in operation, silent (ie. in use but temporarily closed) or mothballed (ie. closed but capable of coming back into operation), and all the distilleries closed since the Second World War. It provides a guide to every malt whisky that is likely to be encountered, bottled as a single; by the distillery owner.

There is always a possibility that individual bottles of malt whisky, made by distilleries that closed before the Second World War, might appear at auction. There is even the chance that, deep in a warehouse somewhere, there lurks a cask of such whisky awaiting discovery.

There are points to look out for when identifying a whisky bottle's contents. By law a malt whisky sold within the European Union must show the brand name, the words Scotch Whisky, the name and address of either the distiller or bottler and the volume of contents and its strength on the label. Some markets require other information. The brand name, usually that of the distillery, almost always appears on the label. However, independent bottlers are sometimes forbidden to state the name of the malt on their labels by the distillery owners. In the past, producers and bottlers often used expressions like "malt whisky", "pure malt", or "vatted malt" to describe mixtures of malts. These are now banned, and replaced by the term "blended malt". Sometimes the region from which a malt comes and its dates of distillation and bottling are declared on the label although this is not always the case.

LEFT A corner of Loch Fyne Whiskies in Inveraray, Argyll, one of the best whisky shops in Scotland. It stocks some 500 brands and expressions.

USING THE DIRECTORY

NAME
Some distilleries once had different names, and others market their whisky under a brand name. Hence the "aka" – also known as – or former name of a distillery attached to headings. In some cases where the name (often Gaelic) of the distillery might be difficult for non-Scots to interpret I have given phonetic pronunciation.

ADDRESS/REGION
The town or village and county is supplied, and the style of whisky, following the regional breakdown in the previous chapter – ie. North Highland, Speyside, Central Highland, East Highland, West Highland, Campbeltown, Island, Islay and Lowland.

OWNER
Several of the companies listed as owners are themselves subsidiaries of other companies or part of conglomerate groups.

Chivas Brothers is the Scotch whisky division of Pernod Ricard, which acquired The Chivas Glenlivet Group from Seagrams in 2001 and part of the Allied portfolio in 2005.

Burn Stewart Distillers is owned by CL World Brands of Trinidad (owners of Angustura Bitters).

Glen Grant Distillers is owned by Campari of Milan.

John Dewar & Sons is owned by Bacardi and owns William Lawson Distillers.

Morrison Bowmore is owned by Suntory of Japan.

Inver House Distillers was bought by Thaibev plc (SE Asia's largest alcoholic beverage company) in 2001 and is now part of its international division, InterBev.

The Edrington Group owns Highland Distillers and 50 per cent of Macallan distillery.

Whyte & Mackay is owned by the United Breweries Group of India.

STATUS
"Blenders Rating" (Top, 1st, 2nd, 3rd Class) for the Highland malts is an historic measure of their desirability for blending, not necessarily their attraction as single malts, although often

the two coincide. It is taken from the classifications used by a major blender in 1974. Visitor centres vary in size and facilities. The largest might include a restaurant, a museum and a shop. The smallest might be simply a room full of memorabilia. Guided tours are available at all the distilleries with visitor centres, and some by arrangement as noted.

THE ENTRY

I have supplied a necessarily brief account of each distillery's history – its date of foundation, owner, peculiarities, current status and so on.

Since the focus of this book is on flavour and where it comes from, I have also remarked on any aspects of production – such as ancient equipment, unusual stills, worm tubs etc. – that might influence the flavour of the whisky.

The general abbreviations I have used are for The Distillers Company Limited (DCL) and Scottish Malt Distillers (SMD). The latter was founded as a group of Lowland malt distilleries in 1914, joined DCL in 1925 and became the holding company for all of its malt distilleries. It amalgamated with Scottish Grain Distillers in 1988, to become United Grain and Malt Distillers (UGMD). Diageo plc is DCL's succesor. IDV is Independent Distillers and Vintners (the distilling division of Grand Metropolitan). United Distillers and Vintners (UDV) was formed by the merger of Grand Metropolitan and Guinness in 1997.

TASTING NOTES

In this column I have supplied an indication of the style of the new-make spirit and of the mature whisky where applicable, but in some cases a generic note is given. Clearly the flavour of the mature whisky will vary greatly with age, and according to whether the casks are American or European oak (ex-bourbon, ex-sherry), so the notes are for guidance only. Wherever possible, the choice of mature whisky is based on the "standard" bottling from the distillery owner (usually at 12 to 15 years, and at 40% to 43% ABV) and not independent bottlings, which are more variable.

ABERFELDY
Aberfeldy, Perthshire, CENTRAL HIGHLAND
Current Owner: John Dewar & Sons
Status: In production; 2nd Class; visitor centre

The distillery was built between 1896 and
'98 by John Dewar & Sons, on a site that had
been occupied by an earlier distillery. It was
ideally located, having a branch railway line
at its door, which provided a direct link to
Dewar's blending and bottling plant in Perth.
The water used in production comes from the
Pitlie Burn. Aberfeldy has continually remained
in production apart from the war years and
was largely rebuilt in the 1970s. It is the heart
malt for Dewar's famous White Label blend,
the number one Scotch in the USA. The Dewar
brands and four distilleries were bought by
Bacardi in 1998, and Aberfeldy single malt is
now much more widely available. The standard
bottlings are at 12, 21 and 25 Years.

An outstanding visitor centre, Dewar's
World of Whiskies was opened here in 2000.
Described by *Whisky Magazine* as the ultimate
whisky visitor centre, it tells the story of
Dewar's and Aberfeldy.

Tasting Note
Sweet and estery, with Ogen melon and heather
honey. The taste is fresh and fruity (pears,
melon, bruised apples), with some maltiness.
Predominantly sweet, with light waxiness and
a medium body.

ABERLOUR
Aberlour, Banffshire, SPEYSIDE
Current Owner: Chivas Brothers
Status: In production; 2nd Class; visitor centre

Aberlour distillery was founded in 1826 on
the site of a holy well dedicated to St Drostan,
who became Archbishop of Canterbury in 960,
and who once had a cell here. It was rebuilt
after a fire in 1898, extended in 1945 and
modernised in the 1970s by Pernod Ricard,
that bought it from S Campbell & Sons in 1974.
It uses only Scottish barley and has uniquely

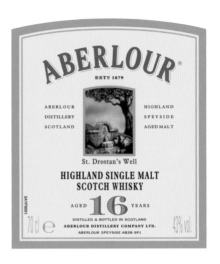

broad-based stills; the product is matured
partly in sherry-wood, partly in bourbon.
Cork bungs are used, not the usual wooden
ones, which allow any residual harsh vapours
to evaporate more easily. Aberlour's popularity
is evidenced by the amount bottled. It is
especially popular in France and is bottled
by its owner at 10, 12 and 16 Years, and also
as *a'bunadh* ("the original" in Gaelic) at cask
strength. It is the heart malt for the
Clan Campbell blends.

Tasting Note
Malty, sweet, fruity and spicy. A viscous mouth-
feel; honey and nutmeg and a thread of smoke
in the finish. Smooth and medium-bodied.

ALLT-A-BHAINNE "Alta-vanya"
near Dufftown, Banffshire, SPEYSIDE
Current Owner: Chivas Brothers
Status: In production

The distillery, founded in 1975, was the
fourth distillery built in Scotland by Seagrams.
Fully automated, it requires a staff of only
two people, and can produce one million
gallons (4.5 million litres) of spirit a year.

It stands on the northern slopes of Ben Rinnes, the mountain that dominates this part of Speyside, and its name translates as "the burn of milk". There are two pairs of stills and the new-make spirit is tankered to Keith for filling. This malt is not bottled by its proprietor and remains very rare, found only in independent merchant bottlings.

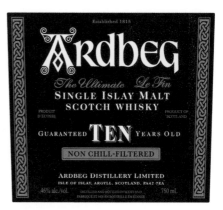

Tasting Note
Sweet and grassy, with vanilla and toffee in the taste. Medium length.

AN CNOC aka Knockdhu
Knock, Banffshire, EAST HIGHLAND
Current Owner: Inver House
Status: In production; 2nd Class

The brand was previously named Knockdhu after the distillery, but was re-named "An Cnoc" in 1994 to avoid confusion with Knockando. Exactly a century before this in 1894, it was the first malt distillery to be built specifically for the Distillers Company Ltd, as a showpiece under licence to Haigs. Knockdhu is situated by the River Isla, beneath Knock Hill (from a spring on which it draws its water) close to the fertile Laich o'Moray which provided abundant barley. Its two original stills are still used today. The distillery was closed in 1983, and sold to Inver House in 1987, which bottles its product at 12 and 16 Years, with occasional limited editions.

Tasting Note
Fruity-floral, estery, with lemon notes, but added body from the use of worm tubs. Light Speyside in aroma – buttercups, vanilla cream biscuits, light lemon notes. The taste is sweet, with cooked apples and lemon meringue pie. Light-bodied.

ARDBEG
near Port Ellen, ISLAY
Current Owner: Glenmorangie
Status: In production; visitor centre

Ardbeg was built in 1815, on the site of an earlier distillery, by John MacDougall. The absence of fans in the pagoda-roofed maltings produced a heavily peated malt, and although these are no longer in operation, the distillery specifies the same from Port Ellen Maltings. After the Macdougalls ceased to control Ardbeg (in 1959) it had a stop-start existence under several owners before being bought by Glenmorangie in 1997. The new owner restored the run-down distillery buildings, installed an excellent visitor centre and restaurant and resumed full production. Where previously Ardbeg's high reputation was based on only around 200 cases a year, now many expressions are available, some chosen by "The Ardbeg Committee", the friends of the distillery. Ownership of the distillery passed to the French company Louis Vuitton Möet Hennessy in 2004 with its acquisition of Glenmorangie.

Tasting Note
Peaty, medicinal, salty, dry, but with a surprisingly sweet taste, followed by a blast of smoke and sometimes hints of liquorice. Full-bodied.

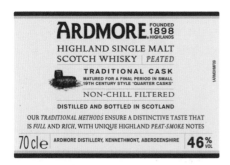

ARDMORE
Kennethmont, Aberdeenshire, HIGHLAND
Current Owner: Fortune Brands Inc
Status: In production; 2nd Class

Built between 1898 and 1899 by Teacher's to secure fillings for its major blend (Highland Cream), Ardmore is set deep in the farmland of "the Garioch", near the River Bogie and the village of Kennethmont. Teacher's was bought by Allied Breweries in 1976, but Ardmore was not bottled as a single until the distillery changed hands once again, 30 years later. The present owner is Fortune Brands, of America (owner of Jim Beam bourbon), who have offered a non-aged, non-chill-filtered expression since 2007.

Tasting Note
Exceptionally smoky for a Highland malt (12 to 14ppm phenols), the new-make is also sweet and spicy. All these come through in the mature whisky – mellow and buttery; sweet and malty, with distinct smoke. Robust and full-bodied.

AUCHENTOSHAN
Dalmuir, Dumbartonshire, LOWLAND
Current Owner: Morrison Bowmore
Status: In production; visitor centre

Founded in 1800, this is one of the few Lowland distilleries still in operation today. Situated just outside Glasgow, Auchentoshan overlooks the River Clyde, with its back to the Kilpatrick Hills and is the only distillery that

continues the traditional Lowland practice of "triple-distillation". It was bombed during the Second World War, rebuilt, sold to Tennent's in the early 1960s and sold again in 1969 to Eadie Cairns, who thoroughly modernised it. Then it was bought by Morrison Bowmore in 1984, and again overhauled. "Auchie", as it is known affectionately, has long described itself as "The Glasgow Malt". A major re-vamp of liquids and packaging took place in 2008, and now the range includes: Classic (no age statement), 12, 18 and 23 Year Old; Three Wood (a mix of ex-bourbon, ex-oloroso and ex-Pedro Ximinez casks) and occasional limited editions. New visitor centre installed at the same time.

Tasting Note
Delicate, fruity and zesty as new-make, with a floral-fragrant, light cereal and citric nose when mature. Smooth mouth-feel, sweet, then dry with roast almonds, fruits and butterscotch. Short finish.

AUCHROISK "Ath-rusk"
Mulben, Banffshire, SPEYSIDE
Current Owner: Diageo plc
Status: In production

This distillery, opened in 1974 by IDV, has won several architectural awards. Its subsidiary, Justerini & Brooks, the London wine merchant (which placed the first-known advertisement for Scotch whisky in 1779), launched the first bottling of Auchroisk (aka The Singleton of Auchroisk). The first word an archaism for "single malt", it translates as "ford of the red stream") in 1986. Since then it has won awards

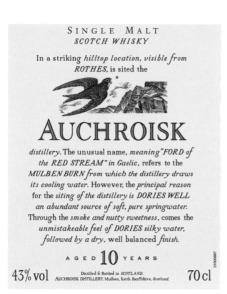

SINGLE MALT
SCOTCH WHISKY

In a striking *hilltop location, visible from ROTHES,* is sited the

AUCHROISK

distillery. The unusual name, *meaning "FORD of the RED STREAM" in Gaelic,* refers to the *MULBEN BURN from which the distillery draws its cooling water.* However, the *principal reason for the siting of the distillery is DORIES WELL an abundant source of soft, pure springwater.* Through the *smoke and nutty sweetness,* comes the *unmistakeable feel of DORIES silky water, followed by a dry,* well balanced *finish.*

AGED **10** YEARS

43% vol   Distilled & Bottled in *SCOTLAND.*
AUCHROISK DISTILLERY, Mulben, Keith, Banffshire, *Scotland.*   70 cl

such as the IWSC trophy and gold medals in 1992 and 1995. Water used comes from Dorie's Well, a local spring rising through granite and sandstone. The Singleton was a vatting of ex-bourbon casks, re-racked into ex-sherry casks for two years. Auchroisk is now bottled at 10 Years Old in Diageo's "Flora and Fauna" series.

Tasting Note
Light and grassy as new-make, the mature whisky is sweet and lightly honeyed (Sugar Puffs), with baked apples in the taste. Light- to medium-bodied.

AULTMORE
Keith, Banffshire, SPEYSIDE
Current Owner: John Dewar & Sons
Status: In production; Top Class

Built in 1896 by Alexander Edward, the owner of Benrinnes distillery, Aultmore is situated between Keith and the Moray Firth, a district that had long been popular with illicit distillers on account of its proximity to the springs of the Foggie Moss, from which the Aultmore

distillery draws its water.

Edward suffered severe losses following the crash of Pattisons of Leith and Aultmore was sold in 1923 to John Dewar & Sons for £20,000. Dewar's joined DCL in 1925 and from then until 1998 (when Dewar's and its associated distilleries were sold to Bacardi) it was managed by SMD, who modernised it in the late 1960s/early 1970s. Ranked "Top Class", the make was not bottled by its owners until 1996, and is still uncommon, bottled only at 12 Years.

Tasting Note
Delicate, fruity and zesty as new-make, with a floral-fragrant, light cereal and citric nose when mature. Smooth mouth-feel, sweet, then dry with roast almonds, fruits and butterscotch. Short finish.

BALBLAIR
Edderton, Ross & Cromarty, NORTH HIGHLAND
Current Owner: Inver House
Status: In production; 3rd Class

Said to have been founded in 1790, Balblair's original owner, Andrew Ross, built a new distillery on the present site in 1872. The location of the original distillery is uncertain, but its present owner claims Balblair to be the second oldest in Scotland. It is certainly one of the most charming; some of the buildings are of eighteenth-century origin and the rest are little changed in 100 years.

The distillery stands close to the village of Edderton, sometimes known as "the parish of peat", on account of the fact that the peat here is rather curiously dry and crumbly. The production water trickles through this peat, which may account for the whisky's distinctive

BALBLAIR
Established in 1790
VINTAGE
19 **75**
Highland Single Malt
Scotch Whisky
70cl.℮ 46%vol.

spicy character. Closed between 1915 and 1947, Balblair was bought by Hiram Walker in 1970, and a third still was added. Walker's successor, Allied Distillers, sold Balblair to Inver House in 1996, who resumed production.

Tasting Note
Full-bodied, waxy and nutty, with fresh fruit notes as new-make, the spirit carries all these characteristics into the mature whisky. Medium-sweet to taste, with an attractively thick texture. Medium-bodied.

BALLECHIN (see EDRADOUR)

BALMENACH
Cromdale, Morayshire, SPEYSIDE
Current Owner: Inver House
Status: In production; 1st Class

The distillery was first licensed to James McGregor, a renowned illicit distiller, in 1825. Following his death in 1878 it was taken over by his brother and the business continued to flourish, although it narrowly escaped destruction the following year in the great storm which blew down the Tay Bridge.

In 1897 the Balmenach-Glenlivet Distillery Ltd was formed; this joined SMD (DCL) in 1930. The distillery was closed in 1993 and sold to Inver House Distilleries in 1997. In 2009 Inver House began to produce occasional batches of pot-still gin at Balmenach, named Caorunn (Gaelic for "rowan-berries"). The make is currently not bottled by its owners.

Tasting Note
Full-bodied, meaty and oily as new-make, its rich character makes it appropriate for sherry-wood maturation, and these have a fruit-cake style, with a whiff of sulphury smoke. Medium sweet, rich and dry in the finish. Full-bodied.

EST? 1892
SINGLE MALT SCOTCH WHISKY
Distilled at
THE BALVENIE®
Distillery Banffshire
SCOTLAND
SIGNATURE
David Stewart
THE BALVENIE MALT MASTER

AGED **TWELVE** YEARS

THE BALVENIE SIGNATURE is an exposition of the TRADITIONAL ART of our Malt Master, David Stewart. He *skilfully* marries aged Balvenie from the finest first fill bourbon, refill and sherry casks to create this *signature malt*, characterised by honey, spice and *subtle* oak.

LTD RELEASE - BATCH Nº 002

70cl 700ml ℮   THE BALVENIE DISTILLERY Cº DUFFTOWN, BANFFSHIRE SCOTLAND AB55 4BB   40%vol 40%alc/vol

BALVENIE
Dufftown, Banffshire, SPEYSIDE
Current Owner: Wm Grant & Sons
Status: In production; 1st Class; tours by arrangement

Balvenie was originally founded in 1892 by William Grant, near his recently built Glenfiddich distillery. It stands in the shadow of Balvenie Castle, once owned by the notorious "Black Douglases" and later forfeited to the Crown. It is still owned by William Grant's descendants and is unusual in that it grows some of its own barley, and has a maltings, a coppersmith's forge and a cooperage.

The original stills were from Lagavulin and Glen Albyn, and have much longer necks than those at Glenfiddich. Their number was increased to eight during the 1960s and '70s. The make was first bottled by its proprietor in 1973, and it is currently offered at 12 Years (Founders' Reserve), 12 Years (Doublewood, ie. racked into oloroso casks; Signature, a mix of cask types), Portwood 21 Years. Single Barrel Vintages 15 and 25 Years and occasional Vintage Casks.

Tasting Note
Fruity and full-bodied, with honeycomb,
Christmas cake, orange peel and sweet malt. A
big, mouth-filling texture, a sweet taste, and a
tannic finish.

BANFF
Banff, Banffshire, EAST HIGHLAND
Status: Demolished; 2nd Class

Founded by James McKilligan & Co in 1824
at the Mill of Banff, close to the ancient town
of that name, the distillery closed in 1863 and
was replaced by one at Inverboyndie. It was
rebuilt in 1877 after a fire and bought in 1932
by SMD (DCL).

A stray bomb caused much damage to the
distillery during the Second World War, and
according to the *Banffshire Journal*, "thousands
of gallons of whisky were lost, either burning
or running to waste... and so overpowering
were the results that even the farm animals
grazing in the neighbourhood became visibly
intoxicated". Banff was closed and demolished
in 1983, so its product is now rare.

BEN NEVIS
Fort William, Inverness-shire, WEST HIGHLAND
Current Owner: Nikka Whisky Distilling Co
Status: In production; visitor centre

The renowned distiller, "Long" John
Macdonald of Torgulbin, built Ben Nevis
in 1825. He named it after the highest
mountain in Scotland and gave a cask
of his whisky, Dew of Ben Nevis, to Queen
Victoria, to be broached on the Prince of
Wales' 21st birthday in 1863. Long John's
son inherited the business.

Ben Nevis remained in production
throughout the nineteenth century and
in 1955 was bought by Joseph Hobbs, the
Scots-Canadian buccaneer. Sadly, the Long
John brand name went elsewhere in the
1920s, but then returned in 1981 when
it was acquired by Long John International

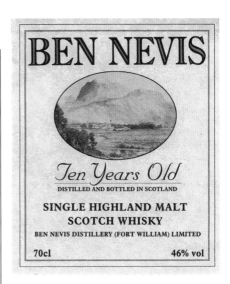

BEN NEVIS

Ten Years Old
DISTILLED AND BOTTLED IN SCOTLAND

**SINGLE HIGHLAND MALT
SCOTCH WHISKY**

BEN NEVIS DISTILLERY (FORT WILLIAM) LIMITED

70cl   46% vol

(Whitbread & Co). Subsequently, in 1991,
the distillery was sold to Nikka, the Japanese
company.

Tasting Note
Malty and robust, with a trace of smoke. The
nose is of cooked fruits, malt and dark chocolate;
a creamy texture, with a sweet, caramel-like
start and a trace of sulphury smoke. Medium- to
full-bodied.

BENRIACH
near Elgin, Morayshire, SPEYSIDE
Current Owner: The BenRiach-Glendronach
Distilleries Co
Status: In production; 1st Class; visitor centre

Built by John Duff & Co Ltd in 1897, at the
end of the whisky boom, BenRiach then
closed between 1900 and 1965, when it was
rebuilt by The Glenlivet Distillers. Since 1985,
when the number of stills was doubled
(to six), BenRiach has been producing in
the region of three million litres of whisky
per annum; it still has its own floor maltings
(currently closed but it is planned to reopen
them, this year, next year, some time…).
Until recently this malt was rare as a single
and most went into Chivas' Queen Anne

MATURED IN THE HEART OF SPEYSIDE

AGED 12 YEARS

CAREFULLY CONTROLLED MALTING, DISTILLING & MATURATION USING AGE OLD METHODS

ESTABLISHED 1898

THE BenRiacH

HEART OF SPEYSIDE

SINGLE MALT
SCOTCH WHISKY

BENRIACH 1898

70cl e   DISTILLED & BOTTLED IN SCOTLAND
THE BENRIACH DISTILLERY Co LTD., MORAYSHIRE, IV30 8SJ   40%vol

Special blends. From 1995 it was promoted as a single malt, and such promotion has increased substantially since the distillery was sold to a private consortium in 2004, including peated and wine- or rum-finished expressions.

Tasting Note
The traditional BenRiach is a robust Speyside, sweet and fruity, with apples and green bananas and some cereal notes. Sweet and creamy to taste, with vanilla. Light- to medium-bodied.

BENRINNES
Aberlour, Banffshire, SPEYSIDE
Current Owner: Diageo plc
Status: In production; Top Class

Standing on the northern slopes of the mountain of the same name at over 200 metres (656 feet) above sea level, the distillery was built in 1826 and licensed in 1834. In his account of his tour of Scottish distilleries Alfred Barnard described the Scurran and

Rowantree burns, from which the distillery draws its water, as rising "from springs on the summit of the mountain and can be seen on a clear day, some miles distant, sparkling over the rocks on its downwards course, passing over mossy banks and gravel, which perfectly filters it." Benrinnes was bought in 1922 by John Dewar & Sons, who took it into the DCL fold three years later. Major refurbishment and modernisation took place in 1955, and in 1966 the number of stills doubled to six. They are operated in such a way as to perform a partial triple distillation.

Tasting Note
The new-make is heavy and meaty, and the mature whisky has a big, robust character, with burnt caramel and dried fruits. The texture is velvety and the taste sweet then mouth-drying, with a long finish. Full-bodied.

BENROMACH
Forres, Morayshire, SPEYSIDE
Current Owner: Gordon & MacPhail
Status: In production; 3rd Class; visitor centre

Founded in 1898 on the outskirts of Forres, by a partnership of the distiller Duncan MacCallum and Leith whisky broker, FW Brickman, who were encouraged by the well-known promoter of Scotch whisky and Speyside distiller Alexander Edward. Yet, following the bankruptcy of Pattisons of Leith in 1900, the distillery closed and Brickman was forced to withdraw his involvement.

The distillery remained silent from 1909 to 1939 when it was bought by Joseph Hobbs. He sold it to National Distillers of America from which it was acquired by DCL in 1953. Production ceased in 1983 and in 1992 the distillery was sold to Gordon & Macphail, the long-established family owned firm of blenders and independent bottlers in Elgin. They refurbished it and resumed production in 1998. A visitor centre opened in August 1999.

MATURED IN HAND
SELECTED OAK CASKS

single

SPEYSIDE

malt

S C O T C H

W H I S K Y

25 YEARS OLD

BENROMACH
DISTILLERY

70cl 43%vol

DISTILLED AT BENROMACH DISTILLERY, FORRES, SCOTLAND.
BOTTLED BY THE PROPRIETORS, GORDON & MACPHAIL
A FAMILY BUSINESS FOR OVER 100 YEARS.

Tasting Note
Light Speyside in style, with fresh fruits and
hedgerow flowers. A creamy mouth-feel and
a sweet overall taste with light cereal notes.
Light- to medium-bodied

BEN WYVIS (1) aka Ferintosh
Dingwall, Ross & Cromarty, NORTH HIGHLAND
Status: Demolished

This distillery was built in 1879 by DG Ross
and sold to Scotch Whisky Distillers Ltd
in 1887. In 1893 its name was changed to
Ferintosh, after the Forbes' eighteenth-century
distillery, although its situation (in the village
of Ferintosh near Dingwall) is across the
Cromarty Firth from the original.

Ownership passed to the Distillers Finance
Corporation Ltd of Belfast, which was sold
to DCL in 1922. It was then licensed to
John Begg Ltd and later closed in 1926; the
warehouses (that still stand beside the railway
line) were used until 1980. The distillery itself
was demolished in 1993 to make way for a
residential development. Not available
for tasting.

BEN WYVIS (2)
Invergordon, Ross & Cromarty,
NORTH HIGHLAND
Status: Demolished; 3rd Class

Established in 1965 with two stills, as part of
the Invergordon grain distillery complex on
the northern shore of the Cromarty Firth. The
distillery was closed in 1977 and dismantled
soon after. Its product was exclusively used for
blending. I know of only two casks that have
been bottled as a single malt, by Signatory.

BLADNOCH
Bladnoch, Wigtownshire, LOWLAND
Current Owner: Bladnoch Distillery Ltd
Status: In production; visitor centre

Bladnoch was established as a farm distillery
in 1817 by the brothers Thomas and John
McClelland, and operated by the latter's son
until 1905, when production ceased. It was
sold to the Irish distillers, Dunville & Co, in
1911 and on that company's liquidation was
bought by a firm of Glasgow blenders, which
dismantled it, sold the stills to Sweden, and the
stock at below its value (attracting a 100 per
cent "excess profits tax").

The buildings were bought by a local man
who resumed production. In 1966 it was again
sold, and two more stills were installed. Inver
House Distillers owned it between 1973 and
1983, when it was bought by Arthur Bell &
Sons, so it became part of Guinness when the
latter bought Bell's. Two stills were removed
in 1986, and Bladnoch was de-commissioned

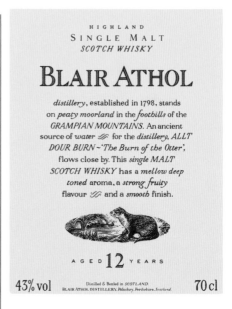

in 1993, then sold to Raymond and Colin Armstrong the following year. They refurbished it and resumed production in 2000.

Tasting Note
The new-make spirit is sweet and grassy, with cereal notes. The mature aroma is pastoral and floral, with light lemon-citric notes. Appetising, with a short finish. Light-bodied.

BLAIR ATHOL

Pitlochry, Perthshire, CENTRAL HIGHLAND
Current Owner: Diageo plc
Status: In production; 2nd Class; visitor centre

The original distillery was founded in the late 1790s by John Stewart and Robert Robertson 17 kilometres (nine miles) south of Blair Atholl village at the town of Pitlochry. It was revived in the mid-1820s and bought by P Mackenzie & Co in the 1880s, when two new granaries and malting floors were added. The water used is from the Allt Dour ("the burn of the otter"), which rises above the snow line. Barnard wrote that it was "of the purest description, sparkling as clear as crystal".

By the turn of the century Blair Athol had a 100,000 gallons (over 454,000 litres) capacity. The distillery was later acquired by Arthur Bell & Sons in 1933 (an event which one whisky writer describes as Bell's coming of age) but remained closed until 1949 when it was rebuilt. Blair Athol is an important contributor to the Bell's blends and, consequently, in 1970 the number of stills was doubled. Constructed in 1987, the visitor centre at Blair Athol is popular with visitors to Pitlochry.

Tasting Note
Rich and malty, with caramel, leather and tobacco on the nose. A mix of sweet and dry in the taste, with a shortish finish. Medium-bodied.

BOWMORE

Bowmore, ISLAY
Current Owner: Morrison Bowmore
Status: In production; 50,000 cases; visitor centre

The earliest legal distillery on Islay, and one of the earliest in all Scotland, Bowmore was established in 1779 by John Simpson and was later expanded by James Mutter in 1852. It remained a private company from the 1890s until 1963 when it was acquired by Stanley P Morrison. Many of the buildings were renovated and rebuilt, although the floor maltings were retained and are still used today. Bowmore is gentle and fragrant compared with some Islays, but still distinctly smoky.

The owner bottles Legend (no age statement), 12, 15 and 18 Year Old bottlings; occasional vintage bottlings, and a range of four whiskies for duty free. Black Bowmore, a limited edition from 1964, is something of a legend and extremely rare.

Tasting Note
Smoky and floral in style. Often a lavender note on the nose, with tropical fruits and scented smoke. Sweet to taste, with a blast of smoke in the finish, and often a lingering perfume in the aftertaste. Medium-bodied.

BRAEVAL formerly Braes of Glenlivet
Glenlivet, Banffshire, SPEYSIDE
Current Owner: Chivas Brothers
Status: In production

Braes of Glenlivet distillery was originally built between 1973 and '74 by Chivas Bros Ltd during the expansion of its parent company Seagrams. Originally Braeval had three stills but two more were added in 1975. It is fully automated and can be operated by one man.

The architecture is traditional, including an attractive pagoda roof. It was re-named "Braeval" in 1996, to avoid any possible confusion with its sister distillery The Glenlivet. The malt is rare as a single, since it is not bottled by the owner and today all of the product goes into Chivas' range of blended whiskies.

Tasting Note
Sweet and grassy, with a Speyside character and a fresh, fruity flavour. Medium-bodied.

BRORA formerly Clynelish
Clynelish, Sutherland, NORTH HIGHLAND
Current Owner: Diageo plc
Status: Closed

Founded in 1819 by the Marquis of Stafford, First Duke of Sutherland, as Clynelish distillery (*see* Clynelish). The Duke is better known as the notorious landowner who cruelly ordered the removal by force of 15,000 men, women and children from his estates to make way for sheep, which were more economical.

His distillery was in the heart of good barley growing land and there was a coal-pit nearby to provide fuel – that turned out to be of inferior quality and ran out quickly. James Ainslie & Co acquired the distillery in 1896 but it was almost bankrupted in 1912, after which it joined DCL.

The excellence of the whisky made here was remarked on by Professor Saintsbury, pre-First World War. In 1968 a new distillery was built adjacent, also named Clynelish, and the original was mothballed. It came back into production in 1969 as "Clynelish No 2", but this caused so much confusion that the name was changed to "Brora". Confusion reigned, since both new and mature whiskies were still sold as "Clynelish". It was finally closed in May 1983. True "Brora" malt whisky must have been made between 1975 and 1983 and it is becoming increasingly rare.

BRUICHLADDICH "Brewick-laddie"
Bruichladdich, ISLAY
Current Owner: Bruichladdich Distillery Ltd
Status: In production; visitor centre

The smart whitewashed buildings of Bruichladdich overlook the pebbly shore of Loch Indaal. It was built in 1881 by the Harvey brothers using a newly patented material, "concrete". Much of the equipment dates back to the foundation, including the cast-iron mash tun and a riveted (rather than welded) wash still. In 1929 Bruichladdich was bought by Joseph Hobbs for Associated Scottish

Distillers and after several changes of ownership ultimately became part of the Invergordon Group in 1968. It passed into the ownership of Whyte & Mackay in 1994, and was mothballed the following year.

In 2000 it was sold to a consortium led by Mark Reynier, a wine and spirits merchant from London. The new owners have refurbished the distillery, resumed production and installed a brand new visitor centre, where there are frequent residential master classes. Bruichladdich traditionally specifies un-peated malt, but in 2001 it introduced a peated version, called Port Charlotte, and in 2002 "the world's most heavily peated whisky", named Octomore. Traditional Bruichladdich is now available in a baffling range of expressions. It is bottled on site.

Tasting Note
Light and malty, in its traditional, un-peated, form, with fresh, grassy, even floral notes and a sweet taste, becoming lightly citric and cereal-like. Dry and short in the finish. Light-bodied.

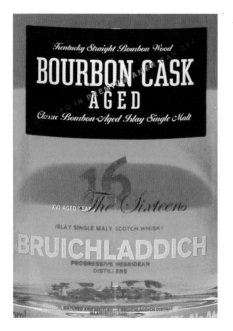

BUNNAHABHAIN "Boona-harvan"
near Port Askaig, ISLAY
Current Owner: Burn Stewart plc
Status: In production; visitors by arrangement

The distillery was established in 1883 as The Islay Distillery Co Ltd by the Greenlees family, who were local farmers. The site chosen was remote and desolate, at the mouth of the River Margadale, where it flows into the Sound of Islay. The Greenlees amalgamated with Glenrothes-Glenlivet distillery four years later, to form Highland Distilleries. The Edrington Group (successor to Highland Distillers) sold the distillery to Burn Stewart Distilleries in 2003.

Bunnahabhain is Islay's most remote and most northerly distillery, and unlike most of the others its make is only lightly peated (two to three ppm phenols). Following trials in 1997, batches of heavily peated Bunna (35 to 40ppm phenols) are now produced each year. Maturation is in a combination of sherry and bourbon casks. Only available as a single malt since 1970 (as a 12 Year Old), 18 and 25 Year Old expressions were launched in 2006.

Tasting Note
Sweet and lightly fruity, traditional Bunna also

has maritime characteristics, and sometimes a whiff of peat-smoke. The texture is soft and smooth, the taste mild, lightly sweet then drying with a hint of smoke. Medium-bodied.

CAOL ILA "Cull-eela"
Port Askaig, ISLAY
Current Owner: Diageo plc
Status: In production; visitors by arrangement

The distillery was constructed in a cove overlooking the Sound of Islay, by a man called Hector Henderson (a partner in Littlemill distillery) in 1846. The site was chosen for its constant supply of fresh water from Loch Nam Bam – of which Alfred Barnard once wrote, "over which ever and anon the fragrant breeze from the heather and the myrtle is wafted". Following Henderson's sequestration in 1857, the distillery was aquired by Bulloch Lade & Co.

In 1927 it passed to DCL who demolished the original distillery in 1972 (apart from the large three storey warehouse) and replaced it with a larger and more efficient building, with a magnificent view across the Sound of Islay (from which the distillery takes its name). Until 1988 Caol Ila was only available in independent bottlings, but it is now released at 12, 18 and 25 Years, and at cask strength, Moscatel-finished and occasionally as a un-peated expression.

CAOL ILA
AGED **12** YEARS
ISLAY SINGLE MALT WHISKY
Out of sight, in a remote cove near Port Askaig lies Caol Ila, hidden gem among Islay's distilleries since 1846. Not easy to find, Caol Ila's secret malt is nonetheless highly prized among devotees of the Islay style.

43% vol   *Caol Ila Distillery, Port Askaig, Isle of Islay.*   70cl e
Caol Ila lies close to Loch nam Ban, source of its pure mash water. The sea provides water for cooling and once brought steamers to collect a whisky appreciated for its *balanced, fresh style* – lighter-bodied than many Islay malts, yet with all their typical peatiness.

Tasting Note
The spirit is smoky; sweet and lightly fruity on the nose, reminiscent of smoked ham, with fragrant smoke and antiseptic cream. Medium-length.

CAPERDONICH
Rothes, Morayshire, SPEYSIDE
Current Owner: Chivas Brothers
Status: Mothballed

This was originally built as Glen Grant No 2 distillery in 1897. Although the water source, malt and distilling practice were the same, it produced a very different spirit from its sister distillery. Owing to the slump in the industry at the turn of the century, Glen Grant No 2 was closed after only three years and only reopened in 1965 when it was reconstructed by Glenlivet Distillers Ltd. It was renamed Caperdonich (after the well that supplies its reducing water). During the refurbishment process the original copper pot stills were retained and two more were added in 1967.

The company became part of Seagrams in 1977, and ownership passed to Pernod Ricard when they acquired Seagram's whisky interests in 2001. Caperdonich was mothballed the following year. The make has only been bottled by its owners twice: a 5 Year Old in the 1970s and a 16 Year Old in 2005.

Tasting Note
Sweet and grassy. A typical light-bodied Speyside, with pear-drops and floral notes and traces of vanilla. The taste is sweet with tropical fruits and nougat.

CARDHU
Knockando, Morayshire, SPEYSIDE
Current Owner: Diageo plc
Status: In production; 1st Class; visitor centre

Original owner, farmer John Cumming, was three times convicted of illicit distilling before he took out a licence in 1824. After his death Cardhu was run by his son (until 1876) and his wife Elizabeth, "the Queen of the Whisky Trade". It was Elizabeth who went on to expand the business dramatically. In 1893 she negotiated a merger with John Walker & Sons, whereby her family retained operational control of the distillery. Her grandson, Sir Ronald Cumming, became chairman of DCL in 1963. Today it is among the world's top ten bestsellers and is Diageo's best-selling single malt. It remains the heart of the Johnnie Walker brands. The visitor centre was refurbished in 2002.

Tasting Note
The new-make is floral; the mature whisky fragrant (rose petals, Parma Violets) and fresh and fruity (apples, pear-drops). Sweet and fresh to taste. Light-bodied

CLYNELISH
Brora, Sutherland, NORTH HIGHLAND
Current Owner: Diageo plc
Status: In production; 2nd Class; visitor centre

A large new distillery was built in 1967 at the side of the old Clynelish distillery (*see* Brora), with a distilling regime which followed the specifications for the earlier distillery. The make is very highly regarded by connoisseurs and blenders alike, with its characteristically scented-wax aroma and texture.

It is often compared to island whiskies, unsurprisingly so except that it has an eastward prospect across the North Sea. Once uncommon as a single, it is now being made more widely available.

Tasting Note
Waxy, with a heathery scent. Both these

characteristics come through in the mature whisky, with herbal notes and fragrant smoke. Teeth-coating in texture, lightly fruity and herbal. Medium-bodied.

COLEBURN
Elgin, Morayshire, SPEYSIDE
Current Owner: Diageo plc
Status: Dismantled

The distillery was built in 1897 by James Robertson & Son, a blending firm based in Dundee. It is situated near the Glen Burn, which provided the water for production, and also near the Great Northern Railway which provided a goods station for the distillery traffic. Coleburn's promoters described the distillery as being "complete in itself, compact and clean with a cleanliness which only can be attained in Highland air". Coleburn was bought by the Clynelish Distillery Co in 1916, and thus joined the DCL conglomerate in 1930.

Although the buildings retain their original appearance, some refurbishment and conversion took place in the 1950s and '60s. It was during this period that the mash house was rebuilt, condensers replaced the worm tubs and the stills were fitted with internal steam coils. The distillery was closed in 1985. The malt is available in occasional bottlings only.

CONVALMORE
Dufftown, Banffshire, SPEYSIDE
Status: Dismantled; 2nd Class

The distillery was built in 1894 by a group of Glasgow businessmen and sold ten years later for £6,000 to WP Lowrie & Co Ltd, in turn controlled by James Buchanan & Co by 1906. Following a serious fire in 1909, a continous still was installed with the capacity to distil 500 gallons (2,270 litres) of wash every hour. However the spirit produced failed to mature properly and the experiment was abandoned. DCL extended the distillery in 1965, mothballed it in 1985 and later dismantled it. The site

was sold to William Grant & Sons in 1990 for warehousing. Convalmore is only bottled occasionally by Diageo.

CRAGGANMORE
Ballindalloch, Banffshire, SPEYSIDE
Current Owner: Diageo plc
Status: In production; Top Class; visitors by arrangement

Established in 1869 by John Smith, who had been manager at the Macallan, Glenlivet and Wishaw distilleries, and who was said to be the most experienced distiller of his day. Cragganmore (named after the hill behind the distillery from which the distillery takes its water for production) was the first distillery deliberately sited to take advantage of railway transport. Smith himself was a great railway enthusiast, but since he weighed 308 pounds (140kg) he was obliged to travel in the guard's van. Following Smith's death in 1923 his widow sold the distillery to White Horse Distillers Ltd and hence into the DCL stable. In 1964 it was expanded from two to four stills. The stills have interesting flat tops rather than swan-necks and retain their worm tubs.

Always well thought of by blenders it was uncommon as a single until the late 1980s, when it was selected for promotion as a "Classic Malt" by United Distillers (now Diageo).

Tasting Note
A big, rich spirit, presenting a complex multi-layered aroma of nuts, saddle-soap, dried fruits, polish. The taste is dryish overall, with walnuts, dried fruit and hard toffee. Medium-bodied.

CRAIGELLACHIE
Craigellachie, Banffshire, SPEYSIDE
Current Owner: John Dewar & Sons
Status: In production; 1st Class

"Restless" Peter Mackie, founder of White Horse Distillers and owner of Lagavulin, formed a partnership with Alexander Edward of Aultmore and Benrinnes to build this distillery in 1898 and bottled the whisky as a single before the First World War. Mackie held his annual meetings here during which he made his views on industry and Empire forcefully known! The distillery became part of SMD (DCL) in 1930 and was rebuilt in the mid-1960s when two stills were added. It passed to John Dewar & Sons in 1999, who have been bottling at 14 Years since 2004.

Tasting Note
Big and meaty and slightly smoky. Speyside fruity-floral on the nose, but with a thread of smoke. Big, creamy mouth-feel; sweet with light acidity and a trace of smoke. Full-bodied.

DAFTMILL
Cupar, Fife, LOWLAND
Current Owner: Francis and Ian Cuthbert
Status: In production

Daftmill distillery was created out of an old meal mill, dating from the late-seventeenth century, on Daftmill Farm, near Cupar. It takes its name from the Daft Burn, so called because it appears to flow up-hill, and is currently the smallest distillery in Scotland, with a capacity of 4,396 gallons (20,000 litres) of pure alcohol per annum. The attractive conversion was done by the owners of the farm, Francis and Ian Cuthbert (whose family have farmed here for six generations), between 2003 and 2005. All the building work was done by local tradesmen, with stills from Forsyth's of Rothes. The malt has not yet been bottled by its owners.

DAILUAINE "Daal-yewan"
Carron, Banffshire, SPEYSIDE
Current Owner: Diageo plc
Status: In production; 1st Class

Situated in the "green vale" between Ben Rinnes and the River Spey – hence its Gaelic name – the distillery was built in 1854 by William Mackenzie, a local farmer. Within 12 years the Strathspey Railway had reached the opposite bank of the river, and when a bridge was constructed close to the distillery Dailuaine could reach its markets easily.

By 1898 Mackenzie's son had joined forces with Talisker distillery in Skye. It was he who successfully and substantially expanded his business, building the Imperial distillery at Carron. He also owned a further grain distillery at Aberdeen. Because of the pressures of the pre-war depression, in 1916 his interests were acquired by DCL.

With six stills, Dailuaine has always been a filling malt and until recently was only occasionally to be found in merchant bottlings.

Tasting Note
Big, rich and meaty in style. Sherry-wood maturation is favoured, and the result is a rich, fruit-cake, Christmas pudding aroma, with a trace of sulphur and sherry. The texture is thick, and the taste starts sweet then dries out, leaving an after-taste of chocolate. Full-bodied.

DALLAS DHU
Forres, Morayshire, NORTH HIGHLAND
Current Owner: Historic Scotland
Status: Museum since 1992

Alexander Edward, the respected Speyside distiller, designed Dallas Dhu in 1899 at the height of the whisky boom. He sold the plans to the blender Wright & Greig, which went on to build it and after a short change of ownership the distillery was acquired by Benmore Distilleries Ltd (which joined DCL in 1929). Production continued until the distillery eventually closed in 1983; it is now a museum.

The malt is available only in rare independent bottlings. The name comes from the Gaelic "*Dail eas dubh*" ("the field by the dark waterfall"). The land hereabouts was granted to one William de Ripley in 1279, who changed his name to "de Dallas". The great Texan city was named after one of his descendants, the US Vice-President George M Dallas, in 1845.

DALMORE
Alness, Ross & Cromarty, NORTH HIGHLAND
Current Owner: Whyte & Mackay
Status: In production; 2nd Class; visitors by arrangement

Founded in 1839, the distillery was taken over by a local farming family, the Mackenzie brothers, in 1878. They had close links with Whyte & Mackay, which used the make as a key component of its blend; this relationship was consolidated in 1960 when the two companies merged.

The distillery overlooks the Cromarty Firth and the Black Isle and uses the water of the River Averon. One of its stills dates from 1874, and has a unique copper jacket around the

neck, which allows water to be sprayed onto the still, in order to increase reflux. It is bottled at a wide range of ages, with 12, 15 and 18 Years as the core. A 62 Year Old bottle (one of only 12, containing whisky from 1868, 1878, 1926 and 1939) was sold for £32,000 in 2005.

Tasting Note

Heavy, oily and musky, with citric notes; favours sherry-wood maturation, when the mature whisky becomes rich and sweet, with fruit-cake, orange peel and marzipan. Big texture; medium-sweet overall. Full-bodied.

DALWHINNIE

Dalwhinnie, Inverness-shire, CENTRAL HIGHLAND

Current Owner: Diageo plc

Status: In production; 2nd Class; visitor centre

The highest in Scotland, Dalwhinnie distillery stands in the Drumochter Pass at the head of Strathspey, in an area steeped in history. Prince Charles Edward Stuart passed down Drumochter after raising his standard at Glenfinnan before the fateful 1745 Jacobite rebellion. A group of men from Kingussie built the "Strathspey distillery" during the boom years of the 1890s. They chose the site for its supply of water from Lochan Doire-

Uaine, above the snow line, and the peat from surrounding moors.

The distillery was sold in 1898, renamed Dalwhinnie and (five years later) was acquired by the largest distiller in the USA, Cook & Bernheimer. Some industry concerns about US ownership in Scotland were dispelled by the Act of Prohibition in 1920, when Dalwhinnie was sold, first to Sir James Calder, then to DCL in 1926. Dalwhinnie is known today as one of Diageo's "Classic Malts".

Tasting Note

The make is robust, sweet, with heather-honey. The nose presents heather pollen and moorland scents. A big, viscous texture, soft and smooth; a sweet taste, drying lightly. Medium-bodied.

DEANSTON

Doune, Perthshire, CENTRAL HIGHLAND

Current Owner: Burn Stewart plc

Status: In production; 2nd Class

Deanston is situated at Doune in Perthshire, just north of the Highland Line and upstream from the ruins of Doune Castle, where the "Bonnie Earl o' Moray" was butchered in 1592. The buildings were adapted from a cotton mill designed in 1785 by Richard Arkwright, the inventor of the "spinning jenny" and one of the "Fathers" of the Industrial Revolution.

The water from the River Teith (which formerly drove the machinery) and the mill's airy weaving halls were ideal for making and

maturing spirit. In 1965 it was converted by the Deanston Distillery Co Ltd and then sold to the Invergordon Group during the industry slump of the 1980s. It closed three years later and was acquired and re-opened by Burn Stewart in 1991. It is bottled at 12, 17 and 30 Years (at 40% ABV).

Tasting Note
The make is light and fruity, and slightly waxy. Malty and slightly oily on the nose, the taste adds fruits and nuts to this, starting sweet and finishing dryish. Light- to medium-bodied.

DUFFTOWN
Dufftown, Banffshire, SPEYSIDE
Current Owner: Diageo plc
Status: In production; 2nd Class

Two young businessmen from Liverpool, Peter Mackenzie and Richard Stackpole, established the Dufftown-Glenlivet distillery in the late 1890s, in an old meal mill. Using barley from the nearby Pittyvaich Farm and fresh water from "Jock's Well" – famous for its quality and quantity – the business prospered and the company, now named P Mackenzie & Co, was able to buy Blair Athol distillery.

It was taken over by Bell's in 1933, which was itself taken over by the DCL in 1985. In the 1960s and '70s some major expansion took place – from two to eight stills (later reduced to six), and it is now Diageo's largest distillery with a capacity of one million gallons (4.5 million litres) per annum. Dufftown is a key filling in the Bell's brands, and is now being widely promoted as The Singleton of Dufftown (12 Year Old) in European markets.

Tasting Note
Malty and nutty as new-make, the mature whisky is Speyside-like – bruised apples, pears, cereal, with some butterscotch. Predominantly sweet to taste, with malt and toffee. Medium-bodied.

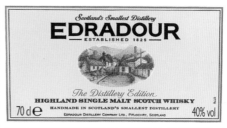

EDRADOUR
Pitlochry, Perthshire, CENTRAL HIGHLAND
Current Owner: Signatory Vintage Scotch Whisky
Status: In production; 3rd Class; visitor centre

Until 2005 Scotland's smallest and, some would say, prettiest distillery was built around 1825 by a group of farmers. William Whiteley, known as "The Dean of Distillers", bought it in 1922 with a view to keeping it exactly as it was. It was he who recognised the high quality of the spirit Edradour produced, which became the heart for his King's Ransom blend – which in the 1920s was claimed to be the world's most excellent and expensive whisky.

Edradour has been conserved with few changes: electricity and a little automation arrived in 1947; plant and distilling regime is traditional. A visitor centre was established in the 1990s. Edradour has a tiny output, and was unusual as a single until the distillery was bought by Pernod Ricard in 1992. In 2002 it was bought by Signatory, the well-known independent bottler, and the range of available expressions vastly increased, including a heavily peated range named "Ballechin".

Tasting Note
Traditional Edradour spirit is fruity and pear-like, with a robust body. Ten different kinds of wine casks are used for finishing or maturing, introducing layers of extractive flavour to the whisky. Medium-bodied.

FETTERCAIRN
Fettercairn, Kincardineshire, EAST HIGHLAND
Current Owner: Whyte & Mackay
Status: In production 3rd Class; visitor centre

Founded in 1824 and established as the
Fettercairn Distillery Co in 1887, with the
father of the renowned Victorian Prime
Minister William Gladstone of Great Britain,
as its chairman. The distillery is situated at
Laurencekirk in the heart of the Mearns, one of
Scotland's most fertile farming areas (providing
some of the best barley), and draws its water
from springs in the Grampian Mountains.
Fettercairn was bought by Joseph Hobbs (the
industry speculator who had made and lost a
fortune in the USA) on behalf of Associated
Scottish Distillers. Hobbs ran the distillery
until 1970, through his subsidiary Train &
Macintyre. In 1973 it was acquired by Whyte &
Mackay, and bottled as "Old Fettercairn". They
repackaged the malt as Fettercairn 1824 in 2002.

Tasting Note
The style sought is butterscotch, nuts and spice.
With maturity, maltiness is evident, with walnuts
and biscuits. The texture is slightly oily, with a
sweet start, drying lightly. Medium-bodied.

GLEN ALBYN
Inverness, Inverness-shire, NORTH HIGHLAND
Status: Demolished; 3rd Class

The Provost of Inverness, James Sutherland,
established Glen Albyn on the site of an old
brewery in 1846 on the Caledonian Canal,
which provided transport to the markets in the
south. A fire badly damaged it three years later,
and soon after this Sutherland went bankrupt.
    The distillery was used as a flour mill for a
time and remained silent for 20 years until in
1884 it was rebuilt with its own private railway
siding, connecting to the main line. Eight years
later, its new owner built Glen Mhor distillery
in collaboration with James Mackinlay. During
the First World War it was used by the US Navy
for the manufacture of mines. In 1920 it was
bought by Mackinlays and Birnie (bought by
DCL in 1972) and they closed the distillery in
1983, subsequently demolishing it to make way
for a supermarket. Glen Albyn was considered
typically Highland and is now rare.

GLENALLACHIE
Aberlour, Banffshire, SPEYSIDE
Current Owner: Chivas Brothers
Status: In production; 2nd Class

Constructed in 1967 by Mackinlay, McPherson
& Co, at the time a subsidiary of Scottish &
Newcastle Breweries, it was designed by
William Delmé-Evans, the leading distillery
architect of the day and the designer of Isle of
Jura and Tullibardine distilleries: modern and
efficient, and very 1960s. It was aquired and
later closed by The Invergordon Group in 1985,
until it was sold to Campbell Distillers, the
whisky subsidiary of Pernod Ricard, in 1989.
Its product is now used by Chivas Brothers
exclusively for blending.

Tasting Note
Sweet, grassy and estery, and some of this comes
through in the mature whisky, with fruity-floral
notes. Clean and smooth texture, with a light,
fresh taste, with vanilla and apples. Light-bodied.

GLENBURGIE
near Forres, Morayshire, SPEYSIDE
Current Owner: Chivas Brothers
Status: In production; 1st Class

Originally known as "Kilnflat, the distillery was founded in 1810 by William Paul. The name was changed to Glenburgie when it was sublet to Charles Hay in 1871. From 1884 onwards several changes of ownership took place, and it remained silent between 1927 and 1935.

Hiram Walker assumed control in 1930 and bought Glenburgie in 1936, after which it was licensed to its subsidiary JG Stodart. In 1958 two Lomond stills were added to the two existing traditional stills, allowing the distillery to produce two different malts (*see* Inverleven); the malt made in Glenburgie's Lomond stills was named "Glencraig" (after Willie Craig, the director of production). Although there remains some of the product in bond, the stills were converted back to traditional Highland malt stills in 1981.

Hiram Walker became part of Allied Distillers in 1987, and when Pernod Ricard bought the bulk of Allied's brands and distilleries in 2005, Ballantine's and Glenburgie distillery were transferred to its operating division, Chivas Brothers. Glenburgie has always been a key filling for Ballantine's, and has only once been bottled as a single by its owner. In 2004 the original distillery was demolished and rebuilt on an adjacent site at a cost of £4.3 million, the new distillery came into production in 2005.

Tasting Note
Sweet, grassy and estery, with maturation in ex-bourbon casks, it takes on vanilla sponge and toffee notes, with tinned pears, sometimes very slightly smoky. Light-bodied.

GLENCADAM
Brechin, Angus, EAST HIGHLAND
Current Owner: Angus Dundee Ltd
Status: In production; 2nd Class

The distillery was built in 1825, a kilometre (0.5 miles) outside the ancient Royal Burgh of Brechin. Following a series of changes of ownership, Glencadam was bought by an established firm of Edinburgh blenders, Gilmour, Thomson & Co Ltd, in 1891. Acquired in 1954 by Hiram Walker, the distillery came under the management of Stewart & Son of Dundee. They went on to use it in the popular Cream of the Barley blend. The distillery was mothballed in 2000, and sold to the privately owned blender Angus Dundee Ltd in 2003, who have gone back into production, and bottle at 15 Years. In November 2007, a large blending plant was installed at the distillery.

Tasting Note
Soft and light, with boiled sweets and pear-drops. Peaches and cream on the nose, with almonds and vanilla. The taste is sweet and creamy, with nuts and traces of cereal. Some detect asparagus and aniseed. Medium-bodied.

GLENCRAIG (see GLENBURGIE)

GLEN DEVERON (see MACDUFF)

GLENDRONACH
near Huntly, Aberdeenshire, EAST HIGHLAND
Current Owner: BenRiach and Glendronach Distilleries Ltd
Status: In production; 1st Class; visitor centre

Built in 1826 by James Allardice, a protegé of the Duke of Gordon, the peer who was responsible for the 1823 Act. It is said that owing to the Duke having introduced its founder to London society, he neglected his duties and as a result, his distillery burnt down in 1837. It passed through three owners, and

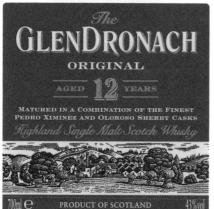

was then bought by a younger son of William Grant of Glenfiddich in 1920. The distillery was sold to William Teacher & Sons Ltd in 1960, which doubled capacity while retaining the traditional production methods, including floor malting and direct fired stills (the latter were retained until 2005, then converted to indirect firing; the former are still there, but have not been used since 1996).

The distillery was closed from 1995 to '97, then sold to Pernod Ricard (Chivas Bros), who sold it on to Billy Walker, owner of BenRiach distillery in 2008. The malt takes sherry-wood maturation well, and is currently bottled at 12, 15 and 18 Years.

Tasting Note
A robust spirit – rich and sweet. The mature character has dried fruits and Christmas cake, but also vanilla and coconut (from ex-bourbon wood). Taste is sweet then tannic-dry. Full-bodied.

GLENDULLAN
Dufftown, Banffshire, SPEYSIDE
Current Owner: Diageo plc
Status: In production: 2nd Class

The last of the original seven distilleries to be built in Dufftown, Glendullan was established by Williams & Sons Ltd of Aberdeen in 1897, close to the River Fiddich, that not only provided water for production but also powered a water wheel. From the outset Williams & Sons used most of the output for its own blends. Special bottlings were said to have been made for Edward VII.

The company merged with Macdonald Greenlees in 1919 and was bought by DCL in 1926. In 1962 the still house, mash house and tun room were rebuilt, and ten years later a completely new distillery with six stills was built on an adjacent site, and now has a capacity of 813,000 gallons (3.7 million litres) per annum. The original distillery was closed in 1985. Glendullan is Diageo's second largest distillery, but because of its importance for blending, was only occasionally bottled by

its owner. This changed in 2007 when The Singleton of Glendullan was released for the North American market.

Tasting Note

Floral and grassy in style, the mature whisky is a typical light-bodied, fruity Speyside. When matured in ex-sherry casks it gains weight – as is demonstrated by The Singleton, which combines European and American casks. Smooth texture and sweet taste.

GLEN ELGIN

Elgin, Morayshire, SPEYSIDE
Current Owner: Diageo plc
Status: In production; Top Class

William Simpson, the manager of Glenfarclas, established the distillery in 1898 during the malt whisky boom. It was the last to be built on Speyside until 1958. During construction, however, one of the main buyers of whisky fillings, Pattisons, went bankrupt and so Glen Elgin ended up a much more modest operation than was originally planned. Production began in 1900, and by 1907 it was sold to a Glasgow blender. Glen Elgin joined DCL in 1936 and was licensed to White Horse Distillers for which it had long been a key filling. Ranked Top Class by blenders it has been bottled at 12 Years in limited quantities since 1977, and joined Diageo's "Classic Malts" portfolio in 2006.

Tasting Note

Fruity and full-bodied as new-make, the mature whisky is a great favourite among blenders. Subtle and complex, at first encounter it is a typical estery Speyside, but with tangerine, honey and sometimes cloves. Smooth and sweet to taste. Medium-bodied.

GLENESK

Montrose, Angus, EAST HIGHLAND
Status: Dismantled

The distillery was converted from a flax mill in 1898 by wine merchant James Isles and was first named "Highland Esk", then "North Esk". It is situated at Montrose close to the Mearns, one of Scotland's great barley-growing regions, and has a ready supply of good water from the River North Esk itself. The distillery was bought by JF Caille Heddle just before the First World War and it remained in production until much of it was later destroyed by fire. It was acquired by Joseph Hobbs for Associated Scottish Distillers in 1938, renamed "Montrose" and converted into a grain whisky distillery. This was sold to DCL in 1954 and reconverted to a malt distillery in 1964 known as "Hillside". It was renamed "Glenesk" in 1980, but closed in 1985 and had its licence cancelled in 1992. A drum maltings was built on an adjacent site in 1968, enlarged in 1973 and closed in 1985. Three bottlings of this whisky have been issued by the proprietor as "Rare Malts".

GLENFARCLAS
Ballindalloch, Banffshire, SPEYSIDE
Current Owner: J&G Grant
Status: In production; 1st Class; visitor centre

This is one of only two major distilleries in Scotland that has remained in family ownership since its foundation. John Grant was first granted a licence to distil in 1865 and the malt enjoyed consistent success under the joint ownership of the Grant family and other investors. The whisky was so popular that by the turn of the century John's son George was shooting with the King's party at Balmoral.

Glenfarclas means "the valley of the green grass" and the distillery stands in meadows at the foot of Ben Rinnes, drawing water from a spring fed by snow-melt in the mountain – soft water filtered through heather and over granite. It was rebuilt in 1897 and in 1973 a visitor centre and shop were opened. Glenfarclas has six of the largest stills on Speyside.

SINGLE
HIGHLAND MALT
SCOTCH WHISKY
AGED 10 YEARS

700ML ℮

40% VOL

The single whiskies are all matured in sherry casks. Its current owners are the great-grandson and great-great-grandson of the founder. They have always bottled their product as a single, now with many expressions: the core range is bottled at 8, 10, 12, 15, 21, 25, 30 and 40 Years, with a special range of annual vintages, "The Family Casks", from 1952 to 1994, all at natural strength.

Tasting Note
The spirit from Glenfarclas's big stills is delicate, sweet and fruity, but it gains weight and complexity during maturation. Sherry-wood is favoured, and suits the spirit admirably, lending a rich, dried-fruitiness, with nuts and leather. A sweetish taste, with tannic dryness. Medium- to full-bodied.

GLENFIDDICH
Dufftown, Banffshire, SPEYSIDE
Current Owner: William Grant & Sons
Status: In production; 1st Class; visitor centre

Glenfiddich produces the world's best-selling malt whisky and was established in 1887 by William Grant. He was the son of a tailor and served an apprenticeship as a "soutar" or cobbler. He later trained as a distiller and using second-hand equipment bought from Cardow/Cardhu distillery, he chose the picturesque field of Glenfiddich, "the valley of the deer", as the site for his distillery.

It has remained in the ownership of his descendants ever since. Everything from malting to bottling is done *in situ*; Glenfiddich still has its own cooperage and coppersmiths and has open mash tuns and Douglas-fir washbacks. It draws its water from the Robbie Dubh spring.

The directors of William Grant & Sons were the first to see the potential of promoting their product as a single malt, in the early 1960s. A visitor centre was opened in 1969, and attracts more than 120,000 visitors a year. There are now 29 stills, producing 2.2 million gallons (ten million litres) of whisky a year. One in every

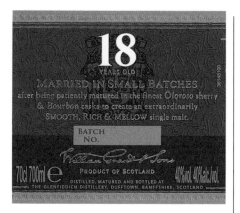

three bottles of malt whisky sold in the world is a bottle of Glenfiddich. The core range is at 12 Year Old, 12 Year Old Caoran (a smoky expression), 15 (matured in three wood-types, then vatted in a solera), 18, 21, 30 and 50 Years Old, with occasional limited Vintage Reserves.

Tasting Note
Light Speyside style of new-make, floral, fruity, estery. The younger mature whisky has a pine-sap freshness, and sometimes a light steam-smokiness. The taste is sweet throughout, with citric, floral and cereal notes. Light-bodied and highly accessible. Older expressions add richness and complexity.

GLEN FLAGLER
Airdrie, Lanarkshire, LOWLAND
Status: Demolished

Built in 1965 within the Moffat grain distillery complex on the eastern outskirts of Airdrie, by Inver House, at the time a subsidiary of Publicker Industries Ltd of Philadelphia.

The distillery operation comprised five continuous stills for neutral spirit and grain whisky production, and two pot stills producing malt whisky. All were housed within a converted paper mill, and the complex was originally known as Garnheath. The distillery was closed in 1985. The product is extremely rare as a single malt and to date I have only found one bottling made by Signatory.

GLENGARIOCH "Glen-geerie"
Oldmeldrum, Aberdeenshire, EAST HIGHLAND
Current Owner: Morrison Bowmore
Status: In production; visitor centre

The Garioch is a 30-kilometre (16-mile) long stretch of fertile land known as "the granary of Aberdeenshire". The distillery is "Glengarioch", its product "Glen Garioch". It was built in 1785, although the current operation dates from 1798. Several of the original buildings are intact, and the distillery retains some of its original floor maltings. Unfortunately the unreliable water source has caused various problems in the past. William Sanderson, the creator of VAT 69, bought Glengarioch in 1884, whence the distillery joined DCL.

It was acquired by Stanley P Morrison in 1970, as part of his bid to build a portfolio of distilleries from each geographical region, and Morrison successfully dug a deep well nearby to secure his water supply, and expanded to four stills in 1973. Morrison Bowmore was acquired by Suntory in 1994, and Glengarioch was closed for periods since then. It is fully operational now; a visitor centre was opened in 2003 and the malt was re-packaged in 2009.

Tasting Note
Medium-bodied, fruity and lightly estery. Given more body by maturation in sherry-wood; sometimes a distinct ginger note, sometimes faint lavender and a whiff of smoke. The taste combines toffee-sweetness and tannic dryness, with still a whiff of smoke.

GLENGLASSAUGH "Glen-glass-oh"
near Portsoy, Banffshire, EAST HIGHLAND
Current Owner: Glenglassaugh Distillery Co
Status: Closed; 2nd Class

The distillery was built around three mills (one of them a rare Scottish windmill) in the mid-1870s by a partnership led by a local businessman, Colonel James Moir. Glenglassaugh was acquired by Highland Distilleries in 1892 and was mothballed between 1907 and 1931. Modernisation and refurbishment came in 1959 when the two stills were replaced. It was the owners' intention to make a Speyside-style malt, but Glenglassaugh stubbornly remained a Highland character, on account of its production water being hard. It was closed again in 1986. Apart from a short period of production in 1998, it remained silent for a further ten years.

In 1998 Glenglassaugh was bought by a Dutch-based consortium, The Scaent Group, after much refurbishment, they resumed production in 2009. Current bottlings at 21, 30 and 40 Years are from old stock; the company has also released two expressions of new-make spirit, The Spirit Drink that dare not speak its name and The Spirit Drink that blushes to speak its name (the last matured for six months in Californian red wine barrels).

Tasting Note
Fruity and sweet, with traces of smoke and an unusually dry and salty finish. I have sometimes detected dry shellfish in Glenglassaugh. The new-make expressions are best drunk with mixers or in cocktails.

GLENGOYNE
near Killearn, Stirlingshire, WEST HIGHLAND
Current Owner: Ian Macleod Distillers
Status: In production; 25,000 cases; visitor centre

Established in 1833 and owned by the McLelland family the distillery was acquired by Lang Brothers in 1876. The sensitive modernisation makes this one of the country's most attractive distilleries; small and compact, tucked into a wooded glen in the foothills of the Campsie Fells..

The Highland Line runs though the distillery, and although technically in the Lowlands (and classified as such until at least the 1970s), water for production comes from above the Line and the whisky's character is Highland. Glengoyne was sold to Ian Macleod & Co (a subsidiary of Peter Russell & Co, the well-known blending company) in 2003. The owner stresses the fact that the malt used for Glengoyne is unpeated and the whisky bottled as a single comes mainly from sherry-wood. The core range is at 10, 12 (cask strength), 17 and 21 Years.

Tasting Note
Fruity with traces of vegetables and nuts, the spirit gains weight with age, especially in ex-sherry casks. The core expressions are from a mix of ex-bourbon and ex-sherry. Malty, with bruised pears; a light sweetness, with some acidity, drying in the finish. Medium-bodied.

GLEN GRANT
Rothes, Morayshire, SPEYSIDE
Current Owner: Campari Milano
Status: In production; Top Class; visitor centre

In 1833 the Grant brothers were partners in Aberlour distillery and in 1840 established Glen Grant. The distillery used the water from the Black Burn close by and the stills were coal-fired; experiments with indirect firing in the 1970s did not work, and the distillery reverted to direct firing by gas until the late 1990s.

In the 1860s the company was called John & James Grant and when the brothers died the distillery was left to James' son. He in turn left the business to his grandson Major Douglas Mackessack who expanded the capacity at Glen Grant. He merged in 1953 with George & JG Smith to become The Glenlivet & Glen Grant Distilleries Ltd, and also developed a huge market for Glen Grant in Italy, where it is still a best-seller. In 1972 further amalgamation with the Edinburgh blender Hill, Thomson & Co Ltd and Longmorn Distilleries took place. Glenlivet Distillers was acquired by Seagrams in 1977, and Seagrams by Pernod Ricard in 2001. The latter were obliged to sell Glen Grant by the European anti-trust authorities, and it was bought by the Italian drinks company

Campari in 2005 for 130 million Euros. Around 30,000 people a year come to visit the distillery and its beautiful Victorian woodlands walk. The proprietor bottles the malt with no age statement, at 5 and 10 Years.

Tasting Note
Sweet and grassy, with green apples. Speyside style. The house style favours refill wood to produce a light-coloured, fresh, summery whisky. The taste is sweet and slightly lemony, with cereal, nuts, apples and pears. Light-bodied.

GLENGYLE
Campbeltown, Argyll, CAMPBELTOWN
Current Owner: Mitchell's Glengyle Ltds
Status: In production

The original Glengyle distillery operated from 1973 to 1925, built by William Mitchell & Company. The site was bought by Bloch Brothers of Glasgow in 1941, who intended to rebuild and resume production. Nothing happened and the site was used as a depot by a farmers' cooperative until it was bought by J&A Mitchell Ltd (owners of nearby Springbank distillery) in 2000; a new distillery was built, and production commenced in March 2004.

Archibald Mitchell of J&A was William Mitchell of Glengyle's father; Hedley Wright, the chairman of J&A is his great-great nephew. Glengyle and Springbank (*see* entry) produce all their own malt, in floor maltings. Current production is only 11,000 gallons (50,000 litres) per annum. Kilkerran Single Malt at 5 Years Old and 46% ABV was released in 2009, named after St Kiaran, "The Apostle of Argyll". Further bottlings are planned over the next four years, as the whisky gains full maturity.

Tasting Note
The style of the new-make is heavier than Springbank, oily and meaty, with sweet cereal notes. These characteristics come through in the 5 Year Old, which is remarkably mature for its age. Full-bodied.

GLEN KEITH
Keith, Banffshire, SPEYSIDE
Current Owner: Chivas Brothers
Status: Mothballed; 1st Class

An old meal mill on the opposite bank of the
Spey from Strathisla distillery in Keith was
converted by Seagrams in 1957 into a modern
distillery complex with the first gas-fired stills
and a highly computerised operation. It was
originally equipped for triple distillation, with
three stills. This was expanded to five in 1970.
Glen Keith provides fillings for Chivas Regal,
Passport and other blends and, until 1994, was
not bottled by its proprietor.

GLENKINCHIE
Pencaitland, East Lothian, LOWLAND
Current Owner: Diageo plc
Status: In production; visitor centre

Founded in 1837 in the heart of East Lothian
by the Rate brothers, beef farmers who grew
and malted their own barley, it was bought and
rebuilt by a consortium of Edinburgh whisky
merchants and blenders in the 1880s. One of
the founder members of SMD, Glenkinchie
joined DCL with it in 1925 and was licensed to
John Haig & Co.

Today Glenkinchie is promoted as one
of Diageo's "Classic Malts" and bottled at 12
Years; it won a gold award in the 1993 IWSC.
The visitor centre was rebuilt and redesigned
in 1996 and includes a detailed model, made
in 1924, of a malt whisky distillery. It is being
further redesigned as this book goes to press.

Tasting Note
Big and meaty as new-make, the mature whisky
is grassy and lemony. The aroma is "rural" –
meadows, hedgerows, cows – with a hint of
smoke. The taste is fresh, starting lightly sweet
and finishing dry, and very short. Light in
character, with a medium-body.

THE GLENLIVET
Minmore, Banffshire, SPEYSIDE
Current Owner: Chivas Brothers
Status: In production; Top Class; visitor centre

George Smith, a well-known illicit distiller in
Glenlivet and a tenant of the Duke of Gordon,
was the first person on Speyside to acquire a
licence under the 1823 Excise Act. He went
into production on his farm at Upper Drummin,
much to the chagrin of his fellow smugglers,
who attempted to burn down his small
distillery, seeing him as a turncoat. The laird of
Aberlour gave him a pair of pistols to defend
himself.

By the mid-1820s his whisky was being
represented by Andrew Usher & Co of
Edinburgh, and by the 1850s Glenlivet was
so famous that many other distillers had
attached the appellation to their own products.
In partnership with his son, John Gordon
Smith, George built a larger distillery nearby
at Minmore in 1858. In 1880, JG Smith was
obliged to take legal action against other
distilleries using the Glenlivet name. The court
ruled that no other whisky could be "The
Glenlivet" although the name could be used as
a suffix.

By 1950 around 27 distilleries were doing
this – "Glenlivet" was synonymous with
"Speyside". The distillery passed to JG Smith's
nephew, George Smith Grant, and to his son
and grandson; it amalgamated with Glen Grant
in 1953 and with Longmorn in 1970; the whole
group was acquired by Seagrams in 1977.

A new visitor centre was opened in 1978 in
a barley loft in the oldest part of the distillery.
It was extensively refurbished in 1996/97,
with a multi-media exhibition and interactive
presentation, ceilidh space, restaurant and

240

GLENLOCHY
Fort William, Inverness-shire, WEST HIGHLAND
Status: Demolished

Founded in 1898 by David McAndie, using water for both power and production straight from the slopes of Ben Nevis. The distillery was silent from 1917 to 1924 and 1926 to 1937, when it was bought by Train and McIntyre for Associated Scottish Distillers. It passed to SMD (DCL) in 1953 and was dismantled in 1983. The maltings and kilns are listed and part of a new leisure complex. Today only rare independent bottlings are available.

GLENLOSSIE
near Elgin, Morayshire, SPEYSIDE
Current Owner: Diageo plc
Status: In production; Top Class

shop, and is now one of the largest and best-equipped distillery visitor facilities in Scotland. Seagrams was sold to Diageo and Pernod Ricard in 2001, with The Glenlivet passing to the latter.

In June 2010 a new still-house was opened at the distillery by the Prince of Wales. At a cost of £10 million, this increased The Glenlivet's capacity by 75 per cent, to 2.3 million gallons (10.5 million litres) of pure alcohol per annum. The core range of expressions is bottled at 12, 15, 15 French Oak, 16 Nadurra, 18, 21 and 25 Years. In addition there are annual special vintage bottlings under the "Cellar Collection" brand.

Tasting Note
A complex Speyside style, with pineapple, tropical fruits and bananas. It develops complexity with age, the younger expressions reminiscent of custard cream biscuits and coconut, the older of dry Christmas cake, burnt orange and dry chocolate. Medium-bodied.

The manager of Glendronach distillery, John Duff, acquired a licence to distil and built the Glenlossie distillery in 1876. It then became the Glenlossie-Glenlivet Company under which name it operated until 1919, when SMD obtained a controlling interest – its first distillery in Morayshire. By 1930 Glenlossie was fully owned by DCL, which undertook a programme of refurbishment and modernisation, including the addition of two more stills in 1962 (now six stills).

A large dark grains plant was also built on the site (1968) capable of processing 2,600 tonnes of draff and 2.3 million gallons (eight million litres) of pot ale each week, from 21 distilleries, to produce 1,000 tonnes of cattle feed. In 1972 a new distillery named Mannochmore (*see* entry) was built adjacent. The make was first bottled as a single in 1990, in UD's "Floral and Fauna" series.

Tasting Note
The spirit style is light and grassy; the mature whisky is fresh, floral, with hair lacquer – typical Speyside. The taste is sweet and perfumed. Light-bodied.

GLEN MHOR

Inverness, Inverness-shire, NORTH HIGHLAND

Status: Demolished; 3rd Class

Glen Mhor was built in 1892 by John Birnie, in partnership with James Mackinlay, a scion of the Edinburgh blending firm, close to Glen Albyn distillery where Birnie was manager.

Neil Gunn, the famous Scottish novelist, was the Excise officer here. In 1906 John Walker & Sons Ltd acquired a 40 per cent interest in Glen Albyn distillery. Later, in 1972, the resulting company was brought into the DCL fold, but the distillery was closed and demolished in 1983.

GLENMORANGIE

Tain, Ross & Cromarty, NORTH HIGHLAND
Current Owner: The Glenmorangie Company
Status: In production; 2nd Class; visitor centre

A world best-seller, Glenmorangie was built on the site of a brewery in 1843, on the southern shore of the Dornoch Firth. It was established by William Mathieson, who was attracted by the unusually hard, mineral-rich water of the nearby Tarlogie Spring. Lacking capital, Mathieson bought a pair of second-hand gin stills, with the tallest swan-necks in Scotland. These have been faithfully reproduced ever since, although heated by internal steam coils since 1887 (Glenmorangie was among the first to introduce this).

The distillery was acquired in 1918 by the Leith blender Macdonald & Muir which rebuilt and refurbished it in 1979, increasing the number of stills to eight by 1993. Although available as a single since at least the 1880s, it was in the mid-1970s that Macdonald & Muir resolved to promote the malt worldwide.

By the mid-1980s, Glenmorangie was experimenting with different wood types and with re-racking into wine barrels. The light style of the spirit does not lend itself to complete maturation in ex-sherry casks, but gains additional layers of flavour when finished

in such casks. A sherry-finished 18 Year Old (introduced 1992) was soon followed by port-wood and a Madeira-wood finishes, and then by more than a dozen different styles. The core range was rationalised in 2007 as: Original (10 Year Old), Nectar D'Or (around 12 Years Old, finished in ex-Sauternes barriques), Lasanta (around 12 Years Old, finished in ex-oloroso casks), Quinta Ruban (around 12 Years Old, finished in ex-port pipes), 18 Year Old, 25 Year Old and a number of special releases.

In 2004 Glenmorangie (now a plc) bought the Scotch Malt Whisky Society, and both were acquired by LVMH. The new owner expanded the stillhouse by a third (to 12 stills) and the tun room with a new mash tun and four new washbacks, increasing capacity by one-third, to 1.3 million gallons (six million litres) per annum.

Tasting Note

The make is light and floral, with a tangerine-citric note. The mature malt is light in character but surprisingly complex. Keynotes are vanilla, almond, mandarin, fresh apple, spice and fresh hay. The texture is soft, the taste lightly sweet, with fresh fruit. Medium-bodied.

GLEN MORAY
Elgin, Morayshire, SPEYSIDE
Current Owner: La Martiniquaise
Status: In production; 2nd Class

Established in 1897, on the western edge
of Elgin, drawing its water from Dallas Moor,
Glen Moray remained silent from 1910 until the
early 1920s when it was bought by Macdonald
& Muir. Expanded in 1958, the malt has long
been well-regarded, but it has only been
bottled and sold as a single malt since 1976.
It is now bottled at 12 and 16 Years; "vintage"
bottlings have been made of 1962, 1964, 1966,
1967 and 1973, but they are now rare.

Glen Moray was bought by LVMH in 2004,
along with Glenmorangie, and Glen Moray
was discreetly put on the market then sold
in late 2008 to the French spirits company,
La Martiniquaise.

Tasting Note
Typical Speyside – fruity and floral – with body.
Maturation adds butterscotch, vanilla and barley
sugar. A creamy mouth-feel and a sweet, fruity
and nutty taste. Medium-bodied.

GLEN ORD
Ross & Cromarty, NORTH HIGHLAND
Current Owner: Diageo plc
Status: In production; 2nd Class visitor centre

The site was chosen to be close to a meal mill,
and uses the same water, from the White Burn
(which is fed by two lochs, the Loch of the
Peats and the Loch of the Birds). The distillery
was first licensed in 1838 to a Mr Maclennan.
The product has been known variously as Ord,
Glenordie and Muir of Ord.

John Dewar & Sons acquired the distillery in
1924 and the following year it became part of
DCL. Glen Ord's floor maltings were replaced
by Saladin Boxes in 1961, and a large drum
maltings was built on an adjacent site in 1968,
supplying its own requirement and that of
Clynelish, Talisker and Teaninich distilleries.
In 1966 the distillery was also rebuilt and
expanded. An attractive and informative visitor
centre and a sizeable shop were opened in
1988. Under a variety of names – Ord, Ordie,
Glenordie, Glen Oran and Muir of Ord – Glen
Ord has been available as a single from time
to time, but only generally available since
1993. In 2006 The Singleton of Glen Ord
(at 12, 18 and 30 Year Old) was released
in Asian markets.

Tasting Note
Sweet and heathery, with distinct waxiness –
typical Highland style. The Singleton has a rich
and complex nose, with fruits (nectarines and
dried orange peel), fudge, almonds, sandalwood
and old-fashioned perfume. A big, chewy texture,
distinctly waxy and slightly mouth-cooling, with
a long finish. Medium-bodied.

THE GLENROTHES
SELECT RESERVE
SPEYSIDE SINGLE MALT SCOTCH WHISKY

43% vol. 700ml
DISTILLED, MATURED AND BOTTLED IN SCOTLAND

CHARACTER *Ripe fruits, citrus, vanilla, hints of spice*
SELECTED *J.M. Sutherland* Distiller
APPROVED *John Ramsay* Malt Master

BERRY BROS. & RUDD
3 ST. JAMES'S ST. LONDON
PRODUCT OF SCOTLAND

GLENROTHES
Rothes, Morayshire, SPEYSIDE
Current Owner: The Edrington Group
Status: In production; Top Class

The City of Glasgow Bank provided the backing for this distillery, but the bank collapsed in 1878 during the building work. The owning company, W Grant & Co, managed to survive, and amalgamated with the Islay Distillery Co (owners of Bunnahabhain) to become the Highland Distilleries Co Ltd.

Glenrothes was eventually completed in 1887, the partners appointing one James Booth Henderson as distiller. Henderson, a well-known judge of livestock, used to stable his horses and cattle in the distillery, much to the distillery owners' displeasure when he was discovered. Glenrothes was expanded to six stills in 1963, eight in 1980 and ten in 1989, at which time the stillhouse was completely rebuilt. In 1987 The Glenrothes brand was licensed to the long-established London wine merchants, Berry Bros & Rudd. They released the first official bottling that year.

The malt was re-packaged in dumpy bottles in 1994 and began to be marketed in earnest with a core expression Select Reserve, regular Vintages (small parcels of casks from single years) and occasional single cask bottlings.

Tasting Note
Sweet, rich and fruity, a heavy style of Speyside. The "standard" bottling, Select Reserve has nuts and nougat, dried fruits, caramel and vanilla sponge on the nose, with a soft mouth-feel, a sweet taste, drying in the finish, and a lingering aftertaste of chocolate. Medium- to full-bodied.

GLEN SCOTIA
Campbeltown, Argyll, CAMPBELTOWN
Current Owner: Loch Lomond Distillery Ltd
Status: In production

This is one of the three remaining distilleries in Campbeltown. Glen Scotia was founded in 1835 by Stewart, Galbraith & Co, sold to West Highland Malt Distilleries in 1919 and acquired by Duncan McCallum in 1924. It was silent between 1928 and 1933 and then bought in 1930 by the owner of Scapa distillery. Both were sold to Hiram Walker in 1954, then sold on Glen Scotia the following year. In spite of being refurbished in the early 1980s, it remained silent until acquired and re-opened by Gibson International in 1989.

Set in this once affluent town, the distillery looks like an elegant townhouse and is reputed to be haunted by a previous owner who drowned himself in Campbeltown Loch.

Gibson International went into receivership in 1994, and Glen Scotia was sold to Glen Catrine Bonded Warehouse Ltd (sister company to the current owner). The distillery is currently in part-time production.

Tasting Note
The new-make has a "maritime" character – seaweedy, briny, oily – and this translates into the flavour of the mature whisky. Its aroma is reminiscent of docks and beaches, with cereal notes and nuts, and a whiff of smoke; the texture is smooth and oily, and the taste sweetish with distinct saltiness, finishing dry. Medium-bodied.

GLEN SPEY
Rothes, Morayshire, SPEYSIDE
Current Owner: Diageo plc
Status: In production; 2nd Class

Built in 1878 by James Stuart & Co – which once owned Macallan distillery – Glen Spey was originally named Mill of Rothes. The distillery was sold in 1887 to Gilbey Vintners, the gin distiller, which maintained production and became part of IDV/Grand Metropolitan in 1962. Glen Spey was rebuilt and expanded to four stills in 1970. A key filling for the Justerini & Brooks' blends, it is bottled by its proprietor in its "Flora and Fauna" series from 2001.

Tasting Note
Malty, nutty and light-bodied, with a floral Speyside notes. The nutty, grassy, cereal character comes through in the mature whisky. The taste is sweet throughout, sometimes with traces of roast chestnuts, and a short finish. Light- to medium-bodied.

GLENTAUCHERS
Mulben, Banffshire, SPEYSIDE
Current Owner: Chivas Brothers
Status: In production

Glentauchers was built in 1898 by a partnership of three blenders, including James Buchanan, who became sole owner in 1906, and took it with him to DCL in 1925. It was completely rebuilt in 1966, when the number of stills was increased to six. The distillery was sold to Allied Distillers in 1989, after four silent years and passed to Chivas Brothers in 2003. It is available in independent bottlings only, mainly from Gordon & Macphail.

Tasting Note
A medium-bodied Speyside, sweet and fruity, maturation adds coconut, almonds and vanilla to the aroma. Light and summery, the taste is sweet overall.

GLENTURRET
Crieff, Perthshire, CENTRAL HIGHLAND
Current Owner: The Edrington Group
Status: In production; 3rd Class; visitor centre

Established in 1775 on the site of an illicit still, Glenturret claims to be the oldest operating distillery in Scotland, although it has been much altered physically since its foundation. Water for production is drawn from the fast-flowing River Turret. Dismantled in the 1920s, the distillery was closed until 1957 when it was

acquired by James Fairlie who preserved the traditional distilling techniques and was one of the first in the industry to develop visitor facilities, and these were expanded into The Famous Grouse Experience in 2002, at a cost of £2.5 million. Situated near Crieff, in picturesque countryside, Glenturret attracts more visitors than any other distillery – 250,000 annually. It became part of Highland Distilleries in 1993 and is bottled at 8, 10, 15 Years, with occasional special releases.

Tasting Note
Fruity (with orange notes), cereal-like and lightly medicinal as new-make, these characteristics are expanded in the younger mature expressions, with a hint of smoke. The taste is sweetish, with honey notes, nuts and cereal, and still a whiff of smoke. Medium-bodied.

GLENUGIE
near Peterhead, Aberdeenshire, EAST HIGHLAND
Status: Demolished; 3rd Class

Built in 1837, close to the sea, 5.5 kilometres (three miles) south of Peterhead, the distillery was converted to a brewery, then rebuilt as a distillery in 1873 (the main distillery building had cast-iron frames, dating from this time).

It changed hands several times before the First World War, was silent between 1925 and 1937 and was acquired by Long John Distillers Ltd in 1956. This company was bought by Whitbread & Co in 1975, which sold Glenugie to a consortium of oilmen the same year. It was closed in 1983 and the buildings were subsequently demolished. Available in rare bottlings only.

GLENURY ROYAL
Stonehaven, Aberdeenshire, EAST HIGHLAND
Status: Demolished; 2nd Class

Built in 1836 by Captain Robert Barclay, MP for the county, and a renowned athlete (he was

the first man ever to walk 1,600 kilometres or 1,000 miles, in 1,000 hours, in 1808). His friend at Court, whom he referred to discreetly as "Mrs Windsor", allowed him the "Royal" suffix. Following his death Glenury Royal was owned by a family in Glasgow and later by Lord Stonehaven from whom it was acquired by Joseph Hobbs for Associated Scottish Distillers in 1938.

In 1953 Glenury Royal was bought by DCL, which rebuilt it in the mid-1960s but ultimately closed the distillery in 1985. The site was sold for residential development in 1992. Uncommon though it is as a single malt, it has been bottled as a Rare Malt by United Distillers, and has won several prizes in the IWSC.

HAZELBURN
Campbeltown, Argyll, CAMPBELTOWN
Current Owner: J&A Mitchell
Status: In production

Hazelburn distillery operated in Campbeltown from at least 1825 to 1925. Today, the whisky is produced at Springbank distillery (see entry), like Longrow (see entry), but unlike Longrow or Springbank it is made from unpeated malt and is triple distilled. Springbank malts its own barley, a portion of which is grown locally, in its own ancient floor maltings, operating steeping and air breaks according to the tides in Campbeltown Loch (into which the steeps empty). The distillery has three stills, but for Springbank and Longrow does not operate a complete triple distillation; the former is 2.5 times distilled, the latter twice.

Hazelburn single malt was first released in 2006 at 8 Years Old, and small batches have followed. It is highly sought after by collectors and connoisseurs. It is only issued in limited amounts, since the distillery (which has a capacity to make 104,000 gallons/472,000 litres) of alcohol per annum) currently only produces 33,000 gallons (150,000 litres), owing to the fact that the staff spend periods of time malting and operating Glengyle distillery (see entry).

Tasting Note
The make is light and sweet, with malty, hay-like notes. These come through in the young whisky. Light-bodied.

HIGHLAND PARK
Kirkwall, Orkney, ISLAND
Current Owner: The Edrington Group
Status: In production; visitor centre

Founded in 1798 by Magnus Eunson, but not actually licensed until 1825, Highland Park distillery overlooks Orkney's principal town, Kirkwall. Eunson, an elder of the Kirk, was said to have hidden his early contraband spirit under the pulpit. The first licensee was Robert Borwick, who ran the distillery until his death in 1840, when it passed to his son, George, and grandson, the Rev. James Borwick. The latter sold it, believing distilling to be "incompatible with his calling as a minister".

The whisky has enjoyed a high reputation for many years. In 1883 it was served to the Emperor of Russia and the King of Denmark and was "pronounced by all to be the finest they had ever tasted". The distillery has its own peat banks and floor maltings, and blends 20 per cent of its own peated malt with imported, unpeated malt to achieve around 15ppm phenols. The washbacks here were used as bath-tubs for the troops stationed on Orkney during the Second World War. Highland Distilleries began to promote

Highland Park as a single in 1979 (at 12 Years Old) and installed a visitor centre in 1986. In 1997 18 and 25 Years Old expressions joined the 12, and over the past five years a number of limited and old bottlings have been released.

Tasting Note
The style of the new-make is malty and slightly smoky. The mature whisky expands upon this hugely: heather pollen and spun honey, caramelised oranges, light oakiness and peat-smoke. The texture is smooth, the taste sweetish, slightly salty, then dry, with toffee, spice (ginger and cinnamon) and a twist of smoke. Medium-bodied.

HUNTLY
Huntly, Aberdeenshire, EAST HIGHLAND
Current Owner: Huntly Distillers Ltd
Status: Under construction

In the heart of good arable farmland, Huntly was once a centre of distilling – at the end of the eighteenth century there were 14 small licensed operations in the district. The site chosen for this new distillery is adjacent to the former "Huntly distillery" (1824 to 1967), and was once a granary (the existing granary buildings are being re-furbished to house the new stillhouse).

The project is the brain-child of Euan Shand, owner of the respected independent bottlers, Duncan Taylor & Company (see "Buying Malt Whisky", page 222). It is his intention to produce gin and vodka, as well as malt and grain whisky, and also to develop the site as the first entirely "green" distillery.

It had been hoped that Huntly distillery would open in 2010; the projected date for commencing production is now early 2012.

Tasting Note
The style of spirit sought is "robust Highland".

IMPERIAL
Carron, Morayshire, SPEYSIDE
Current Owner: Chivas Brothers
Status: Closed; 3rd Class

Thomas Mackenzie already had a share in the Dailuaine and Talisker distilleries when the company which owned them both built Imperial in 1897 (the year of Queen Victoria's Diamond Jubilee, hence the name). Unfortunately the distillery closed in 1899, following the fatal crash of the Leith firm Pattisons. It remained silent until 1955, except for its maltings and apart from the years between 1919 and 1925.

The distillery was then sold to DCL (1982) and subsequently to Allied Distillers (1985), which reopened the distillery four years later, but mothballed it again in 1998. In 2005 ownership passed to Pernod Ricard (Chivas Brothers). It is uncommon except in independent bottlings.

INCHGOWER
Buckie, Banffshire, SPEYSIDE
Current Owner: Diageo plc
Status: In production; 3rd Class

The distillery was built in 1871 by Alexander Wilson in order to replace Tochineal distillery at nearby Cullen which had been established in 1824. Inchgower remained in production until 1930 and was owned by Buckie Town Council between 1936 and 1938; it was then acquired by Bell's for £3,000. The new owner extended the complex in 1966, adding two stills and a large new bonded warehouse to house whisky from its other distilleries. Since 1979 Bell's has been the best-selling blended Scotch in the UK market, and Inchgower remains a key filling. Accordingly, it is not promoted as a single malt, although it was released in 1991 in UD's "Flora & Fauna" range.

Tasting Note
Nutty-spicy and malty as new-make, the nose of the mature spirit becomes more cereal-like and

SPEYSIDE
SINGLE MALT
SCOTCH WHISKY

The *Oyster Catcher* is a common *sight* around the

INCHGOWER

distillery, which stands *close* to the *sea* on the mouth of the *RIVER SPEY* near *BUCKIE. Inchgower*, established in 1824, produces *one* of the most *distinctive single* malt whiskies in *SPEYSIDE*. It is a malt for the *discerning drinker* ~ a *complex* aroma precedes a *fruity, spicy* taste with a hint of *salt*.

AGED **14** YEARS

43% vol   Distilled & Bottled in *SCOTLAND.*
INCHGOWER DISTILLERY.
Buckie, Banffshire, *Scotland*   70 cl

caramelised, but is dry overall. Sometimes coffee and chocolate notes are discernable. The taste is sweet then dry, with a hint of salt. Medium-bodied.

INCHMURRIN (see LOCH LOMOND)

INVERLEVEN
Dumbarton, Dumbartonshire, LOWLAND
Status: Demolished

Inverleven was established in 1938 by Hiram

Walker, the Canadian distilling giant, as a part of its massive grain whisky complex at Dumbarton. The operation was built on the site of the old Clydeside McMillan shipyard and was the largest distillery in Europe at that time.

From the outset the malt distillery supplied fillings for Ballantine's blends almost exclusively, so it has only rarely been available as a single malt. In 1959 a pair of innovative "Lomond" stills were installed alongside the existing two stills. These had squat necks, housing adjustable rectifying plates, and allowing different styles of spirit to be made in the same stills. Hiram Walker went on to install similar stills at Glenburgie, Miltonduff and Scapa (Scapa still retains its Lomond-style wash still). Neither Inverleven nor Lomond were ever bottled by their owner.

ISLE OF ARRAN
Lochranza, Isle of Arran, ISLAND
Current Owner: Isle of Arran Distilling Co
Status: In production; visitor centre

The Isle of Arran distillery opened in 1995 at Lochranza, a pretty bay in the northwest of the island, with a ruined castle in its midst. It was the brain child of Harold Currie (former managing director of Chivas Bros and Campbell Distillers) and the Isle of Arran Distilling Company. Money and public support was raised through a "bond-holders" scheme, which investors could join for £450, receiving five cases of mature malt in 2001, and five cases of Lochranza blended whisky in 1998 (all ex-duty). Malt comes from the mainland and is mashed in a two-tonne lauter tun. The small stills (1,560 and 945 gallons/7,100 and 4,300 litres) were modelled on those at Macallan. Maturation is done on site, at Invergordon and at Campbeltown. The single malt was first released at 3 Year Old in 1998; Founders' Reserve followed at 5 Year Old, and the core range of 10 Year Old (46% ABV), 100 Proof (57% ABV) and Robert Burns Single Malt – the company owns the "Robert Burns" brand, and is a patron of the International Burns Club

network – followed in 2001 and 2006. There are also a number of wine-finished expressions and special releases.

Tasting Note
Sweet and fruity – the intention was to make a Speyside style. The mature whisky has flowers, pear-drops, green apples and citric fruits. The taste is sweet and fresh, with light cereal and crisp acidity. Light-bodied.

195

ISLE OF JURA
Isle of Jura, Argyll, ISLAND
Current Owner: Whyte & Mackay
Status: In production; visitor centre and apartments

The first distillery on Jura was founded as early as 1810, not far from the site of the present distillery, at the island's only village, Craighouse. It was licensed to the laird, Archibald Campbell, and managed by a succession of his tenants, the last of whom abandoned the site in 1901, taking the distilling equipment (which he had paid for) with him, with the tenancy still having 17 years to run. The distillery fell into ruin.

It was revived by two local landowners, with the help of Mackinlay & Macpherson & Co, blenders in Leith, who wanted to bring employment to the island. The new distillery was designed by William Delmé-Evans, who had designed Tullibardine and would go on to design Glentauchers (see entries), and was considered the leading distillery architect of the day. He wrote: "It was our intention to produce a Highland-type malt, differing from the typically peaty stuff produced in 1900".

It was expanded in the late 1970s to four stills and passed to Invergordon Distillers then to Whyte & Mackay, with Mackinlays. It was first bottled as a single in 1974, at 10 Year Old, and since 2000 there have been many expressions, including the successful Superstition (a mix of 13 and 21 Year Old malts), Legacy and 21 Year Old, together with some limited releases from the 1960s, '70s and '80s.

Tasting Note
The new-make spirit is oily, earthy and piney, with citric notes. These flavours come through in the mature whisky as nut oil (and dry nuts), pine sap and orange zest. The taste is oily and malty, sweetish to start, becoming dry with a dash of salt. Medium-bodied.

KILCHOMAN
Rockside Farm, Isle of Islay, ISLAY
Current Owner: Kilchoman Distillery Co Ltd
Status: In production, visitor centre

There is good reason to believe that the secrets of distilling were brought to Scotland in 1300 by a family of "learned physicians" named Macbeatha (Anglicised to "Beaton") who arrived from Ireland in the marriage train of an Irish princess. She was to marry Angus Og Macdonald, whose descendants became the Lords of the Isles, and whose Court was at Finlaggan on Islay. The Macbeatha's were granted lands at Kilchoman, on Islay's west coast, where there still stands a magnificent medieval carved monument in their honour.

The opening of a small farm distillery here in 2005 (22,000 gallons/100,000 litres per annum capacity) might thus be considered a revival of an ancient practice! It was the brain child of Anthony Wills, wine and spirits merchant, who moved to Islay in 2000, having married Cathy Wilks, a local girl, some years earlier. A year later he leased and renovated some derelict farm buildings at Rockside Farm, Kilchoman.

The distillery was opened in June 2005 and went into production later that year. It has its own maltings and sources as much of its barley requirement as possible from Rockside Farm, the rest coming from Port Ellen Maltings. The whisky is bottled on site. There is a charming café and shop on site, run by Cathy Wills, and the whole enterprise has a family feel about it.

In 2010 John MacLellan, long-time manager at Bunnahabhain distillery, joined the team.

Tasting Note
A rich spirit, sweet, fruity and lightly smoky. The whisky, although only 4 to 5 Years Old, is remarkably mature for its age. The skilful cask selection has filled out and enhanced the new-make character. Medium- to full-bodied.

KILLYLOCH
Airdrie, Lanarkshire, LOWLAND
Status: Demolished

Killyloch was a second pair of stills at Moffat distillery, installed in 1965 and producing a malt for blending purposes only (*see* Glen Flagler). It should have been called "Lillyloch", after the name of the water source, but the cask stencil was wrongly applied and the misnomer remained with the whisky permanently! The whisky was intended for blending only and is thus extremely rare: the only known bottling was made by the Edinburgh independent, Signatory, in 1994. Closed in 1985.

KINCLAITH
Glasgow, LOWLAND
Status: Demolished

Long John International, the subsidiary of the US company Seager Evans, built Kinclaith in 1958 as part of its huge Strathclyde grain distillery complex; the last distillery to be built in the City of Glasgow, using water from Loch Katrine. When Long John International was bought by Whitbread & Co Ltd in 1976 Kinclaith distillery was dismantled to expand the grain distillery. Bottlings as single malt are very rare.

KNOCKANDO
Knockando, Morayshire, SPEYSIDE
Current Owner: Diageo plc
Status: In production; 2nd Class; visitors by arrangement

John Tytler Thomson, the founder of Knockando distillery, was a spirit broker and whisky merchant in Elgin with big ideas. He acquired the site, described by the local paper as "most beautiful", on the steeply sloping north bank of the Spey, within Knockando parish, and employed Charles Doig, the leading distillery architect of the day, to design and build it. This he did most elegantly, installing the first electricity supply on Speyside.

It opened in May 1899, only months before the whisky industry crashed, closed in 1900 and was sold to W&A Gilbey Ltd (the well-known London wine and gin merchants) in 1903 for £3,500. When Gilbeys joined IDV/Grand Metropolitan in 1975, the distillery was expanded from two to four stills. Knockando – the name means "the little dark hill" – is a key

filling for J&B Rare, and was first bottled as a single malt in 1977, for export only. Currently bottlings are at 12 and 18 Year Old.

Tasting Note
Malty and cereal-like as new-make, the mature spirit is reminiscent of breakfast cereals, with honey and walnuts, and a hint of olive oil. The taste is sweet and simple, with cereal and nuts. Light-bodied.

KNOCKDHU (see AN CNOC)

LADYBURN
Girvan, Ayrshire, LOWLAND
Current Owner: William Grant & Sons
Status: Dismantled

The distillery was opened in 1966 by William Grant & Sons as part of its massive Girvan distillery complex. Apart from some single bottlings exported to the USA, it was used entirely for blending and occasionally available in independent bottlings. The distillery was finally closed in 1975 and then dismantled in 1976. In 2001, the owners discovered and bottled a couple of casks.

LAGAVULIN
near Port Ellen, ISLAY
Current Owner: Diageo plc
Status: In production; visitor centre

Lagavulin distillery overlooks the ruins of Dunyveg Castle, in a little bay on the southeast coast of Islay, where the Lord of the Isles kept his fleet of galleys. In Gaelic the name means "the hollow of the mill" and in the late 1700s there were around ten illicit stills operating in the bay. The first licence was taken out in 1815 by John Johnston; in the 1820s he acquired a neighbouring distillery, Ardmore, and his son combined them in 1837 as Lagavulin. Much of the present distillery was built in the early 1850s by the Graham brothers, in partnership with James Logan Mackie, who took over in 1860. JL Mackie's nephew, Peter (later Sir Peter), trained at Lagavulin and went on to create the brand "White Horse", his company becoming one of the Big Five by 1910. Following a feud with his neighbour, Laphroaig distillery, Peter Mackie – described as "one third genius, one third megalomaniac and one third eccentric" – established a small sub-distillery within Lagavulin to make whisky with the same flavour as Laphroaig, which he named "Malt Mill". It operated until 1962.

In the late nineteenth century Alfred Barnard remarked in his journal that "there are only a few distillers that can turn out spirit for use as single whiskies, and that made at Lagavulin can claim to be one of the most prominent." In 1927, three years after Mackie's death, the company joined DCL but retained the licence to Lagavulin distillery.

Lagavulin 16 Year Old was chosen as one of United Distillers' "Classic Malts" in 1989, and has proved the most popular of the range. Supplies are under allocation. It was joined by a Distillers' Edition (finished in ex-Pedro Ximenez casks) in 1998, a 12 Year Old (cask strength) and a limited edition 25 Year Old both in 2002.

Tasting Note
The style is rich, sweet and very smoky. The mature whisky is highly complex, with berries, sweet seaweed, linseed oil, wax polish, camphor, carbolic and scented smoke. A big mouth-feel, sweet taste to start, with scented smoke in the finish and long aftertaste. Full-bodied.

LAPHROAIG "La-froyg"
near Port Ellen, ISLAY
Current Owner: Fortune Brands Inc
Status: In production; visitor centre

The stretch of coast between Port Ellen and
Ardbeg boasted at least five distilleries in the
early nineteenth century. This distillery, on
the Kildalton shore in the southeast of Islay,
was founded in 1815 by Donald Johnston,
whose father had founded Lagavulin distillery.
Several of Laphroaig's original buildings remain
intact, including the floor maltings that are still
in use today. The distillery remained in the
ownership of the Johnston family until 1962
(being managed betwen 1954 and 1972 by
Mrs Bessie Campbell), when it was acquired
by Long John Distillers Ltd. Although not the
most heavily peated malt, Laphroaig is the most
pungent. Bottled at 10 Years (40% ABV and
cask strength), 15 Years, 25 Years (40% ABV
and cask strength) and, since 2004, Quarter
Cask (re-racked into small, active American oak
casks for seven months).

Tasting Note
Sweet, spicy and very smoky. The nose is
pungent with coal-smoke, coal-tar and iodine.

The taste is surprisingly sweet to start, then salty
and dry, with billows of tarry smoke and sweet
seaweed. Full-bodied.

LEDAIG (see TOBERMORY)

LINKWOOD
near Elgin, Morayshire, SPEYSIDE
Current Owner: Diageo plc
Status: In production; Top Class

Built by Peter Brown in 1821, by 1835 Linkwood's unusually large stills were producing up to 20,000 gallons (91,000 litres) per annum. (The Glenlivet distillery was producing half this amount in 1839.) Completely rebuilt in 1873, it became a public company in 1898 and was acquired by SMD (DCL) in 1936. Until 1963, when it was again rebuilt, the mill and other machinery were driven by a water-wheel. At this time the distillery was managed by a man of unremitting vigilance who ensured the stills were replaced with exact replicas, with all their dents, so as not to risk changing the character of the spirit. It is said that even the spiders' webs in the distillery buildings were left intact.

A new distillery, with four stills, was added in 1973. The original two-still distillery operated in parallel with the new one until 1985, when it was mothballed. The spirits from both were vatted prior to filling into cask. A highly rated malt, Linkwood is bottled by Diageo in their "Flora & Fauna" range, at 12 Year Old.

Tasting Note
The new-make style is floral – light Speyside. The aroma of the mature spirit is estery, with bubblegum, acetone, lemon sherbet, tea-roses – clean and fresh. The taste is sweet, with traces of white wine, lemon-zest and sherbet. Light-bodied.

LINLITHGOW (see ST MAGDALENE)

LITTLEMILL
Bowling, Dumbartonshire, LOWLAND
Status: Dismantled

Founded in 1772 on the site of a fourteenth-century brewery, this was one of the oldest distilleries in Scotland, making use of water drawn from above the Highland Line in the Kilpatrick Hills. However, it has been through many changes of ownership and several silent periods. In 1931 the distillery was bought by an American, Duncan Thomas, in partnership with Barton Brands of Chicago. They went on to build Loch Lomond distillery (*see* entry) in 1965/66. Both distilleries were mothballed in 1984; Loch Lomond was sold next year to Glen Catrine Bonded Warehouse Ltd, and Littlemill three years later to Gibson International.

The distillery was modernised and production resumed in 1989, when Gibson also bought Glen Scotia distillery. Following a management buy-out and liquidation, Gibson's assets were bought by the owners of Loch Lomond distillery in 1994. Two years later it was dismantled and part of the site cleared for housing development; the remaining buildings deteriorated and in 2004 many were destroyed by fire. The rest were demolished in 2005.

Littlemill was long bottled as an 8 Year Old,

then at 12 Years, but is now uncommon. In the past, two other different styles were made at the distillery for blending: Dumbuck (heavily peated) and Dunglass (lightly peated).

LOCH LOMOND
Alexandria, Dumbartonshire,
WEST HIGHLAND
Current Owner: Loch Lomond Distillery Co Ltd
Status: In production

The distillery was created in 1965/66 by converting a former dye works, the United Turkey Red Company, by American-born Duncan Thomas in partnership with Barton Brands of Chicago, owners of Littlemill distillery (*see* previous entry). The latter bought out the former's interests in 1971. At this time Loch Lomond was producing two makes, Inchmurrin and Rosdhu (the former continues, the latter has been replaced by Loch Lomond single malt), from a single pair of stills fitted with rectifying heads in the "Lomond" style (*see* Inverleven). It was mothballed in 1984 and sold the next year to Inver House Distillers, who immediately sold it to Glen Catrine Bonded Warehouse Co Ltd, owned by Sandy Bulloch, a drinks wholesaler and retailer in Glasgow.

A second pair of stills, copying the first pair, were added in 1992 and a Coffey still for grain whisky in 1994. These were followed in 1998 by a third pair of pot stills, a fourth pair in 2007, and a modified Coffey still (to make malt whisky) in 2008. The range of stills at Loch Lomond, combined with different peating levels, allows the company to produce eight different styles of malt whisky and a grain whisky, and makes it almost self-sufficient as a blender.

Tasting Note
The distillery's website states, "We produce a full range of malts from heavily peated (typical of Islay), to complex fruity (typical of Speyside), to full-bodied fruity (typical of Highland) and also soft and fruity (typical of Lowland)".

LOCHSIDE
Montrose, Angus, EAST HIGHLAND
Status: Dismantled

Lochside was originally established by Macnab Distilleries in 1957 on the site of the old Deuchar & Sons brewery at Montrose. The founder had been backed by Joseph Hobbs, the colourful owner of Ben Nevis distillery (*see* entry), who soon took over, trading as Macnab Distilleries Ltd. His original intention was to make grain whisky, to which end he installed a Coffey still, but when the large Invergordon grain distillery opened, he also installed four pot stills for malt whisky production (in 1961), as he had done at Ben Nevis.

The dual-production regime ceased after his death in 1964, and in 1973 Lochside was sold to the Spanish company Destilerias y Crianza del Whisky (DYC). The latter was acquired by Allied Domecq in 1992 and production ceased. The distillery was dismantled five years later and demolished in 2005, following a fire.

AN INITIAL BIG MALT FLAVOUR THAT COMMANDS A PAUSE, REVEALING A SILKY RICH NATURALLY SWEET AND QUIETLY COMPLEX CHARACTER. LONGMORN. *Aged in Oak for sixteen years* Speyside (aged 16 yo) single malt) NON CHILL FILTERED ESTᴰ 1894

LONGMORN
SINGLE MALT SCOTCH WHISKY
AGED 16 YEARS
48%vol The Longmorn Distilleries Limited LONGMORN DISTILLERY ELGIN MORAYSHIRE IV30 3SJ PRODUCT OF SCOTLAND 70cl ℮

LONGMORN
near Elgin, Morayshire, SPEYSIDE
Current Owner: Chivas Brothers
Status: In production; Top Class; visitors
by arrangement

The name "Longmorn" may come from the Old British word *"Lhanmorgund"*, meaning "place of the holy man". A warehouse now stands on what was reputed to be the site of the chapel itself, which was later replaced in the fifteenth century by an early water wheel. John Duff, the founder of Glenlossie, built two distilleries on this site in 1897, called Longmorn and BenRiach. The area had an ample supply of local peat and abundant spring water from the Mannoch Hill. It was also close to the railway. Longmorn opened in 1897 and has remained in production ever since.

Owned by "The Longmorn Grants" until 1970 when they merged with the Grants of Glenlivet and the "Glen Grant Grants" to become The Glenlivet Distillers Ltd, which was acquired by Seagrams in 1977 and passed to Pernod Ricard in 2001. First released as a 15 Year Old in 1993, this was replaced by a 16 Year Old (48% ABV) in 2007.

Tasting Note
The new-make is Speyside-fruity, with body. The nose is rich and fruity (oranges and dried figs), with traces of sherry, cinnamon and nutmeg. A big, smooth mouth-feel, sweet, with traces of caramel and malt, then drying in the long finish. Medium- to full-bodied.

LONGROW
Campbeltown, Argyl, CAMPBELTOWN
Current Owner: J&A Mitchell
Status: In production

Longrow is produced in the stills at Springbank distillery in Campbeltown, but it is utterly different to Springbank itself. It is made from heavily peated malt – the distillery has its own maltings, and uses local peat – and the resulting whisky is powerfully phenolic. In blind tastings it is usually mistaken for an Islay.

There was originally a distillery called Longrow on the site now occupied by Springbank distillery (*see* Springbank) but the Longrow whisky was only introduced in 1973, produced so that the owner would not have to buy in Islay malt for blending purposes (for its Campbeltown Loch brand, mainly).

Longrow is produced twice a year, in the

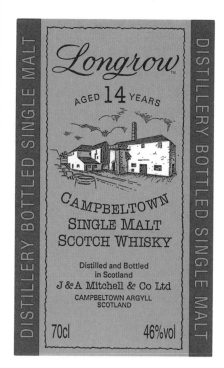

DISTILLERY BOTTLED SINGLE MALT

Longrow™
AGED 14 YEARS
CAMPBELTOWN
SINGLE MALT
SCOTCH WHISKY
Distilled and Bottled
in Scotland
J & A Mitchell & Co Ltd
CAMPBELTOWN ARGYLL
SCOTLAND
70cl 46%vol

DISTILLERY BOTTLED SINGLE MALT

spring and autumn, in small quantities. The core ranges comprise bottlings at 10, 10 (57% ABV) and 14 (sherry matured) Years, with limited edition "Vintages".

Tasting Note
The make is heavy, sweet, oily and smoky. The mature whisky is maritime, (salty, seaweedy), with fruity notes and grubby smoke. The taste is sweet and salty, with smoke in the finish – an "old-fashioned" style. Medium-bodied.

THE MACALLAN
Craigellachie, Morayshire, SPEYSIDE
Current Owner: The Edrington Group
Status: In production; Top Class; visitor centre

The Macallan was originally a farm distillery established in the eighteenth century at Easter Elchies, on a drove road from the Laich o' Moray to the south, near one of the few fords across the River Spey. The cattle-drove roads had obvious advantages to any distiller, providing a constant source of custom for the contraband spirit.

The first licence was taken by Alexander Reid in 1824. His distillery was built of wood and changed hands several times until bought by James Stuart of Glen Spey distillery in 1886, when it was rebuilt in stone. In 1892, Stuart sold it to the Elgin merchant and owner of Talisker distillery on Skye, Roderick Kemp, and it remained under the control of his descendants until 1996, when two of its shareholders, Highland Distilleries and Suntory achieved a controlling interest.

Highland Distilleries assumed the name of its holding company, Edrington, in 2001 and took The Macallan out of public ownership the same year. The distillery had become publicly quoted in 1967 in order to lay down stock and finance the building of a separate stillhouse, doubling capacity. This closed in 1990, but was re-opened in September 2008. The Macallan has always had a high reputation among blenders, but only a small amount

was bottled as single malt by the owner until 1980, when a 10 and 12 (export only) Year Old were launched. 18 Year Old followed in 1983, 25 Year Old in 1987 and 30 Year Old 1998. Since then there have been numerous expressions. Traditionally, The Macallan was matured in ex-sherry wood, then in 2004 a parallel range, drawn from a mix of American and European refill casks was introduced, named "Fine Oak".

Since 1996, the company has also released a number of bottlings, replicating Macallans from 1874, 1876, 1861 and 1841, and also a "Fine and Rare" range of bottlings of whisky distilled between 1937 and 1972.

Tasting Note
The Macallan new-make is rich, robust, fruity and oily. "Traditional" Macallan, from ex-sherry butts is rich with dried fruits and orange peel, sherry, nuts and baking spices, sometimes with a trace of suphur. Texture is smooth; taste sweetish to start, but tannic-dry overall, with sherry, toffee and charred Christmas cake. Full-bodied.

MACDUFF aka Glen Deveron
near Banff, Banffshire, EAST HIGHLAND
Current Owner: John Dewar & Sons
Status: In production; 2nd Class; visitor centre

Macduff distillery was constructed in 1963 by a consortium, Glen Deveron Distillers Ltd, and sold ten years later to William Lawson Distillers, today a subsidiary of The Bacardi Group. In 1998, Bacardi acquired John Dewar & Sons (together with five distilleries) from Guinness. The product is used for William Lawson's Finest blend and is also sold as a single called Glen Deveron, after the local water source, the River Deveron, that divides the Eastern Highlands and Speyside. Independent bottlings still name it Macduff.

Tasting Note
The new-make is malty and cereal-like. Glen Deveron is sweet, with cereal and light sherry notes. The taste is sweet, with baked apples and pears, and traces of tropical fruits, drying into nuts and cereal. Medium-bodied.

MALT MILL (see LAGAVULIN)

MANNOCHMORE
near Elgin, Morayshire, SPEYSIDE
Current Owner: Diageo plc
Status: In production

The distillery was built in 1971 by SMD and licensed to John Haig & Co Ltd, adjacent to its distillery at Glenlossie, a few kilometres south of Elgin, during a brief peak in the fortunes of the whisky industry. Mannochmore draws its water from a different source than Glenlossie and is a large, modern complex containing three pairs of operating stills. It has the capacity to produce one million gallons (4,500,000 litres) per annum.

Mannochmore was mothballed in 1985, but re-opened in 1989 and almost all of its product goes as fillings for Haig's blends. A small amount has been available as a single since 1992, and in 1996 more was made available

under the name of Loch Dhu, a malt that was heavily coloured with spirit caramel and as dark as Coca Cola (designed for the youth market, to be drunk with a mixer). Currently, small amounts are bottled in the "Flora & Fauna" series.

Tasting Note
The new-make is grassy in style, the mature whisky of a light Speyside character – fresh, floral-fruity, with traces of cereal. A creamy mouth-feel; sweet to taste, with fresh fruits and some woody dryness in the short finish. Light-bodied.

MILLBURN
Inverness, Inverness-shire, NORTH HIGHLAND
Status: Demolished; 2nd Class

Said to have been founded as early as 1807, and originally called Inverness distillery, by the end of the nineteenth century Millburn had been completely rebuilt. In 1892 it was bought by two members of the Haig family, who extensively refurbished it. Millburn was then sold to Booth's, the gin distiller, in 1921. Destroyed by fire a year later, it was rebuilt and sold to DCL in 1937. Closed in 1985 and converted to a "Beefeater" steakhouse.

MILTONDUFF aka Mosstowie
near Elgin, Morayshire, SPEYSIDE
Current Owner: Chivas Brothers
Status: In production; 1st Class; visitors
by arrangement

This was established in 1824 close to
Pluscarden Priory, which at one time was said
to produce the finest ale in Scotland – so good
that it "filled the abbey with unutterable bliss".
The Benedictine monks drew their water from
the Black Burn which had been blessed by
a saintly abbot in the fifteenth century. It
was extended in 1896 by Thomas Yool & Co,
which continued to operate the distillery until
1936, when it sold to Hiram Walker, which
licensed the distillery to George Ballantine &
Sons. Allied Lyons acquired Hiram Walker in
1996/97, and Pernod Ricard (Chivas Brothers)
bought most of Allied, including Miltonduff,
in 2005.

Miltonduff continues to be a key filling in
the Ballantine blends. Largely rebuilt in 1964,
including the installation of a pair of Lomond
stills. Miltonduff was bottled by its proprietor
in the 1970s and '80s, but is now only available
from independents; even then it is rare.

Tasting Note
The spirit is sweet, grassy and fragrant, with light
spice. The nose of the mature whisky is grainy
and malty, with notes of honeysuckle and roses.
A smooth texture, the taste is sweet, with fruit
and nuts. Medium-bodied.

MORTLACH
Dufftown, Banffshire, SPEYSIDE
Current Owner: Diageo plc
Status: In production; Top Class

The distillery was built in 1823, in an area
renowned for an excellent smugglers' spring,
"Highlander John's Well". Until 1887 it was
the only distillery in Dufftown; today there
are seven. A later owner, John Gordon, sold
the site as a brewery but he reverted to
distilling and sold his product in Glasgow

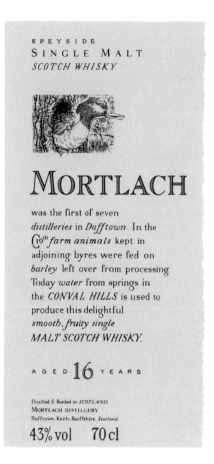

SPEYSIDE
SINGLE MALT
SCOTCH WHISKY

MORTLACH

was the first of seven
distilleries in *Dufftown*. In the
C19th *farm animals* kept in
adjoining byres were fed on
barley left over from processing.
Today *water* from springs in
the *CONVAL HILLS* is used to
produce this delightful
smooth, fruity single
MALT SCOTCH WHISKY.

AGED **16** YEARS

Distilled & Bottled in *SCOTLAND*.
MORTLACH DISTILLERY.
Dufftown, Keith, Banffshire, *Scotland*.

43% vol   70 cl

as "The Real John Gordon". He took on
George Cowie in 1854 and it was he who
went on to establish its reputation. The
distillery was expanded from three to six stills
in 1897 and was bought by John Walker & Sons
Ltd in 1923, thus joining DCL in 1925, which
re-built it in 1964, retaining the original stills.

Unusually, Mortlach uses a form of
partial triple-distillation. It is still licensed to
George Cowie & Sons and is a part of the
Walker blends. Mortlach is bottled in small
amounts by its proprietor, as part of the
"Flora & Fauna" series and with occasional
special releases.

Tasting Note
The style is heavy and meaty, producing a big, rich whisky, typically matured in ex-sherry casks. The aroma is of Christmas cake, with burnt edges, moistened with Madeira and with a sprinkle of nutmeg. Soft and mouth-filling, the taste is sweet then tannic-dry, with some allspice in the long finish. Full-bodied.

MOSSTOWIE (see MILTONDUFF)

NORTH PORT
Brechin, Angus, EAST HIGHLAND
Status: Demolished; 3rd Class

The Guthrie family were established arable farmers and local bankers in Brechin, one of whom had been a provost of the town. They founded the distillery in 1820. In 1922 DCL acquired the entire shareholding in partnership with Holts, a Manchester wine merchant. It was licensed to Mitchell Bros Ltd of Glasgow, closed in 1983 and later demolished.

OBAN
Oban, Argyll, WEST HIGHLAND
Current Owner: Oban
Status: In production; 2nd Class; visitor centre

The prosperity of Oban was greatly enriched by the Stevenson brothers in the late eighteenth century; entrepreneurs who invested in housebuilding, slate-quarrying and ship-building. They established the distillery in 1794. It was bought by Walter Higgin in 1883 who implemented a programme of modernisation and enlargement, which included blasting into the cliff face behind the distillery. By this time Oban was a prosperous port with much trade going on between Liverpool and Glasgow.

Later Oban distillery was sold to Dewars in 1923 and then amalgamated with DCL in 1925. It was silent from 1931 to '37 and from 1969 to '72, when a new stillhouse was built. A visitor centre was installed in an old maltings in 1989,

the year after Oban was selected for promotion as a "Classic Malt". Since then it has become hugely popular in the USA – so much so that allocations are rationed.

Tasting Note
The new-make is fruity and lightly maritime. The mature spirit continues this: fresh, with seaweed and salt behind light fresh fruits, and a suggestion of smoke behind that. The texture is soft and slightly oily; the taste sweet and fruity and very slightly spicy, with a trace of salt and smoke. Medium-bodied.

PITTYVAICH
Dufftown, Banffshire, SPEYSIDE
Status: Demolished; 3rd Class

In the 1970s Arthur Bell & Sons embarked on a huge extension and modernisation programme. As part of this it built Pittyvaich distillery next door to its Dufftown distillery. Pittyvaich is situated in the Dullan Glen, draws its water from the Convalleys and Balliemore springs and has four stills. Its make was not bottled as a single until the 1990s, in UD's "Flora and Fauna" range. Pittyvaich closed in 1993 and was demolished in 2003.

PORT ELLEN
Port Ellen, ISLAY
Status: Dismantled

The attractive village of Port Ellen grew up
around the pier and distillery established there
in the 1820s, both supported by the local laird,
Walter Frederick Campbell, and named after
his wife, Elleanor. The distillery began as a
malt mill, but was making whisky by 1825.
In 1836 John Ramsay, aged 21, was installed
as manager. An enterprising man, he was
the first to make use of the spirit safe and
persuaded the government to allow whisky for
export to be bonded free of duty and shipped
in 80 gallon (360 litre) casks. He also became
a leading agriculturalist, Chairman of the
Glasgow Chamber of Commerce and an MP.

The distillery was continued by his widow
and son, who sold it to their agent, James
Buchanan & Son, in partnership with John
Dewar & Sons in 1923, and so passed to DCL
ownership with these companies. In 1830 it
was closed – although its maltings continued to
operate – and only reopened in 1967, entirely
rebuilt within the original buildings. A large
drum maltings was built along side in 1973.

Port Ellen distillery closed in 1983 and was
dismantled in 1987. The original buildings still
stand, some converted into small business
units, and some of the old warehouses are still
used by Lagavulin distillery.

PULTENEY aka Old Pulteney
Wick, Caithness NORTH HIGHLAND
Current Owner: Inver House
Status: In production; 2nd Class; visitor centre

Pultney town is the fishing port of Wick in
the far northeast of Scotland. It was built as
a model village around 1810, by the British
Fisheries Society, designed by Thomas Telford
("The Father of Civil Engineering") and named
after Sir William Pulteney, Director General
of the BFS. By the mid-nineteenth century
it was the largest herring port in the world
by weight of catch.

The distillery was built in 1826 by James
Henderson, whose family continued to own
it until 1920 when it was sold to James Watson
& Co of Dundee and thence to John Dewar &
Sons. Mothballed in 1930, it was bought by a
local solicitor in 1951, then by Hiram Walker,
who rebuilt it in 1958. In 1995 it was bought
by Inver House Distillers.

The single malt has long been known as
Old Pulteney; the core expressions are at 12,
17 and 21 Years, with some special bottlings.

Tasting Note
**A heavy style, with malt, fruit and almond oil,
it becomes lighter with maturation and gains
distinct maritime notes behind lychees and fresh
fruit. The taste is dry overall, fresh, sherbet-like
and distinctly salty, with nutty notes. Medium- to
light-bodied.**

ROSEBANK
Falkirk, Midlothian, LOWLAND
Status: Dismantled

The distillery was converted in 1840 by an
established local wine and spirits merchant,
James Rankine, from the maltings of Camelon
distillery, on the bank of the Forth-Clyde Union
Canal. It became enormously popular with
blenders to the extent that Rankine was the
first distiller to charge warehouse rents for
stocks in bond. In 1914 he became one of the
founders of SMD, which subsequently became
part of DCL.

The spirit was triple-distilled, in the Lowland
manner. Unusual features at Rosebank included
a cast-iron, copper-covered mash tun and a
traditional worm tub on the wash still. The
distillery was mothballed in 1993 and the site
sold for re-development in 2002. As part of the
buildings are listed, they have remained.

ROYAL BRACKLA
Nairn, Inverness-shire, SPEYSIDE
Current Owner: John Dewar & Sons
Status: In production; 2nd Class

This distillery was founded on the Cawdor
Estate in 1812 by Captain William Fraser
of Brackla, in an area made famous by
Shakespeare's Macbeth, Thane of Cawdor
before he became king. It was the first distillery
to be granted a royal warrant, by William IV in
1835, renewed in the 1850s by Queen Victoria.
After several changes of ownership, it was sold
to two Aberdeen wine and spirits merchants,
who rebuilt it in 1898.

In 1926 it was sold to the Leith blending
company, John Bisset & Co, which joined
DCL in 1943. A major refurbishment took

place in 1964/65, when a second pair of stills
was installed, and again in 1997, although it
had been mothballed from 1985 to 1991. In
1997, United Distillers was obliged to sell the
distillery to Bacardi, along with John Dewar
& Sons and four other distilleries, when the
company merged with Independent Distillers
and Vintners to form UDV/Diageo. The malt is
not currently bottled by its owner.

Tasting Note
Malty and fruity as new-make, the mature spirit
becomes lighter and fresher, more floral and
grassy, with light coconut notes and a hint of
smoke. A smooth texture and a sweet taste, with
apples and pears and light spice.
Medium-bodied.

ROYAL LOCHNAGAR
Crathie, Aberdeenshire, EAST HIGHLAND
Current Owner: Diageo plc
Status: In production; 1st Class; visitor centre

The present distillery was built by John Begg
in 1845, on the Balmoral Estate, leased from
Gordon of Abergeldy. Queen Victoria moved
into Balmoral Castle, nearby, in 1848 and three
days later, she visited the distillery accompanied
by Prince Albert who was passionately interested
in all kinds of manufacture, and the young

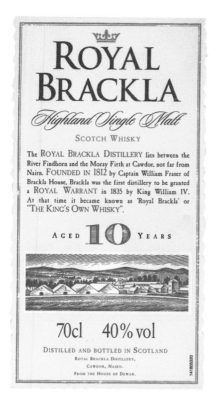

Prince of Wales, Princess Royal and Prince Alfred. After their tour, Begg produced a bottle of mature whisky and they all tasted it – even the children. A royal warrant was granted, with an order for more whisky, only days later.

By the 1880s, most of the product was sent to his friend William Sanderson as heart malt for VAT 69, and Begg himself produced his own blend, John Begg Blue Cap, which he sold with the slogan "Take a Peg of John Begg". His company joined DCL in 1916. Until the 1980s Royal Lochnagar was rare; the owner now bottles it at 12 Years and Selected Reserve (only 3,000 bottles available). The visitor centre opened in 1988 and is now one of the leading attractions on Royal Deeside.

Tasting Note

Although the small stills and worm tubs employed by the distillery would be expected to make heavy spirit, they are operated in such a way as to make light and grassy new-make. The mature whisky had light toffee, planed hardwood, pine, varnish and linseed oil. The taste starts sweet, then acidic, then dry, with sandalwood in the aftertaste. Medium-bodied.

ST MAGDALENE aka Linlithgow
Linlithgow, Midlothian, LOWLAND
Status: Dismantled

The renowned Lowland distiller Adam Dawson founded the distillery on the site of an old hospital in 1797. The town of Linlithgow had been an important brewing and distilling centre from medieval times and there were once five distilleries based there.

By the nineteenth century it had its own wharf on the Forth-Clyde (Union) canal, and such easy access to transportation helped its sales in the south. A&J Dawson was bought by DCL in 1912 and was one of the original members of SMD. Production continued until its closure in 1983. St Magdalene is now highly sought after. The distillery buildings have been redeveloped as residential flats.

SCAPA
Kirkwall, Orkney, ISLAND
Current Owner: Chivas Brothers
Status: In production; visitors by arrangement

This is one of only two distilleries on the Orkney Islands, the other being Highland Park. Built by John Townsend in 1885, it was described by Alfred Barnard as "one of the most complete little distilleries in the Kingdom". It stands on the north shore of Scapa Flow, where the German High Seas Fleet scuttled itself at the end of the First World War.

Total destruction of the distillery by fire during the First World War was averted with the assistance of naval ratings billeted in the district, who arrived by the boatload to assist in putting out the blaze. Scapa was acquired by Hiram Walker in 1954 and rebuilt five years later, incorporating a Lomond-style wash still. The plates within this were removed in 1978.

Ownership passed to Allied Distillers in 1986, and Scapa was mothballed in 1994, then a £2.1 million refurbishment was undertaken 2004/05, during which ownership passed to Chivas Brothers, who resumed production, repackaged the malt at 14 Year Old and started a fan club. A 16 Year Old was released in 2008.

Tasting Note

The new-make presents heather pollen, honey and light spice, but gains maritime characteristics during maturation, with grassy notes and scented wood. The taste is dryish and lightly spicy, with vanilla notes and some salt. Medium-bodied.

THE SINGLETON (see AUCHROISK, DUFFTOWN, GLENDULLAN, GLEN ORD)

SPEYBURN
Rothes, Morayshire, SPEYSIDE
Current Owner: Inver House
Status: In production; 2nd Class

Originally built by John Hopkins & Co in 1897, in a narrow wooded glen at Rothes during the year of Queen Victoria's Diamond Jubilee. The owner was keen to go into production before the year was out, so that its first casks of whisky could bear the historic date. In the end, it only managed to get one cask filled in the last week of the year!

The distillery was the first in the industry to use drum maltings. These closed in 1968. Hopkins & Co had joined the DCL in 1916, and that company's successor, United Distillers, sold Speyburn to Inver House Distillers in 1991. First bottled in the "Flora & Fauna" series as a 12 Year Old in 1990, the current owners bottle at 10 and 25 Years.

Tasting Note
Estery, floral, grassy and citric, but with a heaviness coming from the use of worm tubs. If anything the spirit becomes lighter during maturation, with green apples, pear-drops and herbal-heather notes. Sweet to taste. Light-bodied.

SPEYSIDE
Kingussie, Inverness-shire, SPEYSIDE
Current Owner: Speyside Distillery Co
Status: In production

After being demobilised from the Royal Navy in 1946, George Christie became a whisky broker in Glasgow. In 1955 he founded the Speyside Distillery & Bonding Company and began to look for a site to build on. He found it the next year 5.5 kilometres (three miles) from Kingussie, close to the source of

the River Spey, a barley mill dating from the eighteenth century that had been in operation until 1965. Restoration began in 1967, done by one stonemason, and the first spirit flowed from Speyside distillery in December 1990. The company bottles Speyside at 10 and 12 Years and also a younger expression (no age statement) called Drumguish (pronounced "Drum-ooish"). It also bottles a range of malts at cask strength from different distilleries at different ages under the "Scott's Selection" label.

Tasting Note
New-make is light, soft and sweet, with a trace of liquorice. The mature whisky is predominantly cereal-like, with fruity notes, and this character is echoed by the sweet taste. Light-bodied.

SPRINGBANK
Campbeltown, Argyll, CAMPBELTOWN
Current Owner: J&A Mitchell
Status: In production; visitors by arrangement

Still in the ownership of the descendants of its founder, Springbank was built in 1828. The original buildings are still in use, as are its floor maltings and cast-iron mash tun. An ancient and unique wash still heated by both steam coils and oil fires employs a "rummager" to prevent the yeast scorching on the base of the still. This continually exposes small areas of clean copper in the still and may affect the flavour. Other unusual factors are a worm tub on the No 1 spirit still, a cast-iron rake-and-plough mash tun and the use of a third, "doubling" still (ie. two spirit stills), although this is not truly triple-distillation, since not all the spirit is distilled three times.

In short, it is the most traditional of distilleries. It has also been making the peaty Longrow regularly since 1990 (qv. an early batch was made in 1973/74, released in 1985), and the unpeated, triple-distilled Hazelburn, distilled 1997 (*see* entry). Both Longrow and Hazelburn were once distilleries in Campbeltown. All the whiskies are matured and bottled at the distillery, without chill-filtration and reduced with production water.

Many expressions of Springbank have appeared in recent years, including a number of limited and long-aged "vintages" and, since 2002, some wood-finished whiskies from ex-port, sherry, rum, Tokaji and Barolo casks. The current core expressions are at 10, 10 (57% ABV) and 15 Years. A 32 Year Old 1966 cask strength bottling, made from locally grown barley, is highly sought after. J&A Mitchell has owned the bottling house, William Cadenheads Ltd, since 1969. Cadenheads also bottle at the distillery and sell through specialist shops in Edinburgh and London.

Tasting Note
The new-make is sweet and heavy; oily, with a light smokiness. It benefits from long maturation, gaining body and complexity: fruity aromas (cherries, strawberries and bananas), maritime notes (seaweed and hot sand), machine oil. The texture is creamy, and the taste has sweet butterscotch, fresh mint and grubby smoke in the finish. Medium- to full-bodied.

STRATHISLA
Keith, Banffshire, SPEYSIDE
Current Owner: Chivas Brothers
Status: In production; 1st Class; visitor centre

Founded in 1786 as Milltown distillery, this is the oldest continuously operating distillery in Scotland. It was established by George Taylor, a wealthy businessman who invested in distilling as an alternative to the waning fortunes of the flax dressing industry.

He was leased the land by the Earl of Seafield. In the 1820s Taylor suffered a riding accident, and by 1830 the distillery was owned by William Longmore, banker and grain merchant in Elgin. He began to offer "Strathisla", as the make was called (the distillery was still "Milton"), as a single and by the 1880s it was being sold in "immense quantities" by Sir Robert Burnett & Co in London, according to a local newspaper report in 1885. Longmore brought his son-in-law into the business, which was incorporated as William Longmore & Co Ltd.

From 1940 the company was controlled by a shady London financier named James Pommeroy, who was convicted in 1949 of evading £111,038 in tax by selling its make under different names on the black market. Two years later it was acquired by James Barclay of Chivas Bros (which had itself been bought by Seagrams in 1949), and the name became Strathisla once more, during the 1950s.

Seagrams immediately expanded production, installing another pair of stills in 1965, disconnecting the waterwheel that drove the rummagers in the original wash still (the wheel is still there) and building warehouses nearby, but Strathisla remains a charming traditional distillery. The visitor centre was refurbished in 1995, and the malt is bottled at 12 Years.

Tasting Note

The new-make is sweet, fruity and estery, with good body. The mature whisky is rich and deeply fruity, with apricots and plums, sweet malt, sandalwood and a thread of smoke. Mouth-filling, with a sweet, sherried taste, drying in the finish. Medium-bodied.

STRATHMILL
Keith, Banffshire, SPEYSIDE
Current Owner: Diageo plc
Status: In production

The original buildings were built as a meal mill in 1823. It was later converted into a distillery called "Glenisla-Glenlivet" in 1891. Four years on Gilbey's, the London wine merchant and gin distiller, bought it as part of its acquisition of interests in the Scotch whisky industry. In 1962 Gilbey's merged with United Wine Traders (including Justerini & Brooks) to become Independent Distillers & Vintners, and in 1968 Strathmill was expanded to four stills.

The distillery joined Diageo in 1997. The make was for blending purposes (particularly for J&B Rare). It first became available as a single in 1993 (a bottling for Oddbins), and was first bottled by its owner in 2001.

Tasting Note

Light, grassy and malty in character, the nose is sweet and estery, with floral and fresh-fruit notes (tangerine, sweet apple, orange). Light-bodied, with a sweet fruity taste.

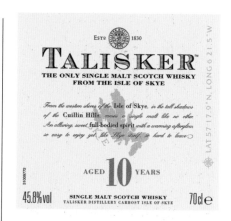

TALISKER
Carbost, Isle of Skye, ISLAND
Current Owner: Diageo plc
Status: In production; visitor centre

Robert Louis Stevenson mentions Talisker in a poem he wrote in 1880 as the "King o' drinks, as I conceive it". The distillery was established by Hugh and Kenneth Macaskill in 1830 at Carbost on the shore of Loch Harport, set in the lee of Cnoc-nan-Speireag (Hawkhill). Hugh was a tacksman, (a gentleman tenant-farmer who leased land to others) and he himself acquired the lease of Talisker House and estate from Macleod of Macleod, the chief laird in Skye. Having cleared the land of people to make room for sheep, he established the distillery. However, it did not prosper and the lease was taken up by the bank in 1848.

In 1857 it was bought by one Donald Maclellan (for £500), who was married to Macaskill's daughter, but he was sequestrated in 1863. Soon after, it was bought by the distillery's Glasgow agent, John Anderson, who invested heavily in it. In spite of the good reputation Anderson had in the trade, he too was bankrupted in 1879.

Talisker was bought and rebuilt by Roderick Kemp and Alexander Grigor Allan (the former would buy Macallan distillery) in 1892 and the latter merged Talisker with Dailuaine distillery in 1898. The distillery was extended

in 1900 and the pier and cottages built. It came under the control of DCL and "The Big Three" (Walker's, Dewar's and Buchanan's) in 1916, and was licensed to John Walker & Sons. Following a devastating fire in 1960, much of the distillery was again rebuilt. Unusually, it has five stills and continues to have worm tubs rather than column condensers.

Talisker has long been available as a single, is highly regarded by connoisseurs and has won numerous awards. It was chosen as the "Island" representative in United Distillers' "Classic Malts", at 10 Years Old. This has been joined by a Distiller's Edition (finished in amoroso sherry-wood) and 12, 20, 25 and 30 Year Old expressions.

Tasting Note
Smoky and spicy, with maritime notes. The mature whisky is elemental and maritime – beaches, seaweed, salt – with spice, dried fruits and wood-smoke. The taste is sweet, with rich fruits and fragrant smoke and a unique chilli-pepper "catch" in the finish. Medium- to full-bodied.

TAMDHU
Knockando, Morayshire, SPEYSIDE
Current Owner: The Edrington Group
Status: Mothballed; 2nd Class; visitors by arrangement

Tamdhu was built in 1897 by a consortium of blenders and The Highland Distilleries Co Ltd, on a site selected for its proximity to the railway and for its excellent supply of water from the "Smuggler's Glen". This was one of the most modern distilleries of its age; it still has its own Saladin maltings – the only Speyside operation to malt all its own barley. Tamdhu was forced to close for over 20 years owing to difficulties regarding the disposal of spent wash (the effluent produced from distilling) but production restarted in 1947.

Tamdhu is an important ingredient in The Famous Grouse blend, and as that brand grew in popularity, Tamdhu's capacity was increased

from two to six stills in 1975. A visitor centre was built but has been closed.

Tamdhu was mothballed in 2010. It was first launched as a single in 1976 (at 8 Year Old), replaced by a 10 Year Old in 1979. Today's only available bottling has no age statement.

Tasting Note
Fresh apple and honey, with traces of smoke and good body. Sweet and estery as mature whisky, with fresh fruits (Ogen melon), bubblegum and a hint of smoke. Full mouth-feel, with a fruity taste and a thread of smoke in the finish. Medium-bodied.

TAMNAVULIN
Tomnavoulin, Banffshire, SPEYSIDE
Current Owner: Whyte & Mackay
Status: In production

This distillery was built between 1965 and '66. It is one of the most modern operations on Speyside and makes full use of the latest computerised technology. The Gaelic name means "the mill on the hill" and the old mill that stands below the distillery was converted into a visitor centre.

Tamnavulin is in Glenlivet and, despite the general appellation of the district, is the only distillery actually on the banks of the Livet burn. It was mothballed in 1995. Whyte & Mackay bought Invergordon Distillers (owner of Tamnavulin) in 1993 and mothballed the distillery two years later. In January 2007 a major refurbishment was begun, completed by August that year, by which time Whyte & Mackay had been bought by United Breweries of India. Tamnavulin is bottled at 10 Years.

Tasting Note
Light, sweet, grassy and slightly peppery. A fresh, herbal nose, with dried parsley, green vegetables, lemon grass and a hint of camphor. The latter comes through in the cooling mouth-feel, with lemon meringue and camomile tea. Light-bodied.

HIGHLAND
SINGLE MALT
SCOTCH WHISKY

The *Cromarty Firth* is one of the few places in the British Isles inhabited by *PORPOISE*. They can be seen quite regularly, *swimming* close to the shore *less* than a *mile* from

TEANINICH

distillery. Founded in 1817 in the *Ross~shire* town of ALNESS, the *distillery* is now one of the largest in *Scotland.* TEANINICH is an assertive *single MALT WHISKY* with a *spicy*, *smoky, satisfying* taste.

AGED **10** YEARS

43% vol   Distilled & Bottled in SCOTLAND.
TEANINICH DISTILLERY,
Alness, Ross-shire, Scotland.   70 cl

TEANINICH "Chee-an-in-ick"
Alness, Ross & Cromarty, NORTH HIGHLAND
Current Owner: Diageo plc
Status: In production

Teaninich was founded in 1817 by Captain Hugh Munro of Teaninich, and built on his own land near Alness. At this time most of the distilling in the area was illicit and the local barley supply was used for illegal production. Teaninich was acquired by Munro & Cameron, Aberdeen whisky brokers, in 1898. It was taken over by Innes Cameron in 1904. His trustees sold Teaninich to SMD (DCL) in 1933.

Apart from the war years Teaninich has remained in operation, supplying fillings for blending – exclusively until 1992, when United Distillers began to bottle a small amount as a single malt at 10 Years. There were four stills until 1971, when a new stillhouse was constructed with six additional stills. The older part of the distillery (including the four earlier stills) was mothballed in 1985.

Tasting Note
Grassy and oily as new-make, the mature whisky is sweet and slightly waxy, with dandelion, green leaves, green apples and gooseberries. The texture is smooth and mouth-filling, with a hint of smoke. Medium-bodied.

TOBERMORY aka Ledaig
Tobermory, Mull, ISLAND
Current Owner: Burn Stewart
Status: In production; 3rd Class; visitor centre

John Sinclair built Tobermory on the island of Mull in 1795. Sinclair was established as a successful shipping merchant and so was able to transport the barley and fuel necessary for distilling. After two subsequent owners the distillery was bought in 1890 by John Hopkins & Co (part of DCL, 1916) and then fell silent between 1930 and 1972. It reopened as Ledaig distillery and was reconstructed by a Liverpool company, with the help of sherry producer Domecq, only to fall out of production again in 1975. In 1979 it was sold to a Yorkshire property company, which converted some of the old warehouses into flats and resumed sporadic production in 1989. In 1993 the distillery was sold to Burn Stewart Distillers, who release Tobermory (un-peated malt) at 10, 15 and 32 Years, and Ledaig (heavily peated) at 10 Years, Original and Sherry Finish.

Tasting Note
Malty and faintly smoky as new-make. The mature whisky is cereal-like, lightly fruity and maritime on the nose, with a faint oily smokiness. A soft mouth-feel, and a dryish taste, with nuts and a trace of smoke. Light-bodied.

TOBERMORY
EST.
LIMITED **1798** EDITION
AGED 15 YEARS
ISLAND SINGLE MALT SCOTCH WHISKY
Tobermory Distillers Limited

TOMATIN
Tomatin, Inverness-shire, NORTH HIGHLAND
Current Owner: Tomatin Distillery Co
(Marubeni Europe plc)
Status: In production; 3rd Class; visitor centre

Tomatin was once the largest distillery in
Scotland. It was built during the boom years
of the late 1890s by a group of Inverness
businessmen, but struggled to survive the
grain shortages of the war years. And it
was not until the 1950s that full production
was resumed.

Extended from two stills to four in 1956,
by 1961 Tomatin had 11 stills. A dozen more
were added in 1974, giving Tomatin a capacity
of 2.6 million gallons (12 million litres) per
annum, although it never operated to capacity,
and the 11 earlier stills have been dismantled.
Following liquidation of the owners, in 1986
the distillery was bought by its principal
Japanese customers, Takara and Okura.
The latter was replaced by Marubeni in 2000.
The company bottles at 12, 18 and 25 Years,
with occasional limited bottlings.

Tasting Note
Light, fresh and grassy, with vanilla notes. The
nose is sweet and malty, with floral scents; the
taste sweet to start, with cereals and caramelised
fruits and nuts. A very faint smokiness. Medium-
bodied.

TOMINTOUL "Tom-in-towel"
near Tomintoul, Banffshire, SPEYSIDE
Current Owner: Angus Dundee Distillers plc
Status: In production; 1st Class; visitors by
arrangement

Tomintoul is the highest village in the
Highlands, and the distillery was built there in
1965, slightly lower than the village (Dalwhinnie
is the highest above sea level). Two whisky
broking firms in Glasgow, W&S Strong and Hay
& MacLeod, built it and sold to Scottish and
Universal Investment Trust (part of LONRHO)
in 1973. LONRHO bought Whyte & Mackay the
same year, transferred ownership and doubled
capacity (to four stills) in 1974. The same
year it was released as a single malt in small
quantities. Whyte & Mackay sold the distillery to
Angus Dundee Ltd, a London firm of blenders
and bottlers owned by three generations of
the Hillman family in 2000. The new owner
immediately began experimenting with peated
malt, the first expression of whisky is available
as Old Ballantruan (no age statement), named
after the distillery's water source, and have
released expressions of Tomintoul itself at 10,
14, 16, 23, 27 and 33 Years.

Tasting Note
Light, fragrant and fruity in the Speyside style, now also with a smoky variant. The nose is fragrant and delicate, grassy, lemony; the taste sweet, with breakfast cereal and nuts and a shortish finish. Light-bodied.

TORMORE
Advie, Morayshire, SPEYSIDE
Current Owner: Chivas Bros
Status: In production; 2nd Class

Long John Distillers Ltd built Tormore in 1960. It was designed by Sir Albert Richardson, past President of the Royal Academy, as an architectural showpiece, complete with an ornamental pond and fountains.

It was the first distillery to be built in the Highlands in the twentieth century. In 1972, capacity was doubled (to eight stills) and three years later Shenley International, the owners of Long John, sold the distillery and brand to Whitbread. The latter's spirits division was acquired by Allied Lyons in 1989, and Allied went to Pernod Ricard in 2005. The new owner repaired the conspicuous distillery clock, which plays four different tunes each hour, but which had been broken for many years. The malt was being promoted in the USA by 1981, and was included by Allied in its "Caledonian Malts" range. It is now bottled at 12 Years Old.

Tasting Note
Sweet, fruity and estery as new-make, the mature whisky is malty and nutty, with coconut notes. A smooth texture and a sweet, honeyed taste, drying slightly in the short finish. Medium-bodied.

TULLIBARDINE
Blackford, Perthshire, CENTRAL HIGHLAND
Current Owner: Tullibardine Distillery Ltd
Status: In production; 3rd Class; visitor centre

Tullibardine was designed by William Delmé-Evans in 1949, the first "stand alone" distillery

to be built since 1900. (*See* Isle of Jura and Glenallachie). The site was that of a famous medieval brewery, and the distillery draws its water from the same source, the Danny burn (which also supplies Highland Spring mineral waters). It stands on the northern slopes of the Ochil hills, near the famous Gleneagles Hotel and beside the main road from Glasgow to the Highlands.

The distillery was bought by Brodie Hepburn, the Glasgow whisky broker, in 1953 and was taken over by Invergordon Distillers in 1971. Invergordon became part of Whyte & Mackay in 1993. Tullibardine was mothballed in 1995 and sold to a private consortium in 2003. The new owners bottle at 10 Years Old, and have also released several "Vintage" and "wood-finished" editions. A shop and café opened in 2004.

Tasting Note
The new-make is sweet, fruity and malty. In the mature spirit, the key aromas are malt, peach, melon and orage zest. The taste is sweet to start, then drying, with biscuits and light caramel. Medium-bodied.

BUYING MALT WHISKY

Malt whisky exists to be enjoyed, and people enjoy it in three ways: as consumers, collectors or investors. The categories are not mutually exclusive. Here are some guidelines about what to look for and how and where to buy it.

THE CONSUMERS' GUIDE

People often ask me: "What is your favourite malt whisky?" I reply that it depends on my mood, the time of day, the circumstances in which I am drinking it and the company. It also depends on the bottler, the strength, the age, and, most important, the character bestowed by the individual cask. Given this number of variables it is impossible to identify a favourite.

As I am lucky enough to serve on a number of tasting panels, I have had the opportunity to nose and taste literally thousands of samples of malt whisky. It is always interesting how individual casks of obscure and little-regarded malts can turn out to be excellent. And the reverse: how some bottlings of well-known names can disappoint. So experiment. The old saying goes that there are no bad whiskies; just good ones and better ones. And the better ones for you might well depend on the circumstances in which you drink them. The only thing I would urge is to use the right glass. It is amazing how much more you will discover if you drink malt from a nosing glass, snifter or *copita*, rather than from a whisky tumbler.

Malt whisky is becoming increasingly popular, which means that it is more widely available than ever before, in both the on-trade (pubs, bars, restaurants etc.) and the off-trade (wine merchants, duty-free shops and liquor stores). There is also a growing number of dedicated whisky shops and clubs with large or specialist lists who will supply by mail order.

When choosing malt whisky there are three categories to consider:

Single Malts – Most fall into this category. Each is the product of a single distillery. Traditionally bottled at 40% ABV, there is a current move to bottle at 43% ABV (this is the standard strength in the USA) or higher, up to "natural strength" (ie. the strength at which it comes from the cask, usually around 60% ABV). Each batch is a mix of several casks – around 100 casks for major brands – in order to achieve uniformity of flavour from batch to batch. If the label states the age, this is the age of the youngest whisky used. The Scotch Whisky Regulations 2009 require that single malts must be bottled in Scotland to be named "Singe Malt Scotch Whisky".

Blended Malts – Formerly known as "vatted malts" or "pure malts", these are a mix of malt whiskies from different distilleries. Not to be confused with "blended whisky", which includes a percentage of grain whisky. Master blenders tell me that they are more difficult to create than blended Scotch. A well-made blended malt marries and balances the characteristics of its component malts in order to create something "more than the sum of its parts". Most use a "limited palette" of malts, but some do not: Chivas Century used 100 malts. Until recently, blended malts were uncommon, but currently they are enjoying a growing interest. Leading brands include: As We Get It, Big Peat, Blue Hanger, Cutty Sark Blended Malt, The Famous Grouse Blended Malt (18 and 30 Year Old), Islay Mist, Monkey Shoulder, The Peat Monster, Poit Dubh, Sheep Dip, Isle of Skye Six Isles, Smokehead, Spice Tree and Johnnie Walker Green Label.

Single Cask Malts – These are bottled from individual casks, so the number of bottles in each batch is limited. Since every cask matures its contents slightly differently, these bottlings allow connoisseurs to appreciate subtle differences. Usually the whiskies are bottled direct from the cask (ie. at "cask" or "natural" strength, typically around 60% ABV) and are hand-filtered only. (Most whiskies are chill-filtered, *see* page 97.)

BOTTLERS AND MERCHANTS

The leading brands of malt whisky are bottled in long runs by their owners. Shorter runs of less well-known whiskies, and single casks of both, are bottled by, or for, independent whisky merchants, which may or may not be allowed to declare which distillery the whisky comes from. The reason for this is that the independent bottling may not taste exactly the same as the proprietary bottling, and distillery owners cannot exercise quality control. So, if you find a single malt with a name that is not listed in the Directory, this is the reason.

PROPRIETARY BOTTLINGS

This simply means the whisky has been bottled by the people who make it. For a single bottling run, the owners will vat together several – sometimes hundreds of – casks to achieve the precise character they want their whisky to have. In some cases they will vat whiskies from both sherry and bourbon casks; in others they will add small amounts of older whisky. Having so many casks to choose from, they can pick the ones that marry best, and they will bottle at the age(s) they think the whisky to be at its peak. Quality control is rigorous, so proprietary bottled whiskies are the benchmark, displaying the whisky's characteristics to best advantage, as perceived by its maker.

LEADING INDEPENDENT BOTTLERS

In the past, distillery owners usually used independent bottlers (notable Gordon & Macphail, *see* page 222) to bottle small amounts of their makes as singles. The number of independent bottlers has increased over the past 20 years, with the growing interest in single malts. Listed below are the leading and best-established companies:

The Adelphi Distillery

www.adelphidistillery.com
The original Adelphi was one of the largest distilleries in Scotland, and stood in the heart of Glasgow. It closed down in 1902, but the name was revived in 1993 by the great-grandson of its last owner, James Walker. The company selects around 50 casks of mature whisky a year and bottles at cask strength.

Berry Bros & Rudd

www.bbr.com
The long-established London wine merchant (founded 1698) introduced Cutty Sark to its list in 1923 and since 1987 has been responsible for marketing Glenrothes single malt (the distillery is owned by Edrington). Berry Bros has been offering its own single malt bottlings for many years, but this activity was expanded in 2002 when "Berry's Own Selection" was introduced. The firm currently offers around 30 expresions at any one time.

Blackadder International

www.blackadder.com
Established in 1995 by Robin Tucek and John Lamond, authors of *The Whisky File*, the company is now run by Robin Tucek from Sweden. He bottles around 100 casks a year in a variety of ranges, all untinted and non-chill-filtered, at varying strengths.

William Cadenhead

www.wmcadenhead.com
Established in Aberdeen in 1842 and now based in Campbeltown (with a shop in Edinburgh's Old Town and in Covent Garden, London), Cadenhead is Scotland's oldest firm of independent bottlers. The business is owned by J&A Mitchell, which also owns Springbank distillery. Bottles a range of cask and reduced strength malts under its own label "Cadenhead".

Compass Box Whisky Co

www.compassboxwhisky.com
Founded by a highly creative and innovative former Johnnie Walker US marketing manager, John Glaser, in 2000. He now offers a distinguished range of mould-breaking whiskies, blends, blended malts and blended grains, elegantly packaged with unusual names.

Dewar Rattray & Co

www.dewarrattray.com
The company was founded in 1868, but has

only recently become involved in selecting and bottling Scotch whisky. Currently the company offers a small range of single cask malts, a house malt named after Stronachie distillery (demolished 1930s) and a blend, Ailsa Craig.

Gordon & Macphail
www.gordonandmacphail.com
Founded in 1896, and still family owned and managed, Gordon & Macphail offers the largest selection of whiskies in the world for sale at its shop in Elgin (around 500 brands and expressions). It has also been buying casks of malt whisky direct from the distillery, warehousing and bottling them itself, since the turn of the century. Their Connoisseur's Choice range of about 50 single malts (some more than 30 years old) is exemplary. In 1993, Gordon & Macphail bought Benromach distillery.

Douglas Laing & Co
www.douglaslaing.com
Founded in 1948, and managed by the sons of the founder, Fred and Stewart Laing, the company offers a range of single malts and blended whiskies and trades internationally.

Murray McDavid
www.murray-mcdavid.com
Mark Reynier, Gordon Wright and Simon Coughlin established Murray McDavid in 1995. They offer a narrow, highly selective range, with around ten changes every couple of months. Joined by James McEwan, the partners bought Bruichladdich distillery in 2001.

The Scotch Malt Whisky Society
www.smws.co.uk
The SMWS is a club, established in 1983, and makes its single cask bottlings available to its members at natural strength, without chill-filtration. It is based in Leith, Edinburgh, with additional premises on Queen Street, Edinburgh and in the City of London, and franchised branches in Australia, Austria, France, Italy, Japan, Benelux, Sweden, Switzerland and the USA. The Society was bought by Glenmorangie in 2003 on the recommendation of its board of directors, in order to secure supplies of mature malt whisky, but remains a separate entity. Currently it bottles 150 to 200 casks per annum.

Signatory Vintage Scotch Whisky Co
Tel: (+44) 131 555 4988
Founded in 1988 by Andrew and Brian Symington, Signatory lists some 50 single malts from operating, mothballed and defunct distilleries at any one time. Unlike many independents, Signatory has its own bottling plant, and bottles at cask strength and 43% ABV. Andrew Symington bought Edradour distillery from Pernod Ricard in 2002.

Duncan Taylor & Co Ltd
www.dtcscotch.com
Founded as a whisky broker in 1938, in Glasgow, the company acquired an outstanding collection of casks of mature whisky in 2002 and moved its operation to Huntly, Aberdeenshire. It now offers a list of around 80 whiskies (mainly very old malts and grains). In 2005, the company won four major awards for the excellence of its bottlings.

The Vintage Malt Whisky Co
www.vintagemaltwhisky.com
An independent family company established in 1992 by Brian Crook, formerly export sales manager with Morrison Bowmore. It offers a small range of single malts under its own names – Finlaggan, Tantallan, Glenalmond, etc., and some in "The Cooper's Choice" range.

Wilson & Morgan Ltd
www.wilsonandmorgan.com
Wilson & Morgan was founded in 1992 by Fabio Rossi, whose family firm (wine and olive merchants in Venice and later Treviso) had been involved in importing Scotch to Italy since the 1960s. The foundations of the stock were laid down in the early 1990s.

THE COLLECTORS' GUIDE
Collecting whisky is not as daft as collecting many other things. At least if you become

bored of the subject you can drink your collection! And, unlike wine, whisky remains constant, stored in the right conditions in a sealed bottle, so will taste more or less the same today as it did when it was bottled – even if this was 100 years ago. The right conditions are: upright (unlike wine, which lies to its cork) and away from direct sunlight. In recent years, the prices achieved at auction for old and rare whiskies have been good, and the trend has been upwards. Generally speaking, single malts fetch more than blended whiskies and proprietary bottlings more than independent bottlings. Age, condition (including the level of the liquid in the bottle), label (style and condition) and rarity (limited editions, etc.) all influence price. But one of the attractions of the subject is that you can begin to collect at whatever level you can afford.

COLLECTORS

Collectors of whisky fall into two broad categories: museum collectors, who hoard and display their bottles, and consumer collectors who buy unusual malts for drinking. Many collectors do both, whenever they can, buying a bottle to keep and a bottle to drink; some collectors also own bars or restaurants and sell old whiskies by the glass. The largest whisky list in the world (a staggering 2,500 makes and expressions, some very old) is found at the Waldhaus am See, in St Moritz, Switzerland (www.waldhaus-am-see.ch).

BUYING AND SELLING

Christie's began holding dedicated whisky sales in 1989, reflecting the growing interest in collecting old and rare malts. Prior to this date whisky was simply attached to wine sales. In the late 1990s the company closed its Glasgow office, where these auctions had been held, and now attaches occasional bottles to its wine sales. Their whisky consultant, Martin Green, now advises Bonhams International Auctioneers in Edinburgh (enquiries@bonhams. com), which holds two or three sales each year. He is also the author of the useful price guide *Collecting Malt Whiskies* (Green Blake

Enterprises, 2007). McTears Auctioneers in Glasgow (enquiries@mctears.co.uk) holds four large sales a year. Some specialist whisky shops hold small numbers of old bottles as well as current limited editions. The leading such outlet in the UK is The Whisky Exchange, near London's Heathrow Airport (enquiries@ thewhiskyexchange.com). The largest stock of old whiskies in the world is at Whisky Paradise in Bologna, with the largest and best collection of whisky on the planet (info@whiskyparadise. com). Both are owned by Giuseppe Begnoni, who also bought The Vintners Rooms restaurant, Edinburgh in 2010, which currently offers over 1,200 malts for tasting (the earliest from 1902), as well as other old wines and spirits (info@vintnersrooms.com).

Information about old bottles of whisky can sometimes be obtained on whisky forums and blogs (start with The Whisky Exchange blog, blog.thewhiskyexchange.com), and from John Rose's regular articles in *Whisky Magazine* (whiskymag.com/collecting); www. collectorsencyclopedia.com illustrates over 4,000 bottles from the collection of Giorgio D'Ambrosio at Bar Metro, Milan. I know of no organised collectors' clubs, except for miniature bottles (minibottleclub@cs.com).

INVESTORS' GUIDE

In late 1996 and early 1997 there was a flurry of interest among the media and the Department of Trade and Industry in the activities of a number of companies that were offering to sell casks of whisky as an investment. Several were found to be fraudulent, leaving both their customers and suppliers out of pocket – sometimes to the tune of hundreds of thousands of pounds.

The idea of buying casks of whisky as an investment is not new. There have always been bona fide whisky brokers, buying new-make spirit and selling it back to the industry as mature whisky for blending. The difference in the proposition made by today's "invest in whisky" companies – which are not whisky brokers as the industry understands the term

– rests on the margin between the price of a bottle of new-make spirit and that of a bottle of mature malt whisky. They claim that new spirit costs £1.80 per 70cl @ 40% ABV, bottling and storage over ten years costs £1.10, VAT and duty £7.05 = £9.95. A 70cl bottle of malt in the shop costs around £25, so you make 150 per cent profit. As a matter of fact, the price of new-make spirit quoted between whisky companies is about a quarter of that quoted by such investment companies, so they are making a hefty profit from your investment. Moreover, there is no guarantee that the individual cask you have bought will produce well-matured whisky in ten years. There are no guarantees that tax and duty will be at the same level. Similarly there are none that you will be able to find a bottler, and there are certainly none that you will be able to sell the 300-odd bottles you will get from your hogshead for anything like £25 each. So, take note, those buying casks of whisky as an investment should beware.

The truth is that distilleries do not want to sell their new-make spirit, for many reasons, not least the fact that the HM Customs & Excise paperwork is a headache. Also, distilleries do not have enough single casks of mature whisky to sell direct to private customers. Buying limited edition, old and rare whiskies by the bottle as an investment is a different matter (*see* "The Collectors' Guide", page 222).

SOME PERIODICALS

Malt Whisky Yearbook
www.maltwhiskyyearbook.com
Since 2005, Invar Ronde, a Swedish whisky expert has published (in English; 2010 edition 274 pages) an invaluable annual review of malt whisky distilleries and new bottlings, whisky shops and independent bottlers, news and new books, features on process, essays by well-known whisky writers… Now universally recognised as an indispensable guide, "… an essential companion for anyone interested in the subject and a triumph of good and imaginative writing, photography and design"

(whisky-pages.com), "…a treasure-trove, full of useful information and facts one could not even imagine" (onlymalts.com). Immensely useful, reliable and informative, I can't recommend it highly enough.

Whisky Magazine www.whiskymag.com
Founded in late 1998 by two experienced wine magazine publishers, this immediately became the source of news, information and entertainment for the consumer and the whisky trade, internationally. Published bi-monthly, it embraces bourbon, Irish, Canadian and Japanese whisky, as well as Scotch, and is a bible for whisky enthusiasts. I was its founding editor. A French language edition is published in collaboration with Le Maison du Whisky, under the editorship of Martine Nouet, the leading French whisky writer. In my view this is even better than the original!

Malt Advocate www.maltadvocate.com
This informative quarterly magazine covers the whiskies of the world – as well as some real ale thrown in for good measure. This is essential reading to find out what is happening in the US market, as well as a good and entertaining read. John Hansell is publisher and editor.

The Quaich www.malts.com
Published by Diageo, this is the bi-annual organ of "The Friends of the Classic Malts" – that operates in Scandanivia, Europe and the USA and is free of charge. Although it is focused on the so-called Classic Malts, it contains much information of interest to the whisky lover. It is well-presented and amusingly edited by Jon Allan.

The Spirit Journal www.spiritjournal.com
F Paul Pacult, who founded *The Spirit Journal* in 1991, is a global authority on spirits. His quarterly newsletter, subtitled "*The Independent Guide to Distilled Spirits, Beer and Fortified Wines*", is the leading publication on its subject, not only in the USA, where it originates. Professional, unbiased, independent, authoritative – and carrying no advertising.

Whisky, Etc. www.whiskyetc.nl
This magazine was founded in 2003 by
Wouter Wapenaar, one of the leading lights of
the Dutch whisky world and the impresario
behind the principal Dutch and Belgian whisky
festivals. It appears around twice a year.
Although its website describes it as "the only
Dutch-language magazine highlighting the
enjoyment that whisky provides", this is not
strictly true...

Der Whisky-Botschafter/Whisky Time
www.whiskybotschafter.com
www.whiskytime-magazin.ch
The leading whisky magazine in the German
market, it describes itself as "a journal for
connoisseurs and epicures". It was founded in
1997 by Christian H Rosenberg, Master of the
Quaich and initiator of the major whisky fair,

InterWhisky, in Frankfurt. Seven years later,
he released the magazine *WhiskyTime* to the
German-speaking market in Switzerland.
The articles in each magazine are not exactly the
same, for legal/advertising reasons, and to do
with coverage of local events and news; both
contain information about the international and
the national whisky market. The magazines are
each published four times a year.

De Kiln www.levenswater.nl
De Kiln is the organ of the Usquebaugh Society
of The Netherlands (established 1990; around
500 members). The first issue of the magazine
appeared in 2003, under the editorship of
Marcel Bol, who was succeeded by Tom van
Engelen in September 2009. Four issues a year;
well-researched articles (mainly in Dutch) and
excellent photography.

WHISKY SOCIETIES

There has been a burgeoning of malt whisky
appreciation clubs around the world. So fast
do they arise (especially in Northern Europe)
that it is impossible to give a full list. See Ulf
Buxrud – www.buxrud.se/linklib.htm – for
many more.

The Keepers of the Quaich
keepers@keepersofthequaich.co.uk
The Keepers of the Quaich is the most
prestigious and exclusive whisky society
in the world. It was founded in 1988 by
leading members of the Scotch whisky
industry to honour those who have
contributed significantly to the prestige and
success of Scotch whisky worldwide, and to
advance the standing and reputation of Scotch
and the hospitable traditions of Scotland.
It currently holds bi-annual dinners at Blair
Castle, home of one of the Society's patrons,
the Duke of Atholl, with occasional meetings
around the world. A magazine, *The Keeper*,
is published bi-annually. Membership by
election only.

The Scotch Malt Whisky Society
www.smws.com
Established in 1983, "The Society" has its base
in the oldest commercial building in Scotland,
at Leith, the port of Edinburgh. Here it has
splendid club premises, including the Members
Room, with a bar, open fires and leather
armchairs, the Nosing Room (where dinners
are held), sundry offices and two flats (that
members can rent for short stays). In September
1999, a London Members Room was opened
at 19 Greville Street, Hatton Garden, London,
and in May 2001 a second Edinburgh club was
opened in the former offices of the Chartered
Accountants of Scotland, a handsome Georgian
town house at 22 Queen Street. The Society
selects single casks of unusual malt whisky,
bottles them at cask strength and offers them
for sale to members in its bi-monthly Bottling
Lists. Currently 150 to 200 casks are bottled
each year. It also publishes an instructive and
entertaining quarterly news-letter, presents
tastings all over the UK and runs other events
in Edinburgh and London.

The SMWS has affiliated branches at the following addresses. These are run independently, but purvey SMWS whiskies.
In Austria: www.smws.at
In France: www.smws.fr
In Italy: www.smws.it
In Japan: www.whisk-e.co.jp
In the Netherlands, Germany and Benelux: www.smws.nl
In Switzerland: www.smws.ch
In Australia: www.smws.com.au
In Sweden: www.smws.s
In the USA: www.smwsa.com

Malt Maniacs
www.maltmaniacs.com
www.maltmadness.com
Malt Maniacs grew out of Malt Madness, a website built by Dutch internet expert Johannes van den Heuvel in 1996. As one of the earliest whisky websites, it attracted the attention of a handful of whisky experts from different countries. There are now 25 "certified" Maniacs, scattered across 15 countries, and the site receives around 1,000 visitors a day. Privately we debate a very wide range of issues confronting whisky consumers, publishing the results of our deliberations as "E-pistles" on the site. We also post scores and tasting notes for the whiskies we discover on "The Matrix" (currently over 1,200 malts noted), hold an annual blind assessment of around 150 malts, posting scores and awarding prizes. This is now among the best-regarded competitions in the world.

The Master of Malt
www.masterofmalt.com
This club is associated with the Master of Malt shop in Tunbridge Wells. It was founded in 1988 by John Lamond and Robin Tucek (authors of *The Malt Whisky File*); however they are no longer involved. Annual membership is charged and monthly lists issued, featuring "Master of Malt" bottlings, and other unusual whiskies.

Usquebaugh Society
www.levenswater.nl
www.usqebaugh.nl
Named after the Gaelic word for whisky, the Usqebaugh Society was founded in 1990 by a group of whisky-loving friends. It is now the largest and most influential whisky club in The Netherlands, with over 800 members. The society was instrumental in the rapid success of single malt whisky in The Netherlands, introducing Nosing & Tastings for small and large audiences. It publishes a quarterly whisky magazine, *De Kiln* (*see* page 225).

An Quaich: The Scotch Malt Whisky Society of Canada
www.anquaich.ca
(Managing Director: Jan Davidson)
A non-profit making society, dedicated to encouraging the appreciation and enjoyment of malt whisky. An Quaich was founded by Bernard Poirier in 1983: it now has almost 1,000 members in the province of Ontario. It publishes a newsletter, *Malt Tidings*, holds bi-monthly tasting meetings and dinners and organises annual tours of Scottish distilleries.

The International Order of Companions of the Quaich
www.thequaich.com
Founded by Ed Patrick as a splinter group of An Quaich in 1999, the Companions of the Quaich now comprises 16 Chapters, mainly in Ontario, but also in Calgary, Vancouver and Victoria, and describes itself as "Canada's premier malt whisky society". It is a very active club, and the chapters hold regular dinners, talks and tasings, as well as organising annual visits to distilleries in Scotland.

Lindores Whisky Society
www.lindores.be
The name of the club celebrates the abbey in Fife to which Friar John Cor, from whom King James IV ordered *acque vitae* in 1494, was reputedly attached. The society was founded in 2004 at Alness, Ross-shire, by four Belgian enthusiasts, under the presidency of

Luc Timmermans. Until 2006, membership was limited to 12 but, now that it is firmly established, the LWS is in a position to spread its wings and expand.

Malmoe Malt Whisky Society
www.mmws.se

The name of the club celebrates the city of Malmoe, in southern Sweden, where James Hepburn, Earl of Bothwell and husband of Mary Queen of Scots, was held prisoner for a number of years. The society was established in September 1997 by a core of 20 founding fathers, under the leadership of Secretary General Håkan Rylander. Mr Rylander is still the leading light in the Society, which has grown to 50+ enthusiastic members. The MMWS organizes local tasting events, lectures on Scotland and its whisky, and expeditions to Scotland, and invests in single casks.

Dansk Maltwhisky Akademi
www.dmwa.dk

Founded in 1995 by Jens Tholstrup and Flemming Gerhardt-Pedersen to educate consumers about whisky through a quarterly magazine, *Malten*, study groups, tastings and tours, and also to import whisky, books about whisky and related items. The Akademi also imports Signatory bottlings and acts as a forum for many of Denmark's small whisky clubs and all the country's whisky distributors.

Le Club Maison Du Whisky
www.whisky.fr

The Club was founded by Thierry Benitah in 1995 as an extension of La Maison du Whisky, the successful chain of whisky shops established in Paris by his father, Georges Benitah. La Maison du Whisky dates from 1956 and now supplies other specialist shops with some 950 expressions of Scotch and 220 other whiskies. The club was founded in reponse to customer demands for more information about Scotch, and has around 600 members, over half of them involved in the drinks industry. There is a newsletter published quarterly called *Le Still*, and they hold monthly tastings, each in a different venue, and weekly tastings in Paris at a private club. The hope is to surprise members with the whiskies selected for the tastings.

The Single Malt Club of Scotland (Italy)
www.singlemaltclub.it

Created with the support of Food From Britain and the Scotch whisky industry in 2000. Under the direction of Nigel Brown who established United Distillers, Italy, and Angelo Matteucci, one of Italy's leading whisky experts. The club's aim is to maintain and develop interest in single malts through talks and tastings.

Associação Brasileira dos Colecionadores de Whisky
Rua General Pereira da Cunha 105, São Paulo SP, CEP 05692-060, Brazil
Tel: (+55) 11 3750 0007
(Founder and President: Claive Vidiz)

Claive Vidiz, Keeper of the Quaich, has a considerable collection of whisky – around 3,000 bottles, housed in a purpose-built museum with a private bar attached. He founded the Brazilian Whisky Collectors Association in 1989. It has members all over the country, who meet to hear lectures on the history of whisky and how it is produced, to hold tastings and to compare notes. It publishes a monthly journal, *Double Dose*.

Sociedad Brasilia du Whisky
Av Rui Barbosa 830, Ap 102, Rio de Janeiro, RJ 22250-020, Brazil
Tel: (+55) 21 551 2297
(President: Hector Vignoli)

This distinguished club was established in 1988. It now has over 700 active members and has been recognised by the mayor of Rio de Janeiro with the title "Partner of Rio" for its services to the city. Its president was created a Keeper of the Quaich in 1992. Its headquarters are in Rio, and there are branch offices in São Paolo, Barana, Ceara and Mato Grosso. Monthly meetings and tastings are held in Rio and São Paolo, and quarterly elsewhere. It circulates a monthly publication, *Whisky News*, to members.

WHISKY WEBSITES

When this book was first published in 1997, the worldwide web was in its infancy with regard to whisky. Now there are hundreds of whisky websites – so many that it is impossible to keep track of them. The most comprehensive portal listings may be found at www.whiskysites. com and www.buxrud.se/linklib.htm. Their scope is enormous. The latter breaks down the categories of site as follows: Scotch malt, Scotch blend, non-Scotch malt, non-Scotch blend, bourbon & rye, bottlers and blenders, retailers, public societies, private societies, collectors & collections, pubs & hotels, books, general whisky information, discussion groups, festivals, whisky auctions, personal pages.

www.maltwhiskyyearbook.com
A good round-up of old and new sites.

www.singlemalt.tv
This is a hi-definition TV channel devoted to whisky(ey). It is produced and directed by former Hollywood cinematographer, Rob Draper, and offers a wide range of excellent programmes, live and from the archive.

www.maltmadness.com
Managed by Johannes van den Heuvel, the leading Malt Maniac (*see* below), this is both a personal site and a splendid introduction to whisky.

www.maltmaniacs.org
Malt Maniacs (*see* page 224) is a group of around 25 hugely knowledgeable malt-heads from all over the world. This is my favourite whisky site; interesting discussions, information and tasting notes for over 9,000 whiskies.

www.whiskyfun.com
Serge Valentin's site is knowledgeable and entertaining and reviews rock and roll as well as whisky.

www.scotchwhisky.net
Claims to be "the definitive online guide to whisky", with the objective of providing "the most comprehensive, accurate and up-to-date information" about Scotch and the Scotch whisky industry. I find its "news" section, that reproduces articles from the press, invaluable.

www.whiskymag.com
The site connected to *Whisky Magazine*, which is published six times a year, archives articles and reviews and has a very active forum of over 3,000 registered members.

www.maltadvocate.com
The equivalent site for the long-standing American magazine, *Malt Advocate*. John Hansell, the magazine's owner, also has a blog at blog.maltadvocate.com.

www.thescotchblog.com
Online news and commentaries from an influential New Yorker (now living in Virginia), Kevin Erskine, "one of the more outspoken whisky personalities" and the author of *The Instant Expert's Guide to Single Malt Scotch*.

blog.thewhiskyexchange.com
Connected to the leading whisky retailer, the site is managed by Tim Forbes, whose comments are pithy and close to the bone – and sometimes get him into trouble.

drwhisky.blogspot.com
Sam Simmons' doctorate was on Ezra Pound. Now he is an ambassador in the USA for The Balvenie. His blog is articulate, well-informed and delightfully opinionated.

www.edinburghwhiskyblog.com
The managers of this site, Lucas and Chris, work as guides at The Scotch Whisky Experience in Edinburgh. They offer news, whisky reviews and personal experiences.

www.whiskyreviews.blogspot.com
Ralfy is Glaswegian so his video blog can be relied upon to be entertaining. On it he reviews individual expressions of whisky, visits whisky fairs and conducts interviews with people in the trade. He also has a traditional blog: www. whiskystuff.blogspot.com.

www.whisky-news.com
Patrick Brossard from Switzerland started this site in 2006. It provides news from a variety of sources, tasting notes, distillery and book reviews and useful links to other sites.

www.nonjatta.blogspot.com
Chris Bunting is an English journalist

living in Japan and his blog is devoted to Japanese whisky and culture. His book on Japanese alcohol is scheduled for publication late 2010.

www.caskstrength.net

A well-laid out (indeed award-winning) and cheerful blog from Joel and Neil, reporting their experiences in, and comments about, the world of whisky.

www.thewhiskychannel.com

Leading whisky writer (and former marketing director at Glenmorangie), Ian Buxton, provides his insight and entertaining comments, and manages a portal to other sites.

www.whiskycast.com

Broadcaster and Malt Maniac, Mark Gillespie, hosts the internet's leading whisky-related podcast, with frequent new programmes and interviews. Professional, relaxed and well-informed, it sets the s tandard by which podcasts are judged.

www.whisky-pages.com

Gavin Smith, the first-rate and prolific whisky writer, originally teamed up with wine expert, Tom Canavan, at the short-lived glossy, *Fine Expressions*. Their well-written online magazine provides news, features and regular reviews of recent releases.

www.whiskyforeveryone.com

A well-designed, easily navigated and substantial site from Matt Chambers and Karen Taylor, which presents the world of whisky in an understandable way.

www.forscotchlovers.com

This sets out to be what it says: a community created by Scotch lovers for Scotch lovers, with the avowed goal of making Scotch whisky accessible and fun, and even sexy.

www.whisky-distilleries.info

A French site (in English as well) providing thumbnail sketches of all Scotland's whisky distilleries, in production, mothballed or recently closed.

www.whiskyforum.se

(In Swedish), with more than 1,800 keen members and over 2,000 tasting notes.

www.whiskynyt.dk

(In Danish), with whisky news and an active forum.

www.whisky.de

(In German), Dr Clemens Dillman's well-informed and comprehensive site, linked to his online shop, The Whisky Store.

VISITING DISTILLERIES

The idea of installing visitor facilities in a distillery was pioneered at Glenturret by James Fairlie, a whisky enthusiast who bought the small and ancient distillery in 1957, with a view to "preserving the craft traditions of malt distilling and developing its appreciation". He opened his visitor centre in 1964, and today it receives about 200,000 visitors a year.

The distilleries listed below are all equipped with facilities to welcome and entertain visitors. Some have restaurants or cafés; whisky, gift and book shops; displays and museums, and film theatres. Others simply provide a guided tour of operations.

Most do not charge admission; those that do (in the range of £3) usually give a voucher for this amount, to be redeemed against the purchase of a bottle of their malt whisky.

Some require advance notice for your arrival (these are noted on pages 228–30) although it is wise to check the opening hours in advance, especially when you are bringing a party.

Visiting Distilleries by Duncan and Wendy Graham (Neil Wilson Publishing, 2001) is an indispensable vade mecum, containing essential information on how to get to the distilleries, what to expect by way of facilities and what to look out for during your tour. They provide a useful star-rating system out of seven, followed here.

Aberfeldy Distillery••••••
Aberfeldy, Perthshire
Tel: (+44) 1887 822010
April to October: Sat 1000–1800, Sun 1200–1600
Nov to March: Mon–Fri 1000–1600

Aberlour Distillery••••
Aberlour, Morayshire
Tel: (+44) 1340 881249
Open all year: (shop) Mon–Sat 0930–1700,
(tour) Mon–Sun 1030–1400; winter by appt

Ardbeg Distillery••••••
Kildalton, Nr Port Ellen, Islay
Tel: (+44) 1496 302244
Open all year: Mon–Fri 1000–1600
June to August: Mon–Sun 1000–1700

Auchentoshan Distillery•••••
Dalmuir, Dumbartonshire
Tel: (+44) 1389 878561
Open all year: Mon–Sun 1000–1700

The Balvenie Distillery•••••••
Dufftown, Morayshire
Tel: (+44) 1340 820373
Open all year: (3 hour tour, by appt),
Mon–Thus 1000 and 1400; Fri 1000 only

Ben Nevis Distillery••••
Lochy Bridge, Fort William
Tel: (+44) 1397 702476
Easter to September: Mon–Fri 0900–1700,
Sat 1000–1600
July to August: Mon–Fri 0900–1800,
Sat 1000–1600, Sun 1200–1600
October to Easter: by appt

Benromach Distillery••••
Forres, Morayshire
Tel: (+44) 1309 675968
October to March: Mon–Fri 1000–1600
April to September: Mon–Sat 0930–1700
June to August: also Sun 1200–1600

Bladnoch Distillery••••••
Bladnoch, Wigtownshire
Tel: (+44) 1988 402605
Open all year: Mon–Fri 0900–1700
July to August,Bank holidays: also Sat 1100–
1700, Sun 1200–1700

Blair Athol Distillery••••
Pitlochry, Perthshire
Tel: (+44) 1796 82003
Easter to September: Mon–Sat 0900–1700,
Sun 1200–1700
October: Mon–Fri 0900–1700
November to Easter: Mon–Fri 1000–1600

Bowmore Distillery•••••••
Bowmore, Isle of Islay, Argyll
Tel: (+44) 1496 810441
Easter to June: Mon–Sat 0900–1700
July to mid-September: Mon–Sat 0900–1700,
Sun 1200–1600
mid-September to Easter: Mon–Sat 0900–1700,
Sat 0900–1200

Bruichladdich Distillery•••••
Port Charlotte, Isle of Islay
Tel: (+44) 1496 850221
Mid-March to October: Mon–Fri 1000–1600

Bunnahabhain Distillery••••
Bunnahabhain, Isle of Islay, Argyll
Tel: (+44) 1496 840646
Open all year: Mon–Fri 1000–1600

Caol Ila Distillery••••
Port Askaig, Isle of Islay
Tel: (+44) 1469 302760
Open all year: Mon–Fri by appt

Cardhu Distillery•••••
Knockando, Aberlour, Banffshire
Tel: (44) 1340 872555
5 April–30 June Mon–Fri 1000–1700
1 July–30 September Mon–Fri 1000–1600,
Sat 0930–1630, Sun 1100–1600

Clynelish Distillery••••
Brora, Sutherland
Tel: (+44) 1408 623000
March to October: Mon–Fri 0930–1700
November to February: by appt

Dalmore Distillery••••••
Alness, Ross & Cromarty
Tel: (+44) 1349 882362
Open all year: Mon–Thur 1000–1630,
Fri 1000–1500, weekend group bookings
by appt

Dalwhinnie Distillery••••
Dalwhinnie, Inverness-shire
Tel: (+44) 1540 672219
March to December: Mon–Fri 0930–1630
June to October: also Sat 0930–1630
July to August: also Sun 0930–1630

Edradour Distillery••
Pitlochry, Perthshire
Tel: (+44) 1796 472095
April to October: Mon–Sat 0930–1700,
Sun 1200–1700
November to March: shop Mon–Sat 1000–1600

Fettercairn Distillery•••••
Distillery Road, Fettercairn, Kincardineshire
Tel: (+44) 1561 340205
May to September: Mon–Sat 1000–1430

Glendronach Distillery••••••
Forgue, by Huntly, Aberdeenshire
Tel: (+44) 1466 730202
Open all year: Mon–Fri 0900–1600

Glenfarclas Distillery•••••
Ballindalloch, Banffshire
Tel: (+44) 1807 500257
Open all year: Mon–Fri 1000–1700
July to September: also Sat 1000–1600

Glenfiddich Distillery••••••
Dufftown, Keith, Banffshire
Tel: (+44) 1340 820373
Open all year: Mon–Fri 0930–1630
Easter to mid-October: also Sat 0930–1630,
Sun 1200–1630

Glen Garioch Distillery••••
Oldmeldrum, Aberdeenshire
Tel: (+44) 1651 873450
Open all year: Mon–Sat 1000–1630

Glengoyne Distillery•••••
Dumgoyne, Stirlingshire
Tel: (+44) 1360 550254
Open all year: Mon–Sat 1000–1600,
Sun 1200–1600

Glen Grant Distillery •••••
Rothes, by Aberlour, Banffshire
Tel: (+44) 1340 832103

Mid-March to end-October: Mon–Sat
1000–1600, Sun 1230–1600

Glenkinchie Distillery•••••••
Pencaitland, Nr Tranent, East Lothian
Tel: (+44) 1875 342004
November to February: Mon–Fri 1100–1600
March to May: Mon–Fri 1000–1700
June to October: Mon–Sat 0930–1700,
Sun 1200–1700

The Glenlivet Distillery•••••••
Glenlivet, Ballindalloch, Banffshire
Tel: (+44) 1542 783220
March to October: Mon–Sat 0930–1600,
Sun 1230–1600

Glenmorangie Distillery•••••••
Tain, Ross-shire
Tel: (+44) 1862 892477
Open all year: Mon–Fri 0900–1700
June to August: also Sat 1000–1600,
Sun 1200–1600

Glen Moray Distillery••••••
Tel: (+44) 1343 550900
Open all year: Mon–Fri 0900–1700
June to September: also Sat 100–1600

Glen Ord Distillery••••••
Muir of Ord, Ross-shire
Tel: (+44) 1463 872004
March to October: Mon–Fri 0930–1700
July to September: also Sat 0930–1700,
Sun 1230–1700
November to February: contact distillery
for opening hours

Glenturret Distillery •••••••
The Hosh, Crieff, Perthshire
Tel: (+44) 1764 656565
January: Mon–Fri 1130–1600
February: Mon–Sat 1130–1600, Sun 1200–1600
March to December: Mon–Sat 0930–1800,
Sun 1200–1800

Highland Park Distillery •••••••
Holm Road, Kirkwall, Orkney
Tel: (+44) 1856 874619
April to October: Mon–Fri 1000–1700
July to September: also Sat–Sun 1200–1700

Isle of Arran Distillery•••••
Lochranza, Isle of Arran
Tel: (+44) 1770 830264
Open all year: 1000–1800
November to March: contact distillery for
opening hours

Isle of Jura Distillery•••••
Craighouse, Isle of Jura, Argyll
Tel: (+44) 1496 820240
Open all year: Mon–Fri by appt

Kilchoman Distillery••••••
Rockside Farm, Isle of Islay
Tel: (+44) 1496 850011
Easter to October: Mon–Sat 1000–1700
Nov to Easter (ex Jan): Mon–Fri 1000–1700

Lagavulin Distillery••••••
Port Ellen, Isle of Islay, Argyll
Tel: (+44) 1496 302400
Open all year: Mon–Fri by appt

Laphroaig Distillery•••••
Port Ellen, Isle of Islay, Argyll
Tel: (+44) 1496 302418
August to June: (tour) Mon–Thur 1015
and 1415

The Macallan Distillery•••••••
Craigellachie, Aberlour, Banffshire
Tel: (+44) 1340 871471
Easter to October: Mon–Sat 0930–1630
November to Easter: Mon–Fri 1100–1500

Oban Distillery••••••
Stafford Street, Oban, Argyll
Tel: (+44) 1631 572004
February to December: contact distillery for
opening hours

Pulteney Distillery••••
Huddart Street, Wick, Caithness
Tel: (+44) 1955 602371
April to September: 10.30–12.30, 1330–1530
October to March: by appt

Royal Lochnagar Distillery••••
Crathie, Ballater, Aberdeenshire
Tel: (+44) 1339 742273

Open all year: contact distillery for opening
hours

Strathisla Distillery•••••••
Seafield Avenue, Keith, Banffshire
Tel: (+44) 1542 783044
April to October: Mon–Sat 0930–1600,
Sun 1200–1600
November to March: (shop) Mon–Fri 0930–
1230, 1330–1600

Talisker Distillery••••••
Carbost, Isle of Skye
Tel: (+44) 1478 614308
Easter to October: Mon–Fri 0930–1700
November to Easter: by appt

Tobermory Distillery•••
Main Street, Tobermory, Isle of Mull
Tel: (+44) 1688 302645
Easter to October: Mon–Fri 1000–1700
November to Easter: by appt

Tullibardine Distillery
Blackford, by Auchterarder, Perthshire
Tel: (+44)1764 682252
Open all year: 1000–1700

OTHER WHISKY-RELATED VISITOR CENTRES

Dallas Dhu Distillery•••••
Forres, Morayshire
Tel: (+44) 1309 676548
April to September: Mon– Sun 0930–1730,
October: Mon–Sun 0930–1630,
November to March: Mon–Wed, Sat–Sun
0930–1630

Speyside Cooperage••••••
Craigellachie, Speyside
Tel: (+44) 1340 871108
Open all year: Mon–Fri 0900–1600

The Scotch Whisky Experience••••••
Castle Hill, Edinburgh
Tel: (+44) 131 220 0441
June to August: Mon–Sun 1000–1830
September to May: Mon–Fri 1000–1800

BIBLIOGRAPHY

* indicates leading titles

Andrews, Allen
The Whisky Barons
London, 1977
Angeloni, Umberto
*Single Malt Whisky: An Italian
Passion*
Rome, 2001
Arnot, Hugo
History of Edinburgh
Edinburgh, 1779
Arthur, Helen
Whisky: The Water of Life
London, 1999
Barnard, Alfred
*The Whisky Distilleries of the
United Kingdom*
London, 1887; rep Newton
Abbot, 1969; Edinburgh, 1987*
Begg, Donald
*The Bottled Malt Whiskies
of Scotland*
Edinburgh, 1972
Bell, Colin
Scotch Whisky
Newtongrange, 1985
Birnie, William
*The Distillation of Highland Malt
Whisky*
Private, 1937 and 1964
Bold, Alan (Ed)
*Drink to Me Only: The Prose
(and Cons) of Drinking*
London, 1982
Brander, Michael
The Original Scotch
London, 1974
A Guide to Scotch Whisky
Edinburgh, 1975
*The Essential Guide to Scotch
Whisky*
Edinburgh, 1990
Bronfman, Samuel
From Little Acorns: The Story

*of Distillers Corporation –
Seagrams Limited*
Private, 1970
Broom, Dave
Spirits and Cocktails
London, 1998
Whisky: A Connoisseur's Guide
London, 1998
Handbook of Whisky
London, 2000
Brown, Gordon
Classic Spirits of the World
London, 1995
The Whisky Trails
London, 1993
Bruce-Lockhart, Sir Robert
Scotch
London, 1951*
Burns, Edward
Bad Whisky
Glasgow, 1995
Burt, Captain Edward
*Letters from a Gentleman in the
North*
London, 1754
Cooper, Derek
A Taste of Scotch
London, 1989
The Little Book of Malt Whiskies
Belfast, 1992
The Whisky Roads of Scotland
London, 1982
*A Guide to the Whiskies
of Scotland*
London, 1978
*The Century Companion to
Whiskies*
London, 1978*
Craig, Charles H
Scotch Whisky Industry Record
Dumbarton, 1994
Scotch Whisky Industry Review
Norfolk, 1994*
Cribb, Stephen & Julie
Whisky on the Rocks

Nottingham, 1998
Daiches, David
*Scotch Whisky: Its Past and
Present*
London, 1969*
*A Wee Dram: Drinking Scenes
from Scottish Literature*
London, 1990
Let's Collect Scotch Whiskies
London, 1981
Darwen, James
The Illustrated History of Whisky
Paris, 1992; London, 1993
Distillers Company Limited
DCL and Scotch Whisky
London, 1961; various editions
The DCL Gazette
Dunnet, Alastair
The Land of Scotch
Edinburgh, 1953
Forbes, George
Scotch Whisky
Glasgow, 1995
Gibbon, Edward
*The Decline and Fall of the
Roman Empire*
London, 1776, 1781
Glen Grant Distillery
A Distillation of 150 Years
Aberdeen, 1989
Gow, Rosalie
Cooking With Scotch Whisky
Edinburgh, 1990
Green, Martin
Collecting Malt Whiskies
Ayr, 2007
Greenwood, Malcolm
The Diary of a Whisky Salesman
Argyll, 1995
Grey, Alan S
Scotch Whisky Industry Review
Glasgow, published annually*
Grindal, Richard
The Spirit of Whisky
London, 1992

Gunn, Neil M
Whisky and Scotland
London, 1935, rep 1990*
Hills, Philip et al
Appreciating Whisky
Glasgow, 2000*
Scots on Scotch
Edinburgh, 1991
Holinshed, Raphael
Chronicles of 1577
London, 1577
House, Jack
Pride of Perth: The Story of Arthur Bell & Co
Perth, 1976
The Spirit of White Horse
Glasgow, 1975
Jackson, Michael
The World Guide to Whisky
London, 1987
The Malt Whisky Companion
London, 1989*; 4th Edition, 1999
Scotland and Its Whiskies
London, 2001
Johnson, Dr
Dictionary
London, 1755
Journey to the Western Isles of Scotland
London, 1775
Laing, Robin
The Whisky Muse
Edinburgh, 2002*
Laver, James
The House of Haig
Perth, 1958
McCondach, JP
The Channering Worm
Edinburgh, 1931
Macdonald, Aeneas
Whisky
Edinburgh, 1930*
McDowall, RJS
The Whiskies of Scotland
London, 1967*
McHardy, Stuart
Tales of Whisky and Smuggling
Moffat, 1991

Mackie, Albert David
The Scotch Whisky Drinker's Companion
Edinburgh, 1973
MacLean, Charles
The Robertson Trust
Edinburgh, 2001
The Pocket Whisky Book
London, 1993
Discovering Scotch Whisky
London, 1996
The Pitkin Guide to Scotch Whisky
London, 1996
Scottish Toasts & Graces
Belfast, 1993
Whiskypedia
Edinburgh, 2009
McNeill, F Marian
The Scots Cellar: Its Traditions and Lore
Edinburgh, 1986
Mantle, Jonathan
The Ballantine's Story
London, 1991
Martine, Roddy
Whisky
London, 1994
Scotland: The Land and the Whisky
London, 1994
Milroy, Wallace
The Malt Whisky Almanac
Moffat, 1987; 5th Edition 1992*
Milsted, David
Bluff Your Way in Whisky
London, 1991
Morton, Tom
Spirit of Adventure
Edinburgh, 1992
Morewood, SA
The Manufacture and Use of Inebriating Liquors
Dublin, 1838
Morrice, Philip
The Schweppes Guide to Scotch
London, 1983*
The Whisky Distilleries of

Scotland and Ireland
London, Limited Edition, 1987
Moss, MS and Hume, JR
The Making of Scotch Whisky: A History of the Scotch Whisky Distilling Industry
Edinburgh, 1981*
Moss, Michael
100 Years of Quality: A History of The Highland Distilleries Company 1887–1987
MS, 1987, *et al*
Chambers Scottish Drink Book
Edinburgh, 1990
Scotch Whisky
Edinburgh, 1991
Murphy, Brian
The World Book of Whisky
London, 1979
Nettleton, JA
The Manufacture of Spirit as Conducted at the Various Distilleries of the United Kingdom
London, 1898*
The Manufacture of Scotch Whisky and Plain Spirit
Aberdeen, 1913
Nown, Graham
Edradour: The Smallest Distillery in Scotland
Private, 1988
Oram, Richard
The Glenmorangie Distillery 1843–1993
Private, 1993
Reeves Jones, Alan
A Dram Like This
London, 1974
Rice, Phillip
Scotch Whisky – Too Much or Too Little?
Edinburgh, 1973
Riddell, JB
Observations on the Scotch Whisky Production Cycle
Invergordon Distillers Ltd, 1976
Robb, J Marshall
Scotch Whisky: A Guide

Edinburgh, 1950*

Robertson & Baxter
The R&B Group: Robertson & Baxter
Private, 1990

Ronde, Ingvar (Ed)
Malt Whisky Yearbook 2006–10
Shrewsbury, 2008

Ross, James
Whisky
London, 1970

Saintsbury, George
Notes on a Cellar Book
London, 1920

Schobert, Walter
Malt Whisky Guide
Frankfurt, 1994
Single Malt Note Book
Frankfurt, 1996

Scotch Whisky Association
Scotch Whisky: Questions and Answers
Edinburgh 1957; last reprint 1992

Skipworth, Mark
The Scotch Whisky Book
London, 1987

Shaw, Carol P
Whisky – Collins Gem
Glasgow, 1993

Sillet, SW
Illicit Scotch
Aberdeen, 1965

Simpson, Bill et al
Scotch Whisky
London, 1979

Sinclair, Sir John
Statistical Account of Scotland
Edinburgh, 1791–99

Smith, Gavin D
Wort, Worms & Washbacks
Glasgow, 1999
Scotch Whisky
Stroud, 1999

Whisky Wit & Wisdom
Glasgow, 2000
Whisky: A Book of Words
Manchester, 1993*

Smith, Grant, Captain W
Glenlivet: The Annals of the Distillery
Private, 1924, rep 1959

Spiller, Brian
Cardhu – The World of Malt Whisky
London, 1985
DCL Distillery Histories
London, 1981*
The Chameleon's Eye, James Buchanan & Co Ltd 1884–1984
Private, 1984

Swan and Gray
Specification of American Oak Wood for Use by the Scotch Whisky Industry
Edinburgh, 1988

Thomson, JK
Should Scotland Export Bulk Whisky?
Edinburgh, 1979

Townsend, Brian
Scotch Missed: The Lost Distilleries of Scotland
Edinburgh, 1993

Tullis Russell Ltd
The Story of Scotch Whisky
Guardbridge, 1977

Walker, Johnnie & Sons
The Opening of the New Premises
Kilmarnock, 1956

Weir, Ronald B
The History of the Distillers Company 1877–1939
Oxford, 1995*
The History of the Pot Still Malt Distillers Association of Scotland: The North of Scotland

Malt Distilleries Association 1874–1926
Elgin, 1970
The History of the Distillers Company 1877–1939
Oxford, 1995

Wheatley, Dennis
The Eight Ages of Justerini's
Private, 1965

Whittet, Martin
A Liquid Measure of Highland History
Inverness, 1987

Wilson, GB
Alcohol and the Nation
London, 1940

Wilson, John
Scotland's Malt Whiskies
Gartocharn, 1973

Wilson, Rev John Marius (Ed)
The Imperial Gazetteer of Scotland
Edinburgh, 1854

Wilson, Neil
The Malt Whisky Cellar Book
Glasgow, 1999
Scotch and Water: Islay, Jura, Mull, Skye
Lockerbie, 1985*

Wilson, Ross
Scotch Made Easy
London, 1959
Scotch: The Formative Years
London, 1970*
Scotch: Its History and Romance
Newton Abbot, 1973
The House of Sanderson

Wisniewski, Ian
The Classic Whisky Handbook
London, 1998

www.lochlomonddistillery.com
www.onlymalts.com
www.whisky-pages.com

234

INDEX

Where names of distilleries and whiskies are the same they are indexed together. Distilleries and whiskies which may be spelt as one or two words, eg those beginning with Glen or Loch, are filed together in one sequence. Page numbers in **bold** indicate a directory entry. *Italic* page numbers refer to illustration captions.